egory; (ii) (A) denotes Air Burst; (iii) (S) denotes Surfa

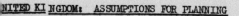

		Missile Weapon yield per target	Aircraft Weapon yield per target
		8 x 1 MT(A)	2 x 500 KT(A)
		2 x ½-1 MT(A)	2 x 500 KT(A)
		2 x ½-3 MT(S)	2 x 1 MT(S)
}		"	"
}	These are	"	"
}	considered to be	"	"
es }	possible, rather	"	"
}	than probable	"	"
}	targets	"	"
}		"	"
		"	"
	)See also	"	"
	)paragraph 2	"	
TLA NT)		2 x ½-1 MT(A)	2 x 1 MT(S)
		"	"
Ho me Station)		"	"
nd)		2 x ½-3 MT(S)	2 x 1 MT(S)
		"	"
and.)		"	"
		2 x 500 KT(A)	2 x 1 MT(S)
		"	"
		"	"
		"	"
		"	"
		"	"
		"	"
		"	"
		"	"
		"	"
		"	"
		"	"
		"	"
		"	"
		"	"
		"	"
		"	"
		"	"
		"	"
		"	"
		"	"
		"	"
		"	"

A - 1

The Secret State

PETER HENNESSY

The Secret State

WHITEHALL AND THE COLD WAR

ALLEN LANE
THE PENGUIN PRESS

ALLEN LANE
THE PENGUIN PRESS

Published by the Penguin Group
Penguin Books Ltd, 80 Strand, London WC2R ORL, England
Penguin Putnam Inc., 375 Hudson Street, New York, New York 10014, USA
Penguin Books Australia Ltd, 250 Camberwell Road, Camberwell, Victoria 3124, Australia
Penguin Books Canada Ltd, 10 Alcorn Avenue, Toronto, Ontario, Canada M4V 3B2
Penguin Books India (P) Ltd, 11 Community Centre, Panchsheel Park, New Delhi – 110 017, India
Penguin Books (NZ) Ltd, Cnr Rosedale and Airborne Roads, Albany, Auckland, New Zealand
Penguin Books (South Africa) (Pty) Ltd, 24 Sturdee Avenue, Rosebank 2196, South Africa

Penguin Books Ltd, Registered Offices: 80 Strand, London WC2R ORL, England
www.penguin.com

First published 2002
1

Set in 10.5/14 pt PostScript Linotype Sabon
Typeset by Rowland Phototypesetting Ltd, Bury St Edmunds, Suffolk
Printed in England by Clays Ltd, St Ives plc

Cover repro and printing by Concise Cover Printers

ISBN 0–713–99626–9

For Frank Cooper, Cold War veteran and
patron of contemporary British history

Although most people, however reluctantly take some interest in war, precious few bother their heads about organising for war in peacetime. It is a subject, like dental care, both dull and mildly repellent.   Professor Sir Michael Howard, 1992[1]

Hardly anyone died in the Cold War, but we lived on a daily basis with the risk that everyone might . . . Our strategy . . . was managed successfully by a small number of dedicated officials, scientists, submariners and other members of the Armed Forces, operating necessarily in conditions of utmost secrecy even within their own organisations . . . As a young man I saw them at work. These were not Dr Strangeloves . . .

Sir Kevin Tebbit, Permanent Secretary,
Ministry of Defence, 2001[2]

Contents

List of Illustrations

Every effort has been made to contact all copyright holders. The publishers will be glad to make good in future editions any errors or omissions brought to their attention. Photographic acknowledgements are given in parentheses.

INTRODUCTION

From Total War to Absolute War?

Neither the saint nor the revolutionary can save us; only the synthesis of the two. Whether we are capable of achieving it I don't know. But if the answer is in the negative, there seems to be no reasonable hope of preventing the destruction of European civilization, either by total war's successor Absolute War, or by Byzantine conquest – within the next few decades.

Arthur Koestler, *The Yogi and the Commissar,*
October 1944[1]

That neither absolute war nor the equivalent of Byzantine conquest happened – at least during the following five or more decades since he wrote – would have struck Koestler and many of his internationally attuned contemporaries as near miraculous. Of course, when he penned those words the number of people in the United Kingdom who knew how far the intensely secret combined US, UK and Canadian atomic weapon programme had progressed was limited to a tiny circle around Winston Churchill[2] – though Stalin knew, thanks to the extraordinarily rich supply of human intelligence from his agents inside the Manhattan Project (the US codename for the bomb programme),[3] whose later discovery, as we shall see, did much to stimulate the construction of a vetting system that was to become an integral part of the British Cold War state.

It is simple to the point of being seriously misleading to suppose that the creation of a nuclear weapons capability on both sides of what became the Cold War divide within four years of the dropping of the atomic bombs on Hiroshima and Nagasaki in August 1945 offers an all-embracing explanation of why the nuclear taboo has not been broken since those devastating blows were visited upon Japan. But whatever the cause, the result has been that my own generation (born in the early postwar years) have enjoyed a kind of 'armistice with history' of the sort attributed by George Steiner to the European *bourgeoisie* roughly 'from the time of Waterloo to that of the massacres on the western front in 1915–16'.[4]

The Cold War had plenty of casualties (physical and psychological), but not only did the unimaginable body counts of Mutually Assured Destruction fail to materialize, no external enemy has launched an armed assault across Europe's boundaries (the Balkans apart) since 1945 either. Nor, since the passing of national military service in the early 1960s, has a young British male been required by being conscripted to die or risk death in the uniform of sovereign and country. The twentieth century as a whole is littered with the corpses of British dead – but not my half of it.

Because what President Kennedy later described to Harold Macmillan as 'the conventions of the international stalemate'[5] were not ruptured to the point where one or both superpowers released nuclear weapons (though Kennedy considered Nikita Khrushchev had broken the conventions by placing missiles on Cuba in 1962), the history of the Cold War can be reflected upon in the kind of tranquillity which may too easily lead to a failure to appreciate the degree of peril generated and the scale of impact involved within the state, society and economy of even a second-rank participant such as the United Kingdom. Yet in British terms what might be called the short postwar – the first twenty or so years after VJ Day – were to an extraordinary degree shaped by the failure of the Potsdam powers to reach a European accommodation in 1945 amid the ruins of Hitler's push for supremacy. It is the Cold War which gives the UK of the late forties, the fifties and the sixties one of its most special flavours and distinguishes it from what came after, even though formally the Cold War had another two decades to run.

The book which needs to be written about it is huge, probably multi-volumed, and some way off. More is required by way of declassification of the official British archives before it can be fully attempted. The process of review and release set in train by the Major Government under the so-called 'Waldegrave Initiative' in 1992[6] does mean, however, that a first stab can be made at an anatomy of the Cold War state which British insiders built alongside the existing one, from roughly 1947 onwards. Describing this construction site, the impulses and thinking behind it, is the purpose of this book.

Apart from the new material (much of it of intense sensitivity when created) which has reached the Public Record Office in successive tranches over the past ten years, this book has enjoyed two other stimuli. The first has been the pleasure of going through swathes of the primary material with the first cohort taking my 'Secret State' undergraduate special subject at Queen Mary, University of London. Their companionship and insights combined to provide a necessary though not a sufficient condition for my writing on this subject. For it was the invitation from Penguin Books and the University of London's Institute of Historical Research to deliver the Penguin Lectures in the autumn of 2001 which caused me to pick up my pen. The theme of those four lectures is also that of this book.

It should be seen very much as work in progress – not mine alone but that of a vigorous platoon of academic colleagues from the Study Group on Intelligence, and from former insiders such as Sir Percy Cradock[7] and Sir Michael Quinlan[8] who are writing or have already written to such great effect. I have not sought either in the compass of the Penguin Lectures or within this book to replicate, for example, Professor Richard Aldrich on the US–UK intelligence relationship or active Cold War operations such as those mounted for counter-propaganda or deception purposes by the Information Research Department of the Foreign Office or the Ministry of Defence's Direct-orate of Forward Plans.[9] Nor have I sought to tackle the history of the Joint Intelligence Committee on the scale of Sir Percy Cradock,[10] or to wrap my mind around the theocratics of nuclear deterrence like Sir Michael Quinlan,[11] or intelligence philosophy in the manner of another former insider, the historian and philosopher of intelligence, Michael Herman.[12]

I entertain the fond hope that it will be one of my students who will, in the fullness of time, direct his or her mind to the great work of synthesis on Cold War Britain. And it is with those who attended the first run of 'Secret State' Monday afternoon seminars in the Mile End Road that my gratitude must begin. Matthew Grant, Samina Malik,

Justine Rainbow, Alban Webb and Helen Welch took it as an undergraduate course. Matt Lyus and Roderick Jones attended as research students. David Frank and Matthew Laban sat in while pursuing their MA in Contemporary British History. The group saw things in the papers that would have remained lost on me. From the first week to the end (when we relived, as it were, the actual Whitehall transition-to-war exercise of autumn 1968), the sessions were events I looked forward to, not least when former Cold War operators came to pool their insights now that a good portion of their old archives had been (legitimately) sprung. Thanks must go to Matt Lyus without whose word-processing prodigies the Penguin Lectures and this volume would have missed their deadlines and to my daughter Polly for producing the map to accompany the 1968 transition-to-war exercise, INVALU-ABLE, and for unearthing some special gems at the Public Record Office.

Peter Hennessy
Walthamstow and Mile End
December 2001

PRELUDE

'The Queen Must Be Told'

We agreed that there is a requirement for the Queen to be
informed, wherever she may be . . . of decisions to implement
the various stages and procedures for a transition to war.
                    Commander J. R. Stephens to Denys Laskey,
                    Cabinet Office, 5 March 1965[1]

Historically speaking, scraps of paper have had something of a bad
press since Neville Chamberlain landed at Heston Aerodrome on 30
September 1938 fresh from Munich and told the waiting newsmen
that 'This morning I had another talk with the German Chancellor,
Herr Hitler, and here is the paper which bears his name upon it as well
as mine . . .'[2] But for those who both devil and revel in archives, their
discovery can bring moments of pure elation and illumination. The
file coded CAB 21/5655 containing the internal exchange quoted
above between Commander Stephens, the keeper of the Government
War Book in the mid-1960s, and his boss, the head of the Cabinet
Office's Oversea and Defence Secretariat, contained a classic of this
kind when, with one of my students, I called at the Historical and
Records Section of the Cabinet Office in Marsham Street, Westminster,
one Friday afternoon in the spring of 2001 to inspect it.

I had long been keen to read the GWB, as it is known – the central
War Book which pulls together all the individual departmental versions
of itself and lays plans for the functioning of a World War III supreme
command built around the Prime Minister and a small War Cabinet.
In correspondence with the head of the Historical and Records Section,
Mrs Tessa Stirling, I had sought access to it and its supporting documentation.

On 26 January 2001 Mrs Stirling (whose staff had worked tirelessly at re-reviewing Cold War material under the 'Waldegrave Initiative' for several years) replied in a moderately encouraging letter but warned me not to be too expectant in this case. 'As to CAB 21/5655,' she wrote,

I have asked my Archives Section to remove the sensitive information so that it can be released in redacted form. From our discussions some while back, you will realise that the file is likely to be extensively sanitised and the result may not be of great interest. The material that is likely to be released deals mainly with matters associated with the maintenance of the Government War Book (GWB) and its circulation rather than a copy of the GWB itself. But as you pointed out to me, every little helps.

The GWB itself is in CAB 134 [the class containing Cabinet committee minutes and papers] and is presently retained under Section 3 (4) of the Public Records Act. This too is under review but I have to say that I think it is unlikely that the review will result in the release of the GWB once it has been completed.[3]

At the time of writing, the outcome of the review of the whole Government War Book is still awaited.

The supporting file, CAB 21/5655, in 'redacted' form as Mrs Stirling had indicated, was quickly made available. And, as my students needed it for their 'Secret State' course, we were kindly allowed to view it at the Cabinet Office before its dispatch to the Public Record Office. At first glance, it was as routine as we had expected, consisting chiefly of correspondence between the Cabinet Office's War Book-keepers – Mrs Beryl Grimble and a succession of military officers for whom she worked – plus Mrs Grimble's correspondence on questions of updating and classification of the GWB (with the General Post Office, for example, about the timing of the erection of protective blocks outside telephone exchanges during a transition to war).[4]

Suddenly, the file came to life, when the war planners realized the following spring, that, though no fewer than ninety-six copies of the GWB were in circulation,[5] Buckingham Palace did not have one. The Queen did not fully know either the drill that, should the stage of a nuclear exchange be reached, would leave her kingdom largely a smoking and irradiated ruin or the plans for carrying on her government in its aftermath. 'It's very strange, isn't it,' Sir Derek Mitchell, the Prime Minister's Principal Private Secretary in 1965, who was involved in putting this right, commented when I talked to him thirty-six years later about the Queen and the potential end of the world.[6] Indeed it was – nearly seventeen years after the Berlin Air Lift (which gave an immense stimulus to contingency planning for a third world war) and over two years after the Cuban Missile Crisis, the Palace was, unusually, very largely in the dark about an important area of state.

The files suggest that it was a new arrival in the top military seat of the Cabinet Office Secretariat, Commander J. R. Stephens, RN, who noticed the omission (perhaps as part of reading his way into the job). For the first trace of 'the Queen must be told' question is a minute from W. I. McIndoe, Private Secretary to the Cabinet Secretary, Sir Burke Trend, to Commander Stephens, dated 22 February 1965, recalling that

You asked me a few days ago whether I knew who was responsible for informing the Palace of decisions to implement the various states and procedures for a transition to war.

I have spoken to Mr Mitchell who tells me that No. 10 have no War Book of their own and are not aware of any obligation to inform the Palace.

You may therefore wish to consider whether our War Book ought to contain some instruction to the effect that we (or some other Department) must inform the Palace of the various steps which are being taken.[7]

After a dash of toing and froing between Stephens and the head of the Cabinet Office's Oversea and Defence Secretariat, Denys Laskey,[8] it was agreed that the Queen should be told of the drills and that the Cabinet Office, rather than No. 10, would be responsible for this.[9] Stephens finished by reminding Laskey that 'You invited me to suggest a list of decisions which should be communicated to The Queen. I attach such a list at Annex.' The annex to this memo of 5 March 1965, however, has been retained under section 3 (4) of the Public Records Act 1958 – plainly still deemed too sensitive for release.[10] Four days later McIndoe in Trend's office wrote to Mitchell in Harold Wilson's following up a telephone conversation 'about our discovery that there appear to be no War Book arrangements for informing The Queen, wherever she may be, of the major decisions taken during the transition to war'.[11]

McIndoe, briefed by the war planners, thought

It should not be necessary to inform Her Majesty of the mass of detailed measures, and we suggest that the decisions which ought to be communicated to Her might be those at Annex. You may wish to suggest additions or deletions. Since the meaning and scope of some of those decisions will not be known to the Queen, a brief guide would need to be provided to her Private Secretary.[12]

No sign of the annex here either.

But there is a god of the archives and he was with us that day in the Cabinet Office reading room. For tucked away in the file and easily overlooked was a scrap of rough paper upon which Stephens had drafted in longhand the decisions to be 'communicated to the Queen'. As can be seen from the photographic section, he has written it out in three sections, in Biro with amendments in pencil. From the Ministry of Defence's 1963 War Book,[13] which was declassified in full some three months before our eyes fell upon CAB 21/5655, it is possible to decode most of it, 'it' being a neat summary of the very Government War Book which is still too delicate for outsiders to read. As Derek Mitchell said when it was described to him (neither he nor Bill McIndoe[14] had any recollection of the episode): 'People had a great gift for summarising.'[15]

It began with the NATO sequence:

NATO

1. Simple Alert. [The 'preparatory measures which will place assigned forces in a state of combat readiness and should bring forces earmarked for assignment to minimum attainable readiness for war'.[16]]

2. Reinforced Alert. [The 'measures necessary to place NATO forces in the best possible position to meet an attack'.[17]]

3. Military Vigilance (ORANGE). ['State Orange . . . comprises the military measures when information received indicates a possible enemy attack within one or more hours.'[18]]

4. Counter Surprise (SCARLET). ['State Scarlet . . . comprises the military

measures when information received indicates an enemy attack within a few minutes.'[19]]

5. Assumption of operational command by NATO Major Commanders.

<u>USA/Russia</u>

1. Any important information concerning transition to war of these countries.

<u>UK</u>

1. MACMORRIS. ['. . . a warning state during which Departments are merely required to have available a responsible officer and a WTN [Whitehall Teleprinter Network] operator who can be contacted by telephone out of working hours'.[20]]

2. FLUELLIN [This should be 'FLUELLEN, which would be instituted, for example, on the declaration of a NATO Simple Alert, when Departments are required to establish immediately and maintain on a 24-hour basis a Departmental Control Point'.[21]]

The creators of codewords have shown a pleasing literary touch here. For Captains Fluellen and Macmorris provide the stage Welshman and Irishman respectively in Shakespeare's *King Henry the Fifth*.[22] Along with Corporal Nym, Lieutenant Bardolph and Ancient Pistol, this pair, as Professor Sir Michael Howard has noted, constitute the first instance of professional soldiers, rather than gentlemanly knights, making their appearance in military literature.[23]

3. Mobilisation [Cabinet decision to order a partial or general mobilisation; proclamations to be issued; Parliament to be informed, if sitting, and messages from Parliament to be conveyed to the Queen; if Parliament is not sitting, 'the Queen to make a Declaration in Council in respect of each Service to be mobilised . . .'[24]]

Here, originally, Stephens had placed at 5 the 'Setting Up of Regional Govt'. In pencil, however, he has moved it down to rest with the 'Dispersal of Central Govt' or, in his redrafted version, the 'manning of TURNSTILE', the central government bunker under the Cotswolds between Bath and Corsham.

So, his revised sequence from 'mobilisation' onwards reads like this (the numbers are now out of kilter so I have not used them).

Assignment of forces to NATO.

Repatriation to UK of dependants overseas.

Dispersal of 'priority classes' [women, children and the elderly] of population within UK.

Originally, alongside 'Dispersal of Central Govt' Stephens had placed 'Reinforcement of BAOR [British Army of the Rhine]'.

'Manning of TURNSTILE' becomes his revised number 9.

Pencilled-in as the last stage of the transition to war is number 10, 'Operation VISITATION', which looks like the early to mid-1960s codename for nuclear retaliation.[25] 'That would be a logical deduction to make,' as one old nuclear hand put it.[26] It has a truly Old Testament ring to it.

So Stephens's summary of the sequence to World War III – Koestler's 'Absolute War' – starts with Shakespeare and ends with the Bible.

Stephens's scrap of paper is, in its way, a remarkable historical artefact. Not only does it give its reader the essence of a very substantial item of evidence he or she cannot yet actually consult, it reflects a huge piece of government apparatus constructed piece by piece since the late 1940s, when the intelligence world, senior officials and military and certain ministers came to appreciate the magnitude of the Soviet 'threat' – that, in Eric Hobsbawm's phrase, 'the strength of the Cold War and its justification was that the potential aggressor to American ideals and interests was a real and formidable superpower'.[27] From the earliest days of the Cold War, it was plain to British war planners that with or without a home-grown nuclear capability, the United Kingdom, as the USA's number one ally in Europe and, from 1948, a forward base for its soon-to-be atomic-capable bombers, would be a prime target for Soviet bloc assault in the opening phase of a global war and that, in the meantime, the Russian intelligence service would expend every effort to penetrate the country's state, military and intelligence machinery. Stephens's draft encapsulated the interlocking measures pieced together to protect as far as was deemed feasible the Queen's (and her father's) realm from the possible attentions of Stalin and his successors. There is no evidence that Her Majesty or her Private Office, on receipt of Stephens's anatomy, asked for a short historical explanation of how her Cold War machine came to be as it was by the spring of 1965. But, if such a volume *had* been requested, it *might* have looked like this . . .

I

Secrets and Mysteries:
the Intelligence Picture

*The long-term aim of the Russian leaders is to build up the
Soviet Union into a position of strength and greatness fully
commensurate with her vast size and resources. They are convinced of the greatness of Russia's future under the Soviet
system. We believe it to be their firm conviction that, within
the next fifty years or perhaps a hundred years (unlike Hitler,
they are not pressed for time), the Soviet Union will inevitably
become the most powerful, the richest and the best ordered
country in the world.*

'Russia's Strategic Interests and Intentions',
Joint Intelligence Committee report, 1 March 1946[1]

*The policy of the Soviet Union can only be understood if it is
realized that she is not merely, like Nazi Germany, a totalitarian
dictatorship engaged in power politics, but a unique and
abnormal member of international society inspired by a
dynamic ideology with a strong international appeal.*

'Soviet Interests, Intentions and Capabilities . . .', Joint
Intelligence Committee report, 6 August 1947[2]

*Neither side would allow themselves to believe the other side
was as frightened as they were.*

Senior British intelligence officer looking back on the
Cold War, 2001[3]

The Cold War was a specialists' confrontation, not a peoples' conflict,
though it aroused fear on a wide scale, not just among rival sets of war
planners and decision-makers. Shortly before the Chinese entered the

Korean War, for example, a Gallup Poll indicated that 14 per cent of those surveyed in the UK thought 'that the fighting in Korea will lead to a Third World War' with 29 per cent returning a 'don't know'.[4] But even though 749 British troops lost their lives during that three-year conflict[5] and the last national serviceman was not called up until 1960[6] (the final batch departing by the end of 1963[7]), it was not a widespread, shared and shaping experience of the kind encountered by previous generations of conscripts. As Denis Healey, a veteran of World War II and a considerable player in the cold one, has put it:

The last two world wars were unique in our history, not least for the cultural shock they inflicted on the whole of our society. Each of them took millions of young men and women away from their families and friends at the most sensitive stage in their lives. It put them into uniform to serve under strict discipline with total strangers in closed communities. It send them abroad to kill other young men and women hundreds or thousands of miles away – in cities, fields, and mountains, in deserts and jungles.[8]

In one way, the Cold War reversed the process observed by Clausewitz early in the nineteenth century whereby wars ceased to be the concerns of professional armies to become conflicts of peoples. Michael Howard characterized the post-1945 world as one in which 'war is now seen as being a matter for governments and not for peoples: an affair of mutual destruction inflicted at remote distances by technological specialists operating according to the arcane calculations of strategic analysts. Popular participation is considered neither necessary or desirable'[9] – though, had the Cold War tipped into World War III, civilian casualties would have mounted on a scarcely imaginable scale. But for these reasons, the Cold War neither socialized large numbers of people into its disciplines, rationales and complexities nor did it, in modern argot, give them a sense of ownership or outcome (apart from the natural relief when without a nuclear or a direct conventional exchange, the Berlin Wall fell in 1989 and Mikhail Gorbachev kept the Red Army in its Eastern European barracks rather than turning its tanks on the rebellious citizens of its soon-to-be-separated satellites). The conduct and the management of the Cold War was largely an insiders' affair, nowhere more so than in its intelligence and counter-intelligence aspects. As one former British operator behind the Iron Curtain put it: 'The hot end of the cold war was espionage.'[10]

Michael Herman, himself a former Secretary of Whitehall's Joint Intelligence Committee,[11] expressed this forcefully in the last days of the great East–West confrontation when he said: 'The Cold War was in a special sense an intelligence conflict . . . Never before in peacetime have the relationships of competing power blocks been so influenced by intelligence assessments. Never before have the collection of intelligence and its denial to the adversary been such central features of an international rivalry.'[12] And to an extraordinary and hugely disproportionate extent, the world sees this clash of the secret worlds through supposedly British eyes. For it has been claimed 'that half the world's population has seen a [James] Bond film . . .'[13]

Certainly the intelligence Cold War in its handling and processing at the Whitehall end was very much a John le Carré phenomenon (as expressed through the mouth of the ghastly Roddy Martindale in *Tinker Tailor Soldier Spy* with 'Little reading rooms at the Admiralty, little committees popping up with funny names . . .'[14]). And if, like George Smiley in his hunt for 'Gerald the mole', you 'go forwards, go backwards'[15] through the now declassified files, it is possible to recontrast most but not all of the considerable Cold War apparatus which was pieced together in the fourteen years between the Berlin Air Lift[16] and the Cuban Missile Crisis.[17]

Not every piece of this infrastructure was part of the British intelligence community but all of it, to some degree, was suffused by the product of the agencies which carried out collection and counter-intelligence as directed by and filtered through what one of its former chairmen has characterized as the 'high table' of British intelligence[18] – the Joint Intelligence Committee, the JIC.

The JIC stood (and still stands) at the apex of the British intelligence process bringing together and analysing intelligence material which flows to it from covert and overt sources: the human intelligence procured by the Secret Intelligence Service (MI6), the signals and electronic intelligence gathered by the Government Communications Headquarters (GCHQ), the counter-espionage intelligence obtained by the Security Service (MI5), as well as material from relatively more open sources gleaned by the armed services' intelligence branches (merged from 1964 into the Defence Intelligence Staff), the Diplomatic Service and the defence attachés stationed within embassies. The JIC's staff undertake an 'all source' analysis (until 1957 the JIC was part of the Chiefs of Staff organization; since then it has been a Cabinet committee and part of the Cabinet Office). At its table sit the heads of the secret agencies plus Whitehall representatives and it reaches agreed views, by consensus, which are then circulated to an inner group of ministers and departmental customers.[19]

As Sir Michael Palliser, a former head of the Diplomatic Service, put it of the postwar years: 'The Cold War is a thread that has run through everything in that period.'[20] And to a very large extent, the Whitehall tapestry of that war, from beginning to end through all its mutations, was continually rewoven by the JIC. In a strange way – given that it was a war which involved neither declaration nor surrender – the JIC has been a concealed surrogate for such missing moments.

The end moment, in terms of the JIC at least, is easier to date than the start-line. It is late August 1991, and the coup against Gorbachev, led by, among others, Vladimir Khryuchkov, the head of the KGB, has just failed. One intelligence insider recalls the formidable and especially influential chairman of the JIC, Sir Percy Cradock, producing champagne for his fellow professionals and toasting the intelligence community as a whole on the demise of the Cold War with the words: 'We *didn't* have a war. We *did* win.'[21] Sir Percy himself, true to form, describes the occasion a trifle less dramatically in his book *In Pursuit of British Interests*:

The Joint Intelligence Committee is an austere body. It rarely rejoices and it lives too close to the dark side of political activity, the plots, revolutions, defections and betrayals, to find much ground for surprise, let alone celebration in the events it analyses. But the proscription of the Soviet Communist Party, which had been the prime object of its study for so many years, was memorable even against that bleak background. After our meeting of 29 August I asked the Committee to join me for a glass of champagne. We drank to the demise of the Party and added a toast to the plotters of 19 August who, in the best Marxist fashion, had given a push to history.[22]

The realization of the magnitude, peril and likely duration of the Cold War – the non-champagne moment, it might be called – is far harder to date.

Scholars such as Professor Richard Aldrich have described the debates in World War II Whitehall about the degree of threat the Soviet Union might pose in the postwar period. The Chiefs of Staff, led by Sir Alan Brooke, the Chief of the Imperial General Staff, were pessimistic compared to some in the Foreign Office, for example.[23] For instance, during the summer of 1944, in the privacy of his diary, Brooke opined that 'Germany is no longer the dominating power of Europe, Russia is. Unfortunately, Russia is not entirely European. She has however vast resources and cannot fail to become the main threat in 15 years from now.'[24] By early 1946, as we have seen, the JIC's assessment of both the magnitude and the imminence of the Soviet threat made Brooke's notion and timescale look positively Pollyanna-ish.

It is important to trace the mutations of the JIC's threat assessments during the early years of the Cold War as it was largely (but not wholly) on these that ministers, civil servants, diplomats and the military based their anxieties about what Stalin and his successors *could*, as opposed to *might*, do – intentions, of course, remained far harder to divine than capabilities. The distinction always to be borne in mind is between the 'secrets' that intelligence could, with effort, skill and no little luck, hope to uncover and the 'mysteries' which, in the near continuous absence of human agents close to the epicentre of the Soviet power structure, were to remain a closed book to the UK's secret world. As Michael Herman put it when reviewing the grand sweep of Western intelligence during the Cold War: 'On a medical analogy, the West by the 1980s had become well informed about Soviet anatomy and physiology; but the windows to the antagonist's mind remained largely opaque.'[25]

But before describing the picture painted by Whitehall's all-source intelligence analysts for their customers from the monarch down (traditionally the no. 1 copy of the 'Weekly Summary of Current Intelligence' goes to Buckingham Palace[26]), it is useful to reconstruct the mixture of images which went into the making of the big picture of the possible threat from the Soviet Union and its allies.

Nearly ten years after the end of the Cold War, the Cabinet Office declassified a particularly fascinating file containing the JIC's warning indicators for 1962 – the 'Red List' ('those preparations which the Soviet Union would consider essential to make before launching a surprise attack on the West') and the 'Amber List' ('the more important of the additional preparations for war which the Soviet Union might make if achieving strategic surprise was not considered possible')[27] together formally titled 'Indications of Sino-Soviet Bloc Preparations for Early War'. These were circulated in 1962, an especially fraught year when the Cuban Missile Crisis took Western intelligence unawares some seven months after the lists were distributed.[28] The document did not deal with the 'warning which we would hope to obtain from the general political situation'.[29] Instead the JIC instead broke down its adversaries' possible preparations for war into three:

(a) those indicating long-term military preparations for war;
(b) those indicating that the whole nation is being prepared for war;
(c) those indicating the bringing of operational units and facilities, and also civil defence, to immediate readiness for war.[30]

The JIC indicators paper concentrated on category (c), breaking it down still further into the two lists.

A very senior intelligence figure, a veteran of the Cold War whose service included spells behind the Soviet bloc lines, going through the declassified Red and Amber lists many years later said they aroused two thoughts in particular:

It's frightfully difficult now to put yourself in the context of 1962–1963. There was a very real feeling of threat. I remember just a few years earlier saying to my wife if it happens, where should we take our children – Chile or New Zealand? It was a well-justified worry. We'd had Berlin and Hungary, and Cuba was to come. So this document must be seen in that context or it's unreal – Dr Strangelove.[31]

The Red List of 1962 contained seventeen indicators which the JIC simply itemized without placing a priority on them. They were these:

1. Unusual flight activity or the lack of flight activity in the Long-Range Air Force which indicates a departure from normal peacetime operations.
2. The bringing to an increased state of readiness of Soviet strategic missile

units wherever they may be, including the movement of the missiles themselves into forward areas; the identification, outside fleet areas, of numbers of missile firing submarines, or, in time of tension, the absence of such submarines from local communication networks.

3. Unusually high state of readiness of all components of the Soviet air defence system, wherever located.

4. Sudden or unexplained redeployment and dispersal of Soviet ground forces, particularly in peripheral areas.

5. Sudden dispersal of naval ships from fleet bases.

6. Increased deployment of Soviet submarines in sea areas of interest to the Western Powers.

7. Dispersal of vital components of Soviet Government headquarters.

8. Redeployment of Soviet air force servicing units to, and build-up of aviation fuel stocks at or near, airfields in East Germany and the Satellites.

9. Issue of nuclear weapons to airfields where they are not normally stored, and issue of nuclear warheads to missile launching sites.

10. Provision of operational servicing facilities at suitable airfields in China to act as forward bases for Soviet medium and heavy bombers and the deployment of Soviet all-weather fighter units to protect these bases.

11. Arrival of Soviet army specialist units in forward areas (especially missile, medical and interrogation units) and military personnel wearing rocket insignia.

12. Redeployment or reinforcement of Soviet army units with a nuclear capability in forward areas.

13. Unusual deployment of missile guidance radar in the Soviet field armies.

14. Unusual signals activity, particularly if this suggests:

   (a) Increased central control of various components of Soviet strategic offensive.

   (b) Increased state of readiness throughout the armed forces. This could take the form of either an abnormally high, or an abnormally low, level of activity.

   (c) Disguise of preparatory measures.

   (d) A widespread and radical change of signal data.

15. Priority for Soviet military traffic, reduction of civil traffic on East German and Satellite railways, unusual concentrations of rolling stock, and the appearance of movement control staff.

16. Sharp increase in air transport flights between guided missile production factories, storage centres and known missile launch complexes.

17. Intensified security measures in the Soviet Union and Satellites.[32]

The Amber List spelt out forty-seven:

(ADDITIONAL SOVIET PREPARATIONS WHICH MIGHT BE MADE AND BLOC PREPARATIONS FOR HOSTILITIES)

ARMED FORCES

Common to All

1. Bringing units up to wartime strength and readiness through:
   (a) Recall of reserve personnel.
   (b) Postponement of demobilisation of trained soldiers.
   (c) Cancellation of leave, confinement of troops at barracks, increase of security patrols in vital areas.
   (d) Reassignment to full military duty of those units employed on civil projects.

2. Redesignation of military districts or formations as fronts and/or their reinforcement by high-ranking officers.

3. Readying of combat headquarters of ground and air units and the setting up of Joint-Services or Operations Headquarters.

4. Increases in the number of high-ranking officers in Soviet and Chinese missions in *bloc* countries. [Even as late as this China and the Soviet Union were treated together for global threat purposes.]

5. Extension of military hospital accommodation at the expense of civil establishments and the formation of emergency stockpiles of medical equipment and drugs.

6. Abnormal censorship of forces mail.

7. Accelerated build-up of missile units.

8. Change in pattern of activities at missile test ranges.

Ground Forces

9. Unusual reinforcing of the striking forces or the movement and concentration of troops to form a striking force.

10. Sudden or unexplained redeployment and dispersal of ground forces.

11. Assembly of airborne units in the vicinity of airfields on which transport planes are, or could be, concentrated.

12. The positioning of bridging equipment ready for use.
13. Building of bridges serving secondary routes.
14. Preparations for unusually large scale exercises involving Soviet Ground Forces being deployed into Satellite countries.

Air Forces

15. Unusually high state of readiness of *bloc* air defences.
16. Bringing into use inactive landing strips and airfields.
17. Dispersal and concealment of military aircraft.
18. Increase in the strength of air units on active airfields and reinforcement of air armies on the periphery of the *bloc*.
19. Unusual activity suggesting an assembly of military and/or civil air transport aircraft and airborne forces.
20. Interference with civil and military flight in the Berlin air corridor and with civil flight over *bloc*-controlled territory.
21. Extension of military control of civil air movement and disruption of *bloc* civil air schedules. The withdrawal of civil transport aircraft for military use.
22. Occupation by Chinese ground staff of North Vietnamese airfields.
23. Movement of bomber and fighter aircraft to airfields within striking distance of pro-Western countries.
24. Increase in aircraft delivery from Soviet Union to China.
25. Increase in POL [petrol, oil and lubricant] supplies to China, North Korea and North Vietnam.

Navy

26. Increased movement of small ships and submarines through the Soviet canal systems.
27. Reinforcement of naval air units; redeployment of Soviet naval units from their normal operating areas, particularly movements of submarines through the Sound or the Belts (Baltic) and from the Straits (Bosphorus).
28. Redeployment of submarine depot ships and support groups from the normal bases.
29. Significant changes in normal commercial maritime traffic. Recall of merchant ships or abnormal decrease of the number of those ships on the high seas.

30. Abnormal concentration in harbours of merchant ships or fishing vessels, adaptable for amphibious and supply operations.
31. Damaging of fixed Western anti-submarine detection systems, *e.g.*, by cutting associated cables.
32. Deployment of Chinese North and Eastern fleet units to southern ports.
33. Abnormal concentration of junks and landing craft in southern Chinese ports.
34. The movement of Chinese naval staff officers into North Vietnamese ports.

Logistics

35. Establishment of dumps in forward areas and increase of stocks, or sudden increases in military stockpiling near frontiers, communication centres, ports and airfields.
36. Change in supplies and distribution to East Germany. Change from long-haul replenishment by rail to local issues from depots and supply points and to increased use of road transport, including the requisitioning of road transport, for military supply in the USSR and the Satellites.
37. Priority for Satellite military traffic, with consequent loss of traffic for civil purposes, and the appearance of movement control staff.
38. Assembly of rolling stock of all types for Satellite forces and particularly of specialised rolling stock in main supply areas and in distribution centres.
39. Increase in the number of hospital trains in service and preparation for service.
40. Unusual movement of special trains for transporting ballistic missiles and/or fuels.

CIVIL DEFENCE

41. Bringing to a state of readiness civil defence measures on a large scale such as initiation of black-out measures and announcement of evacuation.
42. Dispersal of government and administrative headquarters.

SIGNALS

43. Transmission of jamming signals directed against radio communications, radar and missile guidance systems.
44. Setting up of new communication links applicable to specific military operations.

45. The interruption of Western communications by the deliberate cutting of submarine cables.

SECURITY

46. Increased activity of security organisations.
47. Bans on visits to and scheduled flights over sensitive areas, and the forced evacuation of local inhabitants from those areas, when the latter are likely to include ballistic missile launching sites.[33]

As a former senior intelligence operator put it, the 'key to all of the indicators is to (a) notice any change, and (b) to assess its significance. Any change is bad news.'[34]

For historians, the wider significance of this list is how revealing it is of the range of activities carried out by the collectors of British and allied Cold War intelligence. It is dominated by signals intelligence (the interception of military traffic especially) and electronic surveillance (the tracking of Soviet and Warsaw Pact radar). Human intelligence, though a relatively small component, is there, too, such as the number 11 on the Red List – the 'Arrival of Soviet army specialist units in forward areas . . . and military personnel wearing rocket insignia.'[35] (The United States by 1962 was putting its early Corona satellites over Soviet territory, but they could not deliver cap-badge imagery. Agents observing in the field could.) Similarly on the Amber List, the railway sections implied informants in the marshalling yards and, perhaps, number 6, 'Abnormal censorship of forces mail',[36] would best be detected by an agent of Western intelligence serving inside the Red Army.

It is also quite plain from the Red and Amber lists how important was the constant surveillance by Western intelligence of the Soviet bloc's periphery. Michael Herman, an old GCHQ hand,[37] later characterized this as having a touch about it of

a multinational Great Game, played out not only along the German border, but also in Berlin and around the rest of the Soviet periphery – the Baltic, North Norway and the Barents Sea, the Black Sea, the Sea of Okhotsk and elsewhere: tough men rolling for weeks on station in small ships; patient monitors on quiet islands; aircraft of many nations flying every day, packed with technical equipment; and much else.[38]

Herman goes on to observe that 'Much of the timely intelligence produced by the West was, strictly speaking, totally useless; its twenty-four-hour surveillance was a precaution, for warning of an attack that never came.'[39]

Certainly, throughout the bulk of the Cold War, the JIC's 'Weekly Summary of Current Intelligence' began with the words: 'There are no indications of Soviet Military aggression.'[40] Yet, as Herman recognizes, reassurance of this kind *was* hugely – I would say centrally – important: 'American Presidents never believed that they were about to be Pearl Harbored. Western confidence in intelligence warning provided some stability in Cold War management.'[41]

Back in the formative years, however, in the days long before satellites, U2 or even RAF Canberra overflights of Soviet territory, the JIC's preoccupation was with capabilities and indicators. Intentions it would dearly have loved to gauge but the late 1940s assessments were commendably candid about their shortcomings here. In that crucial twenty-five-page assessment of 'Russia's Strategic Interests and Assumptions' of 1 March 1946, the diplomats, civil servants, military and intelligence chiefs on the JIC were quite frank with their customers about 'our difficulties in obtaining intelligence on Russian intentions. Decisions are taken by a small group of men, the strictest security precautions are observed and far less than in Western Democracies are the opinions of the masses taken into account.'[42]

JIC (46) 1 (o) was the first big analysis of the Soviet Union's strategic interests and intentions the committee had produced since December 1944,[43] and it was especially notable as it reflected a sustained surge of pessimism on the part of the analysts since the final months of World War II. Such growing anxiety was reflected, famously, by Winston Churchill during his last weeks in No. 10 when, in Brooke's words, he

gave a long and very gloomy review of the situation in Europe. The Russians were further West in Europe than they had ever been except once. They were all powerful in Europe. At any time that it took their fancy they could march across the rest of Europe and drive us back into our island. They had 2 to 1 land superiority over our forces and the Americans were returning home.[44]

A very great deal turned on those mid- to late 1940s JIC assessments, not just in terms of ministerial perceptions and anxieties about that vast military machine to the east of the Elbe, but in the rationale, perhaps even the imperative, they provided for the sustenance of a sizeable military and intelligence capacity on the part of the UK into the increasingly uneasy peace. As Michael Howard put it, the postwar Chiefs of Staff (to whom, as we have seen, the JIC reported until 1957 when the committee was removed from their orbit into the Cabinet Office, partly to increase the flow of intelligence to senior ministers),[45] continued fighting their own private turf wars, but '[t]his did not matter so long as they had plenty of men and money to dispose of, which, thanks to the Cold War, they had'.[46] Defence spending as a proportion of Gross National Product stood at 7.1 per cent in 1948, and peaked at 9.8 per cent in 1952 thanks to the Korean War-inspired rearmament programme. As late as 1963 it still stood just above 6 per cent and only nudged below 5 per cent in 1969 thanks to the Wilson governments' near perpetual series of defence reviews.[47] And, as the postwar and the Cold War deepened in tandem, successive generations of ministers and officials on the inner intelligence loops came to appreciate, in Sir Burke Trend's words, that 'After the Second World War, it became apparent that we should henceforth have to make our way in the world by influence rather than by power and that political intelligence would henceforth be at least as important as military intelligence, if not more so.'[48]

What was it in those assessments which led to so high a proportion of the UK's national wealth being deployed for so long on politico-military purposes? The opening sections of the 1 March 1946 analysis of 'Russia's Strategic Interests and Intentions' is especially intriguing as it sets out the extent of the collection famine which its compilers had to overcome, before going on to outline the reasons for the report's descent into pessimism since the last big examination of the same theme in December 1944. 'Any study of Russia's strategic interests and intentions,' the JIC warned its inner circle of readers,

must be speculative, as we have little evidence to show what view Russia herself takes of her strategic interests, or what policy she intends to pursue. We have practically no direct intelligence, of a detailed factual or substantial nature, on conditions in the different parts of the Soviet Union, and none at all on the intentions, immediate or ultimate, of the Russian leaders ... Our present appreciation is based, therefore, on the limited evidence which we have, on deductions made from such indications of policy as Russia has given, and on reasonable conjecture concerning the Soviet appreciation of their own situation.[49]

Reprising their portrait of the likely postwar condition and stance of the Soviet Union drawn in the last weeks of 1944, the JIC recalled the stress they had placed on the primacy Stalin and the 'inner circle controlling the Communist Party of the Soviet Union' would give to the 'greatest possible measure of security', with every precaution taken to prevent a future invasion of Soviet territory. To this end: 'She [Russia] would wish to improve her strategic frontiers and to draw the states along her borders, particularly those in Europe, into her strategic system.' Another primary impulse would be the securing of 'a prolonged period of peace in which to restore devastated areas, to develop her industry and agriculture, and to raise the standard of living'.[50]

The JIC had not been overly optimistic, as their armies converged on Germany, that allied co-operation would continue once that great concentrator of collective minds – Adolf Hitler – had received his deserts, but they did believe that Russia

would at least experiment with collaboration with Great Britain and America in the interests of world security. But if she came to believe that we were not sincerely collaborating, she would probably push her military frontiers forward into the border states in Europe, try by political intrigue to stir up trouble in Greece, the Middle East and India, and exploit her interest over the Communist parties in the countries concerned to stimulate opposition to anti-Russian policy.[51]

Despite what Bradley Smith has called the 'record of four years of East–West intelligence co-operation' from Hitler's invasion of the Soviet Union in 1941 to the end of the Japanese War in August 1945, which he describes as 'the most extensive and successful such effort carried out by reluctant allies in the history of modern warfare',[52] the JIC had concluded in December 1944, when these intelligence exchanges were still flowing, that

While Russia would not follow an aggressive policy of territorial expansion, her suspicion of Great Britain and America would continue to cause difficulty, as would also her tactlessness in the handling of international relations. Her relations with us would depend very largely on the ability of each side to convince the other of the sincerity of its desire for collaboration.[53]

The thrust of that late 1944 assessment was that the chances of a post-Axis world of great powers cohabiting and collaborating in wary tolerance of each other were seriously limited but not altogether impossible.

The intelligence community, however, did not wait long to resume operations as usual against Soviet targets. As Bradley Smith has shown, while '[i]t must now be recognised that although the West avoided making serious intelligence attacks on the USSR during World War II, within days of its conclusion, British intelligence was working on Soviet military codes and ciphers'.[54] What persuaded British Intelligence during 'the course of 1945' that the faint hopes for a co-operative, united nations postwar world had been dashed? The JIC adduced four influences which had hardened the mindset of Stalin's inner group:

(a) The speed of the Western Allies' advance, after crossing the Rhine in March 1945 must have given rise to Russian fears that their allies would beat them in the race to Berlin, would then refuse to withdraw into their allotted Zones and so would rob the Soviet Union of many of the spoils of victory.
(b) The use of the atomic bomb disclosed a weapon which seemed to constitute a new threat to that security for which they have been striving ever since 1917 and which, in late 1944, they seemed, at last, to be on the point of attaining.
(c) The attitude both of the Americans and ourselves towards Russia seemed to them to harden after the end of hostilities. Both in South-East Europe and in the Far East, the United States Government seemed to them to be pursuing a policy designed to restrict Russia's aspirations. His Majesty's Government appeared to be pursuing a similar policy in South-East Europe, Turkey and Persia.
(d) On the other hand they must now appreciate that both the British Commonwealth and the United States are incomparably weaker than they were in the summer of 1945. Great Britain is faced with great man-power and financial problems leading to rapid demobilisation, while the United States has let her military forces disintegrate, and since the death of President Roosevelt has an executive which lacks decision.

15

In an intriguing afterthought to this disquisition on what they thought the Soviet leadership had in mind, the JIC, in a sentence surprising to post-Cold War eyes, saw Stalin as a force for relative moderation in the Politburo:

When Stalin has himself intervened in the past in negotiations between Russia and Great Britain and the United States, the result has usually been to make Russian tactics more flexible and accommodating: we cannot tell whether this will continue now that the war is over, but in the event of Stalin's death it is reasonable to assume that the absence of this modifying influence would be felt.[55]

Were the JIC failing to appreciate reality in both Washington and Moscow in the late winter of 1945–6? It is surprising that President Truman could have been regarded as indecisive as late as that. As for Stalin, the former KGB officer-turned-analyst Oleg Tsarev has painted a picture of him as an avid reader of 'intelligence in its raw form',[56] including documents purloined by his human agents in the UK such as Kim Philby, Guy Burgess and John Cairncross, which went to him, dangerously, without the 'evaluation and assessment which would have involved political judgments his aides were too afraid to make', meaning 'that such materials lacked depth and background'.[57]

According to Tsarev, Stalin convinced himself that some of the thinking in the JIC assessments in the early postwar period reinforced his view that the British Empire and the United States were preparing for hostilities against the Soviet Union. Tsarev placed particular emphasis on Russian translations of documents prepared by the UK Chiefs' Planning Staff in June 1945 on imperial defence which probably reached Stalin's desk thanks to Philby.[58] Similarly, late 1940s Western intelligence assessments suggesting the Soviet Union would not be militarily or industrially ready to fight a global war until 1955–7, appear, according to Tsarev, to have been interpreted in the Kremlin as identifying the period in which the US and the UK would 'unleash' war against the Soviet Union.[59]

If this was so, it involved a profound misreading of Chiefs of Staff and JIC material, illustrating how dangerously distorting can be the effects of unprocessed and unassessed intelligence documents, even though they were provided by what was probably as well-placed and rich a seam of human intelligence as one great power has ever enjoyed for use against another. Documents such as JIC (46) 1 (o) bear careful scrutiny for themselves. But read with Stalin's delusions in mind, the fear and sense of vulnerability in the West in 1945–6 were replicated in Stalin's office, and based partly on the very same material which led Attlee's ministers and the British military eventually to conclude that the Cold War was going to be a global, dangerous and prolonged affair. The JIC March 1946 assessment expressed their judgement that

In considering what action she can take, short of a major war, to attain her immediate aims, Russia will no doubt give full weight to the fact that Great Britain and the United States are both war weary, faced with immense internal problems and rapidly demobilising their forces. By comparison, Russia's own forces and industry are still on a war basis. No further demobilisation has been announced, and Russian divisions are being rapidly re-equipped with the latest material.[60]

Not much sign here of an Anglo-American preventive-war-in-the-making.

Could handwritten copies of the vast KGB archive which MI6 spirited out of the Soviet Union, along with its archivist, Vasili Mitrokhin, in 1992 provide part of the explanation for Stalin's determination to convert in his own mind British anxiety into Anglo-American bellicosity? It is one of the greatest paradoxes of intelligence history that the so-called 'Magnificent Five' (Kim Philby, Anthony Blunt, Guy Burgess, Donald Maclean and John Cairncross) came under deep suspicion in Moscow during World War II. As Professor Christopher Andrew, Mitrokhin's collaborator in organizing the archive for publication, has explained:

The problem for the professionally suspicious minds in the [Moscow] Centre was that it all seemed too good to be true. Taking their cue from the master conspiracy theorist in the Kremlin [Stalin], they eventually concluded that what appeared to be the best intelligence ever obtained from Britain by any intelligence service was at root a British plot. The Five, later acknowledged as the ablest group of agents in KGB history, were discredited in the eyes of the Centre leadership by their failure to produce evidence of a massive, non-existent British conspiracy against the Soviet Union. Of the reality of that conspiracy, Stalin, and therefore his chief intelligence advisers, had no doubt.[61]

The Mitrokhin material, therefore, suggests that Whitehall's all-source intelligence analysts were wrongly attributing to Stalin and his intelligence assessors the kind of rationality and detachment to which the JIC themselves aspired.

The short executive summary of JIC (46) 1 (o), designed to meet the needs of busy readers without the time to absorb the full, 127-paragraph report, itself alone dispels any fantasies about either the West itching for war or the Soviet Union trembling on the brink of a westward and irresistible march to the English Channel. It acknowledged that while the long-term aim of the Soviet leaders was to let time and the superiority of their system win for them 'an ultimate position of predominance in the world', the short-term preoccupation of the USSR will be to surround itself with 'a "belt" of satellite states with governments subservient to their policy' behind which Russia would rebuild 'her military and industrial strength to make up fully for her war losses and relative backwardness in the latest technical developments'. Should she perceive the West as seeking to compromise her position inside the protective 'belt', Russia

will retaliate by using all weapons, short of major war, to frustrate these attempts. She will make full use of propaganda, of diplomatic pressure and of the Communist parties abroad both to this end and to weaken foreign countries.

Measures short of war would also be used in an attempt to bring within her 'belt' contiguous areas such as Turkey and Persia which 'she considers it strategically necessary to dominate'. Russia will avoid, however, areas where she would encounter 'firm combined resistance from the United States and Great Britain together'. 'Elsewhere she will adopt a policy of opportunism to extend her influence wherever possible without provoking a major war, leaving the onus of challenge to the rest of the world. In pursuing this policy she will use, in the ways she thinks most effective, Communist Parties in other countries and certain international organisations . . .'[62]

So, in the eyes of the JIC, by late winter 1945–6 the Soviet Union had moved firmly and irrevocably beyond being an awkward partner in world affairs to being a formidable adversary with its own satellite belt and troublesome branch offices in many more countries in the form of indigenous Communist Parties – the whole apparatus operating a twin-track approach to eventual global predominance based on immediate reconstruction and security priorities that would eventually give way to wider ambitions as the sinews of military, political and economic superiority waxed ever stronger. The JIC summed up this Soviet approach as being 'aggressive by all means short of war'.

Would war come, however? In 1946 the British intelligence community answered the question in two parts:

1: The ingredients of a capacity to wage a sustained global war. Oil output would not reach pre-war levels (it was thought) until 1950. It was 'unlikely' that the USSR would possess 'significant quantities of atomic weapons before about 1955–60 . . .' By 1952, Russia would have made up wartime losses in manpower. By about 1955–60 the development of Russian industry will have made her self-sufficient in time of war. [63]

2: As to intentions, the Soviet Union may pursue defensive policies, but 'the tactics will be offensive, and the danger always exists that Russian leaders may misjudge how far they can go without provoking war with America or ourselves'. [64]

Herein lay many of the particles which went into the making of the JIC's Cold War state of mind: an intense concentration on what became the Soviet bloc's capacity to wage war (alongside a persistent underestimation of the speed with which they would make their leaps in military technology); a recognition of the inherent caution of the regime (alongside a sustained appreciation of the danger of war-through-miscalculation). The pattern of analysis, anticipation and anxiety was set. Here was a formidable, totalitarian adversary which differed from the tyranny from which Europe and the world had been delivered so recently in the durability and reach of its threat.

This latter aspect was the subject of a special JIC assessment in the summer of 1946 with quite a considerable input from MI6 (which is evident in its pages) and the codebreakers (which is not). One seasoned MI6 Cold War-hand took particular pride in his service's sustained ability to rub the noses of successive generations of ministers in the sheer nastiness of life in the Soviet bloc: 'The main contribution of MI6, the HUMINT [human intelligence] service at the level of our government,' he said,

was really quite humdrum. We reminded them on a weekly, sometimes a daily basis of the reality of the Soviet and other regimes. They had no chance to have illusions about what life was like behind the Iron Curtain . . . and there were constant reminders of what Soviet espionage was about.[65]

The 23 September 1946 JIC report, 'The Spread of Communism Throughout the World and the Extent of Its Direction from Moscow', very much carries this flavour.

It is difficult to know how much SIGINT [signals intelligence] influenced JIC (46) 70 (0). The defection of the Soviet GRU [military intelligence] cypher clerk Igor Gouzenko, in Ottawa in September 1945, with 'more than a hundred classified documents under his shirt', had exposed a major spy ring in North America.[66] The first breakthroughs into the so-called VENONA traffic, a cache which would rise to nearly 3,000 intercepted Soviet intelligence communications between New York and Moscow from 1940 to 1948,[67] were probably not made by US codebreakers until just after 'The Spread of Communism' document had circulated in Whitehall.[68] By 1950–51, a substantial penetration of the diplomatic and nuclear capacities of both the United States and the United Kingdom had been exposed, albeit to a very limited number of intelligence and counterintelligence experts within the VENONA loop and in the UK, most probably, to Clement Attlee and a small circle of his ministers.[69]

The September 1946 JIC assessment concluded starkly that 'Communism is a serious menace to the interests of the British Commonwealth both outside British territory, and to a lesser extent inside it, and we are of the opinion that it is essential that some immediate counter-action should be taken against this danger.'[70] It was unusual for a JIC paper to make a specific recommendation, but it was heeded, as we shall see in Chapter 3, when Attlee set up first his Cabinet Committee on Subversive Activities in June 1947[71] and a pair of official committees on Communism (Home) and Communism (Overseas) two years later.[72]

The JIC at this stage treated international Communism as if it were one and indivisible. The dissolution of the old Communist International, the Comintern, in May 1943,

appears to have had no effect on the cohesion and discipline of the Communist movement. Minor tactical difference exist between some of the national Parties, but on essential issues (and particularly on those in which the Soviet Union has declared its line) the Communist movement acts as a single whole.[73]

The British analysts, in a curious way, mingled intense dislike with considerable respect for this new adversary:

The appeal of Communism is based on an all-embracing idealogy [sic], to which Communists adhere with religious fervour, and on the promise of a better world free from exploitation and war. The Communist Parties are led by nuclei of able, experienced and devoted men, capable of directing mass movements, and firm in the belief that they are assisting in an inexorable historical process.

Since the Russian Revolution, the Communist movement has been dominated by the prestige and influence of the Russian Communists. The Soviet Union is by far the most powerful element in the Communist movement, and its defence, therefore, is an essential point in all Communist policy.[74]

This was converted directly into an internal threat directed, as it were, from the same source as controlled the Red Army.

Communist Parties accept willingly and loyally the obligations involved in the Soviet Union. In general they lend themselves readily to use as instruments of Soviet policy, if necessary at the expense of their own 'bourgeois' Governments . . . The membership of the Communist Parties provides a ready field of recruitment for agents and informants prepared to serve the Soviet Union, and officials of Soviet Missions have made considerable use of Communist Party members for espionage and subversive political activities.[75]

The fact that until the suppression of the Hungarian uprising by Khrushchev's tanks in the autumn of 1956, the Communist Party of Great Britain sustained a capacity to retain the loyalty of some of the most gifted and charming men and women of high intelligence (and a few thereafter), along with its influence within certain trade unions, gave the CPGB the capacity politically to punch far above its numerical weight, as the British intelligence community plainly appreciated.

Though but a small proportion of the membership could ever be described as agents of the Soviet Union in the intelligence sense, it would be intriguing to know if MI5 was aware of the pitch employed by Harry Pollitt, General Secretary of the CPGB, who would instruct young Communist undergraduates at Cambridge University during the last years of World War II to forget about selling the *Daily Worker* on street corners or the pursuit of lesser jobs out of a sense of solidarity with the proletariat. The Party required them to get Firsts and to secure high positions in the state.[76] The British Security Service may well have been apprised of the Pollitt line as it is quite plain that it had substantial sections of the Party wired up for sound throughout the Cold War (as we shall see in Chapter 3 on the assessment and handling of the internal 'threat'). As late as the start of the twenty-first century, a decade after its 1991 Congress voted to dissolve the CPGB after seventy-one years of political life and to reconstitute itself as the Democratic Left,[77] more than one MI5 officer could be heard to claim that (a) the British Security Service 'had been virtually running the CPGB at the end', and (b) to bemoan how much the pensions of its former agents within the CPGB were absorbing from current budgets![78]

Place the big 'Russia's Strategic Interests and Intentions' assessment of March 1946 alongside 'The Spread of Communism . . .' paper of September that year and you can see the firming up of the British intelligence analysis of this extraordinary threat. Events in Eastern Europe in 1947 and the Berlin Crisis of 1948 set this picture firm and hard for nearly ten years and, in some ways, until the Soviet superpower 'died in the saddle' in 1989–91.

The August 1947 JIC assessment of 'Soviet Interests, Intentions and Capabilities' still stressed the 'preoccupation with security' of the Russian leadership and that it was

unlikely . . . before 1955–60 [that] the Soviet Union will be capable of supporting her armed forces entirely from natural resources and industrial potential under her own control, in any major war, except one of very short duration. Nevertheless, if Russia wished to go to war, economic considerations would not in themselves be enough to prevent her from doing so, in the event of her feeling confident of rapid victory.[79]

And here one found *the* spectre haunting early postwar Western Europe in the '175 divisions' Stalin was thought to have at his command. 'The very scanty evidence at our disposal,' the JIC told its customers in August 1947, just a month after the Soviet Foreign Minister, Vyacheslav Molotov, led the Russian and satellite delegations out of the Marshall Plan discussions in Paris marking the start of the 'high cold war'[80] and a protracted period of peril and confrontation,

indicates that in the event of mobilisation, this total of 175 divisions could be approximately doubled in 30 days, although the proportion of new armoured and mechanised formations is likely to be low owing to limitations of tank production and specialists ... A vast programme of re-organisation and re-equipment is in progress throughout the Soviet Army with the object of bringing a large proportion of its divisions up to Western standards ... [81]

Half-a-mile from the secret world of the JIC, in Transport House a young Denis Healey, then in charge of Labour's International Department, concluded that 'All that the Red Army needed in order to reach the North Sea was boots.'[82]

The JIC agreed, though without the aid of such graphic images to chill the bones of their readers:

The Soviet land forces, with their close support aircraft, are sufficiently strong at the present time, to achieve rapid and far-reaching successes against any likely combination of opposing land forces. The strategic air situation, however, remains adverse to the Soviet Union, in that she has no satisfactory answer either to atomic weapons or to opposing strategic bomber forces. She cannot thus count, as yet, upon a reasonable degree of immunity for her centres of population and industry from serious air attack. Her future readiness to embark upon a major war is likely, therefore, to be conditioned by considerations of her own air power in relation to that of probable opponents.[83]

The nuclear factor was central throughout the Cold War.* Likely, and later, actual Soviet nuclear capabilities were a continual 'Priority I' target for British intelligence from the later 1940s on[84] and represented a considerable failure in forecasting terms, as we shall see in a moment when we examine the JIC's record as Whitehall's primary early-warning mechanism.

---

* We shall examine the importance of being nuclear to Labour and Conservative governments alike from Mr Attlee onwards in Chapter 2.

But first, another element of the big JIC assessment of the summer of 1947 needs to be highlighted. Though the late 1940s JIC had no knowledge of Stalin's devouring of purloined Whitehall documents and fitting of them into his mental picture of aggressive and menacing Western powers, its analysts were aware of the honoured place of the British democratic socialist tradition in the Soviet leader's demonology predicting that

... the Soviet Government will continue their present flow of propaganda designed to set world opinion against imperialist and capitalist governments in general, and against His Majesty's and the United States Government in particular. It should be emphasised that Soviet propagandists continue to represent this country as imperialist and capitalist, despite its Labour Government. In fact the Soviet leaders are especially hostile to 'reformist socialism' which they regard as a dangerous competitor for working-class support in many countries.[85]

No trace here of any of the nonsense which later affected a small part of the British intelligence community, who believed that Labour was soft on Communism and that Harold Wilson was a long-term Communist agent.[86]

A pronounced feature of the JIC's large surveys of Soviet intentions and capabilities was their area-by-area, often country-by-country, examination of Soviet influence and the likely location of potential hot spots. How well did Whitehall's chief window on the Cold War world perform as a predictor of trouble in the early years of the great confrontation? The short answer is, not very. As Alex Craig, the first scholar to attempt a performance assessment of the early Cold War JIC, has written of the committee:

Most importantly, it failed to predict either the Berlin Blockade or the outbreak of the Korean War. [Scholars] have emphasised the extent of JIC culpability for the failure to predict the Soviet atomic test [in August 1949].[87] However, what has not been fully recognised by historians is that these were essentially failures in intelligence *collection* rather than analysis. They resulted from the inevitable post-war famine of good intelligence from deep inside a secretive Soviet Union, rather than from JIC mistakes. The JIC never attempted to conceal from policy-makers gaps in their knowledge and reports frequently contained caveats to indicate their limited information about particular subjects, especially about the Russian atomic and biological weapons programme.[88]

The familiar secrets/mysteries dilemma is at work here as well as a sheer shortage of hard facts.

Berlin was and remained a particular problem. There was nothing secret about the centrality of Germany to the Cold War. In its August 1947 grand-sweep appraisal, the JIC showed itself well aware in macro terms of what a united *and* Communist Germany would mean to the Soviet Union and the East/West balance. On a micro level, British analysts knew that 'the Russians have been training ex-German officers and N.C.Os. with a view to their filling important posts in the future administration of Germany, both in their own Zone and eventually in the Western Zones'.[89]

But whether and when the Russians would move against the isolated Western sectors in Berlin, 100 miles inside the Soviet Zone, was very difficult to divine. The fusing of the full-scale Anglo-American Western Zones and the issue of a new currency for their use, in the teeth of Russian opposition in June 1948, was a certainty in terms of tension-raising. But a military move to sever the road, rail and canal ties could be – and was – effected from a standing start. No revealing build-up of troops was necessary.

As General Sir Brian Robertson, the Military Governor and Commander-in-Chief of the British Armed Forces in Germany, acknowledged at a Chiefs of Staff Committee meeting in the first weeks of the Berlin crisis, 'our intelligence of Russian military movements in the Eastern Zone of Germany was reasonably good', adding that '[h]e could see no sign of any preparations that might indicate that Russia was preparing for war'.[90] This was before special British air reconnaissance operations were mounted to increase surveillance around Berlin from September 1948.[91] Alex Craig is right to describe the Berlin blockade as one of those crises where the JIC was able to exert 'a calming influence on policy-makers'[92] by stressing the unlikelihood of its being the foreplay to World War III. The Berlin experience gave a considerable stimulus to civil defence and war planning in London and to a sharpening-up of the early-warning indicators and processes. At the weekly JIC meetings 'a regular item entitled "Russian Preparedness for War" was added to the agenda', and a personal copy was sent to the Foreign Secretary, Ernest Bevin.[93] As we have seen, virtually throughout the 1950s this was the first line of its weekly 'Red Book', which replaced this particular agenda item. Even during the second Berlin Crisis in the late 1950s, by which time the indicator process was highly developed and Berlin contingency planning immensely elaborate, the Chiefs' joint planners needed to remind their masters that 'The opportunities for physical obstruction are so great that the Soviets/GDR [German Democratic Republic] do not need to use force, and may not do so.'[94]

The failure to predict the invasion of South Korea by Communist forces from the North in the middle of the night on 25 June 1950 cannot be so easily explained away. In this instance, however, it was largely an American one. The secret 1948 UKUSA Agreement had divided up the world between the two countries for eavesdropping purposes. The Korean peninsula was an American target. Christopher Andrew, reflecting on the chaotic procedures which operated in this branch of US intelligence until the National Security Agency was created in November 1952 (and in which immense resources were invested chiefly in response to the inquest into the failure of June 1950[95]), has written that 'largely as a result of the lack of co-ordination, North Korea did not become a priority SIGINT target until after it had attacked the South'.[96] And as Richard Aldrich has pointed out, the North Koreans were good at signals security. The Russians had trained them well. Very little of value was there for the eavesdropping though in terms of what little there was, Western intelligence was 'not well disposed to intercept it'.[97]

Top-flight SIGINT, however, was not the only way to gauge a military build-up, and this one was huge, with some 90,000 troops involved.[98] The CIA station in Seoul had a few agents in the North who reported 'on increased troop movements and armoured build-ups. This had not led to a direct prediction of the invasion. But it had allowed the CIA to circulate warnings on 20 June about North Korean mobilization to members of President Truman's Cabinet . . .'[99]

Tom Dibble has shown how dependent British intelligence remained on the United States throughout the Korean War for its raw material on the conflict.[100] But its assessments of the significance of the shock of Korea were very much its own. In the weeks following the invasion, as South Korean, American, British and other United Nations forces struggled to retain a toehold on the peninsula, the JIC, 'in the light of recent developments', prepared a report for pooling at US/UK/Canada meetings on 'The Likelihood of War with the Soviet Union and the Date by which the Soviet Leaders might be prepared to risk it'.[101] The tone is still generally one of reassurance but a distinctly anxious note is now audible too:

We do not know whether the Soviet Leaders believe that, provided the Soviet Union is strong enough to deter capitalist aggression, world Communism under Soviet hegemony can in the long run be achieved without the Soviet Union becoming involved in a major war with the non-Communist world, but it is reasonable to conclude that they wish to achieve their aims this way.

The shock of 25 June 1950 along the 38th Parallel which divided the two Koreas is reflected directly in the JIC's picture presented to Whitehall and to the UK's foremost intelligence allies:

The Soviet Leaders will, however, continue to press their plans for the extension of Communist influence by political, economic and ideological warfare, and by subversion and civil war.

In a further reference to the Korean case, the JIC warned about the possibility, despite the UN's resistance to the North Korean advance, that the Soviet leadership might once again and elsewhere be tempted 'to press home the advantage of local military superiority even at the risk, which they may underestimate, of provoking armed Western counter-action, always provided that the Soviet armed forces are not directly engaged and that military operations can be localised'.[102]

It was during this particularly risky phase of the East/West conflict (what might be called the perilously high Cold War between the outbreak of the Korean War in June 1950 and the death of Stalin in March 1953) that the more thoughtful members of the British intelligence community became especially anxious about their American counterparts in exactly this area – the possible overreaction to Soviet provocation. Richard Aldrich has discovered that while the Whitehall analysts tried to make sense of what Korea meant in the summer of 1950, one of the figures around the JIC table went so far as to warn those on the inner loop only a year after of the threat the *United States* posed to world peace.

Vice-Admiral Eric Longley-Cook, Director of Naval Intelligence, felt moved in his last weeks of service to prepare a 'Where are we going?' think-piece which eventually found its way to Attlee and, on the demise of the Labour Government in October 1951, to Churchill. His memo reflected the consistent JIC view (despite that surge of concern the previous summer) that the Russians would not pursue their objectives through 'a general military offensive ("Total War")' but through 'economic and psychological' pressure directed against the non-Communist world. From his 'conversations with many responsible and influential Americans who are obviously convinced that war with Russia is inevitable', Longley-Cook had reached the alarming conclusion that they had fixed a date for such a war in their minds 'for mid or late 1952', that it was 'doubtful whether, in a year's time, the US will be able to control the Frankenstein monster which they are creating'. There was 'a definite danger of the USA becoming involved in a preventive war against Russia, however firmly their NATO allies object'.

What is especially interesting about Longley-Cook's summer 1951 reflections is the extent to which he highlights the differences between British and American intelligence assessments of the Soviet threat. He had been alarmed during the combined US/UK intelligence conference in Washington in October 1950 by the degree to which the American equivalent of the JIC produced assessments that 'tend to fit in with the prejudged conclusion that a shooting war with the Soviet Union at some time is inevitable ... Although the Americans were eventually persuaded to endorse a combined appreciation of the Soviet threat, based on reason and factual intelligence, they were quick to alter it to fit their own preconceived ideas as soon as the London team had returned to this country.'

Longley-Cook's paper, clearly reflecting the big JIC threat assessments of the late 1940s (he actually cites JIC (48) 9 (o) of July 1948), concentrates on why the London analysts interpreted the same evidence so differently from their opposite numbers in Washington. Certainly the Soviet leaders had decided 'to retain their war machine at great strength even after the defeat of Germany and Japan'.

As a constant threat, the Soviet war machine plays an important part, but, in considering the size of the Soviet Army, it should be remembered that Russia has always required a very large standing army for the garrisoning of her very long frontiers. It is not primarily intended for offensive purposes, and it should not be allowed to drive the Western powers into attempting an exact balance of military power.

Longley-Cook saw the Americans as interpreting the Soviet war machine as a direct threat to the USA and that their policy was 'based on false reasoning, and on intelligence which it shaped to fit a preconceived idea', and 'a nearly successful attempt at a further Communist advance in the Far East (Korea) brought about the decision of the United States to rearm on a scale never before known in peace time'.

British intelligence, by contrast, knew that war could come through miscalculation and/or each side misinterpreting the other's intentions. But this was unlikely, meaning that the 'struggle between the Western Democracies and the Soviet Block is going to be a very long-term affair' that could not be solved by 'Total War'. This was why, since the big July 1948 assessment of the Soviet leadership's intentions, 'We have invariably stated our opinion that their long term aim is to achieve world domination by all means short of war. But we have at the same time advised that they might be frightened into using their immense army if they felt their last chance of survival had come in the face of the rapid build up of US forces and/or German rearmament on a very big scale.'[103]

At the heart of Longley-Cook's warning were not just the purposes of the immense Red Army but the atomic dilemma too. In the days following the invasion of South Korea, he and his colleagues had based their continuing assumption that Stalin's people would not risk a major war

[s]o long as they estimate that the United States have [sic] a commanding superiority in atomic weapons and that their air defences are unable to prevent the incalculable damage which the highly centralised Soviet system might expect to suffer from atomic warfare, it is not likely that the Soviet Leaders would wish to become involved in a world war.[104]

A year later Longley-Cook's reading of the American mind saw many as arguing that ' "we have the bomb; let us use it now while the balance is in our favour. Since war with Russia is inevitable, let's get it over with now" '[105] (a truly alarming counterpoint to Stalin's misreading of the UK documents purloined for him by Philby and the others).

Intriguingly, Churchill himself was prone to take this view in his gloomier moments. In the summer of 1954 he prepared a fascinating note on the thoughts he wished to present to Cabinet as part of his case for going all out to bring the Soviet Union and the United States together at a summit meeting. He was greatly worried by 'the argument which must be present in many American minds' which he simulated thus:

We alone have for the next two or perhaps three years sure and overwhelming superiority in attack, and a substantive measure of immunity in defence. Merely to dawdle means potential equality of ruin. Ought we not for the immediate safety of our own American people and the incidental rescue of the Free World to bring matters to a head by a 'show-down' leading up to an ultimatum accompanied by an Alert?[106]

Such thoughts continued to plague Churchill in retirement. That accomplished diarist James Lees-Milne penned a particularly vivid entry in September 1957 on a drinks party at Lord Beaverbrook's villa in the South of France, where the Churchills were staying when the shadow of the bomb briefly eclipsed the sunshine:

Sir Winston sitting slumped in an armchair in the middle of the room to whom we talked in turns. A [Alvide, Lees-Milne's wife] told him how much she was impressed by Neville Shute's book On the Beach[107] [about the last survivors of a global nuclear war set in the future – 1961 – in the last days of their lives in and around Melbourne, Australia], which he too had read. He said he was sending it to Khrushchev. She asked would he not also send it to Eisenhower? Sir W.'s retort: 'It would be a waste of money. He is so muddle-headed now' ... He said to Montague Browne [his Private Secretary]: 'I think the earth will soon be destroyed ... And if I were the Almighty I would not recreate it in case they destroyed him too next time.'[108]

Whether the old warrior did or did not send a copy of On the Beach to the Kremlin for the attention of Khrushchev is not known.[109]

The bomb suffused *all* Cold War thinking for the duration of the conflict. Nothing, apart from warnings of imminent attack, surpassed the nuclear weapons question in terms of Cold War intelligence priorities and the intelligence world carried special scars on matters nuclear. Its failure to predict how soon the Soviet Union would cross the nuclear weapons threshold was probably the greatest single failing of Western intelligence in the early Cold War period and explains the preventive-war psychosis which so exercised Longley-Cook and Churchill. For so much rested on Western nuclear superiority that any misreading of Soviet capabilities was bound to fuel the belief that such an advantage could be very short-lived.

From the outset, in the big mid- to late 1940s assessments of the Soviet threat, the United States' monopoly of atomic weapons was seen as trumping Stalin's huge conventional weapons superiority. The JIC's March 1946 paper did not entirely discount the possibility that the Soviet leadership might seek to secure its objectives 'by bluff', but they would estimate carefully the margin of risk involved:

Russia must also realise that America would be unlikely to stand aloof from a major war and that it might, therefore, be one of long duration. She is likely to be deterred by the existence of the atomic bomb.[110]

Central to every subsequent analysis of the big strategic picture, until the Soviet atomic test of August 1949 shook the Russia-watchers rigid, was the forecast of when the Soviet Union would bust America's monopoly.

The March 1946 assessment 'tentatively estimated that the USSR will not have atomic weapons before the early 1950s, and even if new sources of raw materials which are at present necessary be found, that the numbers of atomic weapons possessed by the USSR will not be significant until about 1955–60'.[111] The JIC, however, disagreed with 'American economic experts' who reckoned Russia's postwar economic plans meant that insufficient resources would be available for the development of atomic energy and the creation of a bomb plant: 'In our view . . . it would be dangerous to assume that the Soviet Union cannot develop the economic resources necessary for the building up of atomic bomb production plant and at the same time carry through their planned programme of reconstruction and development.'[112] They were right. On Stalin's behalf, his ghastly secret policeman Lavrenti Beria ensured, from the end of August 1945, that the bomb programme had overwhelming priority, tripling the science budget and building what became in 1948 Arzamas-16, a secret nuclear weapons city some 250 miles east of Moscow, near Sarov.[113]

By the time of their August 1947 *tour d'horizon*, the JIC reckoned that two factors were 'probably' hampering the Soviets' nuclear effort: the 'difficult industrial techniques' required and a 'serious shortage of uranium', which was likely to continue until methods were found of extracting the necessary material from low-grade ores or high-grade ore was discovered within the territory Russia controlled. Their latest estimate was that by January 1952, 'the Soviet Union's stock of bombs is unlikely to exceed 5 though it may possibly reach 25'.[114]

The summer assessment of 1948, just under a year before the first Soviet atomic test in Kazakhstan, saw the JIC reprising for its customers the industrial/uranium refinement problems and concluding that

Existing estimates of the date when the Russians began their programme and of their ability to overcome the technological difficulties involved suggest that they may possibly produce their first atomic bomb by January 1951 and that their stockpile of bombs in January 1953 may be of the order of 6 to 22.

Here a touch of Western technological hubris distorted the estimate still further: 'These figures, however, are the maximum possible based on the assumption that the Russian effort will progress as rapidly as the American and British projects have done. Allowances for the probably slower progress of the Russian effort will almost certainly retard the first bomb by some three years,'[115] i.e. until early 1954.

So, when debris from the 29 August test at Semipalatinsk-21 was picked up after attaching itself to the filters of a US Air Force B-29 on a weather mission over the North Pacific on 3 September 1949, what Lorna Arnold has described as the 'rude shock'[116] both in London and Washington intelligence circles was genuine and profound, as it was to the world generally when President Truman broke the news on 23 September. Why had Igor Kurchatov's team and Soviet industrial capacity been so underestimated? For several years an explanation – alarming and consoling in equal measure – was available. From early

March 1950, when the British physicist Klaus Fuchs, who had worked on the Manhattan Project during World War II and the British nuclear programme thereafter, was revealed as a spy, the explanation seemed as obvious as Chapman Pincher in the *Daily Express* made it appear:

In 90 minutes at the Old Bailey yesterday, a riddle was solved: How did Russia make the atomic bomb so quickly? Dr Klaus Emil Julius Fuchs, confidant and leading member of Britain's atom team, who began a 14-year jail sentence last night, gave them the know-how.[117]

In subsequent years, when the scale of Stalin's human intelligence on the American and British bomb programme became apparent (all-in-all a 'spectacular' element in a huge Soviet effort directed at scientific and technical intelligence,[118] which on the bomb alone left thousands of pages of reports awaiting evaluation in Moscow as World War II ended[119]), Pincher's conclusion was fortified. When interrogated by MI5, Fuchs reckoned that what he had passed to his GRU controller, Ursula Beurton,[120] had accelerated Stalin's bomb 'by one year at least'.[121]

Such a cornucopia of information must indeed have helped enormously, not least by preventing Kurchatov's laboratories from pursuing scientific and technological culs-de-sac. With the ending of the Cold War, a row erupted between the veterans of the 1940s Soviet intelligence and atomic communities – a debate which has been monitored by the official historian of the British H-bomb, Lorna Arnold. Writing in 2001, Mrs Arnold described this as a 'war of words' because

[s]ome of the scientists thought that self-justifying members of the secret services were spreading 'myths and legends,' exaggerating the part played by the intelligence community. On the other hand it was argued that the scientists wanted to minimise the intelligence contribution because it seemed to detract from the brilliance and originality of their own achievements . . .[122]

It may be, as Mrs Arnold suggests, that because the source of intelligence knowledge was kept so tight, scientists outside the loop had not appreciated that some of the most valuable insights promulgated by those within it had been shaped by material purloined by Stalin's atomic friends in the West.

Either way, the creation of the atomic device which went up in the Kazakhstan steppe in 1949 was a huge scientific and industrial achievement. It does seem from recent scholarship that British intelligence was right to see the uranium-processing question as a key factor in the programme's timing. Fuchs himself, as scholars discovered when the transcript of his scientific interrogation in January 1950 was declassified in 2001, expressed himself as 'extremely surprised that the Russian explosion had taken place so soon as he had been convinced that the information he had given could not have been applied so quickly and that the Russians would not have the engineering, design and construction facilities that would be needed to build large production plants in such a short time'.[123] It is plain from the inquest carried out by Eric Welsh, the Naval Intelligence commander who ran the UK's atomic intelligence capacity, that the lack of hard information from human or technical sources meant that Whitehall had made 'a very poor stab of it in the field of Atomic Energy Intelligence. Long distance detection techniques supply History *not* News. Nothing is as stale as yesterday's newspaper. What the JIC want and what the JIC demand is preknowledge of what are the enemies' intentions for tomorrow.'[124]

To be fair to the JIC pre-August 1949, not only did it have scanty information on the Soviet bomb programme from any source, but the immense scale of the KGB and GRU's penetration of the American and British projects had still to be fully appreciated. It took a while for technological hubris to dissipate and the appreciation to harden that a second- to third-world domestic consumer society can coexist with a first-world military economy.

The view of the potential enemy had set hard by the early 1950s, and with it the belief of British intelligence that direct military conflict – World War III – was highly unlikely in large part because of the unarguably catastrophic consequences all round of a nuclear exchange (especially once both sides had become fully fledged *thermo*nuclear adversaries). Much effort was expended, however, on how war might come by inadvertence or miscalculation. Intriguingly, the early 1950s JIC, during the period of what I have termed the high Cold War, thought that those in Washington whose instincts told them World War III had to be fought before the adversary became even more intimidating had their counterparts in Moscow.

In a February 1951 appraisal for its readers on the 'Likelihood of

Total War with the Soviet Union up to the End of 1954', the committee declared:

... we cannot exclude the possibility that the Soviet leaders may consider the immense scale of American rearmament [stimulated by the surge of anxiety following the Korean War] and the rearmament of Western Germany to be a direct threat to the security of the Soviet Union and may decide that their best course is to start a total war before Western rearmament becomes effective. Such a war might be 'preventive' in the strict sense, that is, intended to forestall a Western attack which they genuinely believed to be inevitable; or, alternatively, it might be undertaken because they feared that once Western rearmament became effective, further Communist expansion would be impossible; or for a combination of both reasons.[125]

The JIC saw a malign fusion of timing on the part of the pre-emptive schools of thought within the two superpowers: 'The period of greatest danger appears to be about the end of 1952 when American and West German rearmament cannot yet have become fully effective and by which time the Soviet Union will have in part made good some of its major deficiencies and will have accumulated a stock of atomic bombs.'[126] Despite this nightmare possibility of war for fear of war, the JIC, true to form, reassured its customers that 'Provided the Western Powers can combine resolution with restraint' – i.e. sensible if illusion-free containment – 'there should be no total war during the next four years.'[127]

It took the huge change in destructive power from atomic weapons to hydrogen bombs which by the end of 1954 both superpowers had completed[128] (and the British had decided to take as soon as possible, as we shall see in Chapter 2) effectively to remove from the minds of British intelligence the possibility of deliberate, pre-emptive strikes. In mid-1955 the JIC reckoned that the Soviets' nuclear stockpile was already sufficient 'to cause very major damage to the UK' and to parts of the USA; that the fabled 175 divisions were now well trained, well equipped, well led and in a condition of high morale; that the Soviet Navy was now comparable in size to NATO's though still lacking aircraft carriers. Nevertheless, '[t]he probability is that the present [post-Stalin] Soviet leaders have realised the full implications of nuclear war and have come to the conclusion that general war at present would involve mutual annihilation'.[129]

The JIC had been tasked in 1954 to produce an estimate of the likely H-bomb assault on the UK in such a general war and, strongly influenced by its report on this theme of January 1955, Whitehall's home defence planners rethought fundamentally previous calculations of the prospects for national survival.* And for all the ghastly reassurance the prospect of mutual annihilation might provide (not least by banishing what had been seen in late 1952 as the possibility of resolving the Cold War through pre-emptive strike) the potential for mistakes and misperceptions continued to haunt the JIC assessments, including that of September 1955:

It is unlikely that the Soviet leaders think that the Western Powers will launch a premeditated attack on the Soviet Union. They may think, however, that there is a danger of war breaking out as a result of miscalculation . . .[130]

Just over a year later, the twin crises of Suez and Hungary suggested that a combination of destabilizing events and the rise in global tension that ensued might tip the balance of possibility towards global war. The JIC expressed this with stark clarity in a special assessment amid the ruins of the Hungarian Uprising and the Suez Affair. In mid-December 1956 they informed their customers that

The present world tension comes from civil disturbances and/or war in two areas. The events leading up to the warfare in the two areas were unrelated but the trouble came to a head more or less simultaneously; this has had the effect of heightening the tension and hardening relations between the West and the Middle East have given rise to instability in both areas, which will certainly last for several months and which could last much longer. While this instability exists the incidence of events causing international friction is likely to be greater than it was before last October, and the possibilities of one side taking action, the effects of which might be other than they had expected, will be greater.[131]

Hungary had demonstrated

the view we have always held that the Soviet leaders would go to almost any lengths to retain their hold on the Satellites . . . Any action by the West to

* As we shall see in Chapter 4.

assist a Satellite to free itself from Soviet domination would be likely to result in violent Soviet reaction, and, through a confused series of events, including threats and counter threats made under mounting nervous pressure, could lead up to a global war.

So, according to JIC doctrine, there would be a grave risk in any notion of a liberation crusade if future Hungarys erupted. 'Unless the political situation changes in some completely unexpected fashion (such as through the emergence of more aggressive Soviet leaders)', NATO and the doctrine of containment, whereby 'the West maintains its strength and cohesion and continues to act with restraint', should together hold the peace. The JIC continued to believe in the aftermath of the accumulated traumas of October–November 1956 in the Middle East and Mitteleuropa 'that the Soviet leaders do not want war, but . . . the chances of global war arising through a chain of circumstances and miscalculations have somewhat increased'.[132]

When we examine the simulations and scenarios which underpinned the actual, Whitehall, transition-to-war exercise ('Operation IN-VALUABLE'),* we will see that it was just such a shift to a hard-line leadership in Moscow that triggered the events which culminated in the simulation of the path to World War III with which the exercise finished. By coincidence, though long planned, 'INVALUABLE' was exercised in the aftermath of the next Hungary – the Soviet suppression of the Prague Spring in August 1968.

What of the moment when nervous pressure mounted to greater heights than at any previous or subsequent stage in the Cold War – the Cuban Missile Crisis of October 1962? Alban Webb's researches have shown how, as early as 1957, the JIC envisaged the possibility of a Cuban-style crisis. The committee's forecasters thought the Soviet Union might 'be prepared in extreme cases to send "volunteer" forma-tions' to a sympathetic country outside the bloc and the Russians 'might well feel their policies and prestige would suffer a serious blow if they failed to respond to a request for help . . . by making nuclear weapons available to . . . [a] . . . non-Communist Power'.[133] As Webb noted, the JIC lost sight of the possibility of Russia overreaching in

---

* See Chapter 4.

this fashion, leading to escalation, confrontation and possible global war and did not return to it even after Castro's seizure of power in Cuba in 1959. The focus of the JIC's collective eyes tended to be absorbed by the regular hot spots.

By the early weeks of 1962, when the JIC took a forward look at 'The Likelihood of War with the Soviet Union up to 1966', British intelligence was case-hardened by its constant fixations with the chance of war erupting over Berlin (which had only recently begun to emerge, though not yet fully, from the protracted crisis of 1958–61 when Khrushchev presented the Western powers with a series of deadlines for a conference to resolve all difficulties associated with that city's four-power occupation) and through a possibility of toxic combinations in the Middle East. Despite the recent perils of the Berlin confrontation (armed American and Russian tanks facing each other, feet apart, at Checkpoint Charlie is the image, second only to the Berlin Wall itself, which is scored most deeply into the historical memory[134]), the JIC continued to believe the stakes were vastly too high for either side to contemplate deliberate and major war.

The immense latent power of each other's nuclear arsenals, and their state of readiness, had, by this stage, added new levels to old anxieties. It was the danger of 'accident and miscalculation' which now represented the great preoccupation of British intelligence. In that short hiatus in early and mid-1962 between the Berlin and Cuban crises, the JIC concluded that

Even when there is no particular political tension each side now has a proportion of its nuclear strike forces constantly at immediate alert. There must always be a risk, however remote that by pure mechanical or electrical accident one of the missiles might be launched; or that through misunderstanding one might be launched by human agency without this being the intention of the Government concerned; or that one side might interpret the evidence of its early warning devices to mean that an attack had been launched by the other when in fact this was not so. We believe that the Soviet leaders are as aware as the West of the possibility of such accidents and take equally elaborate precautions to prevent them.[135]

Setting aside the notions of war-by-accident, the JIC, on the assumption 'that the Soviet leaders act rationally', saw the possibility of war-through-miscalculation erupting due to the lighting of three possible fuses:

(a) the Soviet Union or the West in some critical or tense situation were to make a false appreciation of what was considered by the other side to be intolerable; or

(b) the Soviet Union or the West were to believe wrongly that the other had weakened in its determination to use nuclear weapons if pressed too far; or

(c) either side were to fail accurately to foresee the consequences of the policies being pursued by a third party with which it was associated.[136]

Elements of each of these were bound up in the Cuban crisis seven months later, from the moment when US reconnaissance U2 flights suggested that new missile sites under construction in Cuba could be for something bigger and nastier than air-defence weapons.[137]

Interestingly enough, the JIC had included Cuba as an example in its explanatory paragraph on third-party triggers of a war-through-miscalculation. Crises involving third countries created

a particular risk that one side might fail accurately to recognise that the situation was becoming one which the other side would consider intolerable. The chances of such dangerous situations arising in future will be increased if recent Soviet expressions of support for 'national liberation wars' mean a greater willingness to intervene in such disputes. By this term Soviet leaders apparently mean risings against Western colonial powers (eg, Algeria) or rebellion against 'reactionary' pro-Western regimes (eg Castro's revolt). They have described such hostilities as 'just' and 'inevitable' and have said that it is the duty of the Soviet Union to support them, though they have not made clear the nature and extent of this support.[138]

The committee concluded that if 'general nuclear war arose through miscalculation it would probably be preceded by a period of limited hostilities, however short'.[139]

As the Cuban crisis moved into its acute phase on 22 October 1962, when sixteen medium-range ballistic missile sites 'appeared to be operational' to US intelligence,[140] the intolerability of Khrushchev's move on Castro's terrain became obvious to the United States. In the words of a JIC assessment of 26 October, it was apparent that, if nuclear warheads were fitted to them, 'the overall Soviet initial launch capability against the US will have increased significantly to the end of 1962'.[141] Dr Len Scott has emphasized how the routine flight off Alaska of a CIA reconnaissance U2 on 27 October 1962 went wrong when the plane drifted into Siberian airspace causing Soviet Migs to be scrambled to shoot it down and US F-102s sent up to protect it. Mercifully the F-102s reached the spy plane first and escorted it back safely. If they had not, with the level of tension prevailing, who knows what would have happened if the Soviets had treated this as the last reconnaissance flight before a pre-emptive American strike against Russia.[142]

As the JIC compiled its private inquest into Cuba[143] and the war planners began their post-Cuba review of War Book and readiness procedures*, Government ministers admitted in Parliament that 'we were very near the edge'[144] during the crisis that almost came out of nowhere. As an old man, Macmillan suffered recurrent nightmares of Cuba having gone wrong.[145]

British intelligence, however, true to form, was a soother rather than an inflamer of ministerial and military minds during the Cuban Missile Crisis. One of the days of greatest tension, Saturday 27 October 1962, when Macmillan authorized the V-bombers to be placed on Alert Condition 3 (i.e. fifteen minutes' readiness at the end of their Lincolnshire runways),[146] the JIC produced an assessment of 'Possible Soviet Responses to a US Decision to Bomb or Invade Cuba' calculated to defuse any notions that East and West were on an irreversible march to and over the brink. The report could well have reinforced Macmillan's desire to avoid any provocative moves such as ordering the V-bombers to their dispersed airfields or any other overt preparations for war.[147]

The picture the JIC presented was of a Russian leader, Khrushchev, behaving in a 'relatively moderate' fashion over the five days since President Kennedy had gone on television to announce the presence of Soviet missile sites on Cuba and to tell the world that this shift in the balance of power could not be tolerated by the United States. The turning back of their missile-carrying freighters had already amounted

---

* Which we will examine in Chapter 4.

to 'a considerable climbdown and to a loss of face'. It could well be that the Soviet Union's placing of a new offensive capability on Cuba in the first place might have been prompted by its leadership's awareness 'of an overall strategic inferiority vis-à-vis the US'.[148] They did not see Khrushchev's response to a US attack on Cuba as the much planned for snuffing out of the Western position in Berlin 'in view of the clear warning from the US that this would bring about a full confrontation. Indeed, central to Soviet thinking in deciding upon their reply will be their fear of doing anything that might escalate into general nuclear war.'[149]

According to the JIC, the Russians' 'most likely' armed response to a US move against Cuba 'will be a tit-for-tat as nearly parallel as possible to the US action. It seems unlikely, therefore, that they will attack directly either US territory or the territory of the NATO powers. The closest parallel would appear to be a US base in some third country or an attack on some major US naval vessel.'[150] Here, as at so many other moments after 1945, one sees the antithesis of any crude portrayals of British intelligence as the captive of inflamed cold warriors. The files, taken together, do justify the overall conclusion of their earliest appraiser, Dr Alex Craig, that 'There was . . . no attempt to demonise the Soviet Union in JIC analysis.'[151] Though well aware of their failure to *predict* many of the great Cold War episodes except, at best, in terms of general possibility, Craig none the less was right to emphasize 'the broad success of JIC threat assessment' during the early and middle Cold War years: it was neither 'alarmist', nor did it 'underestimate the scale of the Soviet threat'.[152]

Much of the inflamed view of British intelligence as a force for reaction comes from the notion of the character and political thinking of some secret service figures such as George Kennedy Young, who reached the number two position in MI6,[153] or Peter Wright, still the most notorious counterintelligence officer MI5 has ever produced.[154] There is something in this unnerving portrait. A very accomplished Whitehall figure, with long association with the secret world, has said of some parts of the 1950s and 1960s Secret Intelligence Service, 'they were very right wing' (he had particularly in mind a section called Special Political Action which tried to influence the press).[155]

Imagery is a problem for any treatment of the Queen's secret servants. Quite apart from our own rich and widely read spy literature and the reach and grip of the Bond films on the global imagination, other intelligence professionals have a certain idea of the British secret services. I have heard a senior figure in the secret world of an allied country declare, once the senior intelligence operators of East and West began to pool experience in the early 1990s, that MI6 was the service the Russians regarded as their toughest and worthiest opponent.[156] Ten years after the end of the Cold War, the head of a secret service in a former Soviet bloc country talked to me of his huge admiration for 'the British intelligence services, with their great traditions, which have been on the winning side in the *three* wars of the twentieth century'.[157] A former chief of SIS once explained to me what a huge asset such impressions remain. Such is the image of the service around the world that when one of his officers, after a long and careful cultivation of a potential agent, finally revealed himself or herself and made the pass, the object of their attention would often 'virtually stand-to-attention, such was the honour'.[158]

There is one former member of his service who, I think, I would place alongside the best of the JIC's analysts in terms of balance and restraint. He was the MI6 officer, operating undercover in the Moscow Embassy in the autumn of 1962, responsible for running the most important human agent the West possessed throughout the Cold War, Colonel Oleg Penkovsky. Veterans of those days still describe Penkovsky in terms of pure gold and stress that 'we had him at the crucial time'[159] of hyper-anxiety about nuclear weapons and the possibility of war as a bolt-from-the-blue. Penkovsky had been arrested by the Soviet authorities on 22 October 1962 at the moment the world became aware of the possible linkage between Cuba and Armageddon. The KGB did not immediately announce his capture. But various things convinced his MI6 controller that something was amiss and he ignored messages which would normally have summoned him to a crash meeting with Penkovsky.

On 2 November 1962, nearly a week after the Cuban Missile Crisis had eased (but when British V-bombers still stood on Alert Condition 3[160]), a prearranged set of noises came down the MI6 officer's telephone which Penkovsky was to use if and when a Soviet nuclear attack on the West was imminent (three blows of breath, repeated in another

1 Sir John Winnifrith: designed the 1950 plan to keep Stalin's Brits out of the Secret State

2 Whitehall reminder, 1962: the pursuit of perpetual security

3 (*left*) Sir William Strath: planning for ultimate catastrophe and the survival of the state

4 (*below*) If the bomb had dropped: official government poster

5 Air Chief Marshal Sir Kenneth Cross: to him could have fallen the decision to bomb Russia

6 Air Vice-Marshal Bobby Robson (*left*): 'We would have done it unhesitatingly'

7 Practising the last 'scramble': aircrews race towards Vulcan bombers at RAF Scampton, August 1960

8 Sir Michael Cary: contemplating the 'nightmarish gavotte' of a transition to nuclear war

9 The Cary memorandum of May 1962

10 Gervase Cowell: MI6 man in Moscow running Penkovsky who did not believe the fake attack-imminent signal

NATO

1. Simple Alert
2. Reinforced Alert
3. Military Vigilance (VXANXXX)
4. Counter Surprise (SCARLET)
5. Assumption of operational command by NATO Major Commanders

US A / Russia

1. Any important intervention concerning transition to war of these controls

UK

1. MAENOYERIS
2. KLAXXIN
3. Precautionary Stage
4. Mobilisation
5. Setting up of Regional Govt
6. Assignment of forces to NATO
7. ~~Evacuation~~ Repatriation to UK of dependants overseas
8. ~~Evacuation~~ Dispersal of population within UK
9. 10. Dispersal of Central Govt Reinforcement of BAOR

11 A first draft of the 1965 doomsday drill – By Royal Appointment

call one minute later). Shortly before he died, I asked Gervase Cowell, the SIS man who took the call, what he did on hearing those sounds. Certain that Penkovsky was captive and had had information extracted from him about call-signs, rendezvous and so on, Cowell decided to do nothing. He neither alerted his ambassador, Sir Frank Roberts, nor his chief in London, Sir Dick White.[161] Mr Cowell, a small, humorous, unassuming man, delivered himself of this recollection without personal grandeur or historical drama. He is, however, the only man I have ever met who has found himself in such a precarious and classically Cold War position. For the bomb made error so terrible and potentially terminal, from virtually the beginning to the end of the East/West confrontation. It was the nuclear question, and what it might mean to the UK as either the receiver or the deliverer of the ultimate weapon, that placed an awesome, mushroom-shaped shadow over the Cabinet Room from Attlee's time onwards.

2

The Importance of Being Nuclear: the Bomb and the Fear of Escalation

We must do it. It's the price we pay to sit at the top table.

Winston Churchill, 1954, on being told what would be
necessary for the UK to manufacture its own hydrogen bomb[1]

Over port and brandy Harold [Macmillan] held forth. The great thing for a country was to be rich as we were in the nineteenth century, he mused; and why should we not give up spending millions on atom bombs, why should we not give up Singapore, sell the colonies, sell the West Indies too to America, and just sit back and be rich?

Harold Macmillan, as recorded by Cynthia Gladwyn, after
dinner in the British Embassy in Paris, December 1956,
shortly before becoming Prime Minister[2]

Because with the submarine [Polaris] system the deterrent remains constantly at sea, a blunting attack against the fleet is not feasible. Nor would attack against communications frustrate retaliation ... there is very much to be said for a system which is quietly unobtrusive, secure in a relaxed way and ultimate in its bulldog-like determination to retaliate if the homeland is attacked. The submarine system seems in every way compatible with the British character. Let us have it.

JIGSAW, 'U.K. EYES ONLY', 'A New Strategic
Deterrent for the UK', June 1960[3]

The Committee has been told that Polaris or Polaris-type missiles do not have Union Jacks or Stars and Stripes on them.

Lord Rothschild, minority opinion appended to the
Kings Norton Report, July 1968[4]

Singapore has gone, the colonies and the West Indies too, long disposed of, if not actually sold. Yet as the twentieth century turned into the twenty-first, there was still a highly sophisticated nuclear submarine being driven in a thoroughly British way by a Royal Navy crew somewhere between Scotland and Murmansk, armed with a sheaf of Trident missiles, not one of which, if fired, could be distinguished by Russian (or anybody else's) radar from their US Navy counterparts. Continuing secrecy still prevents a precise costing of the British nuclear weapons programme from the moment Attlee's Cabinet committee, GEN 163, authorized the manufacture of the first UK bomb in January 1947, to now. But, by the late 1980s, it had probably absorbed between £40 and £50 billion all told.[5] The nuclear impulse plainly had become and remains part of what the anthropologist Clifford Geertz might have called the 'deep play'[6] of successive British governments. No UK administration would now seek to acquire a nuclear weapons capability if the UK did not possess one, but, so far, it has never seemed quite the right moment to dispose of it, even though in the mid- to late 1960s there was a group of ministers for whom abandonment was at least a possibility, as we shall shortly see.

I have written elsewhere on the inner group/machinery of government aspects of the handling of nuclear weapons policy from Attlee to Blair.[7] For the purposes of this book, I shall concentrate on the reasons given at various stages in the years between 1947 and 1968 for the importance of becoming (and remaining) nuclear. In the UK context, this was (and still is) significant in several senses. A nation is changed both when it decides to make a nuclear bomb and at the point it acquires a serious capability to deliver usable weapons in strength (roughly speaking 1947 and 1957 in the British case). Secondly, and more widely, the Cold War, like no conflict before it, was soaked in the nuclear factor in a manner that everyone, expert or inexpert, could understand. If it came to it, and the nuclear taboo which had held since the atomic bomb fell on Nagasaki on 9 August 1945 was broken, the world, or at least what was left of it if East and West had unleashed their arsenals against each other, would have been transformed for ever. Thirdly, the question arose in 1947 (and still does) of the utility to the UK of retaining an individual nuclear weapons capability usable, as a last resort, outside the NATO alliance (which came into being just over two years after Attlee and his Cabinet committee had decided to make an atomic bomb). And finally, the capacity to retaliate against a Soviet bloc attack with nuclear weapons became the political, psychological and, above all, financial reason for *not* creating a serious civil defence system in Britain. This imperative held good from the anxious weeks following the start of the Berlin Air Lift in the summer of 1948 (as we shall see in Chapter 4) to early October 1989 when Mikhail Gorbachev told the East German leader, Erich Honecker, that Soviet troops based in the GDR would *not* be available for internal repression (the rupture of the Wall following on 9 November).[8]

In 1945 the new Labour Prime Minister, Clement Attlee, knew full well that the bombs dropped on Hiroshima and Nagasaki, to whose research and construction the British had made a considerable contribution,[9] had changed the world. By the end of August 1945 he had put his thoughts on paper: 'It is difficult for people to adjust their minds to an entirely new situation . . .', he wrote. 'Even the modern conception of war to which in my lifetime we have become accustomed is now completely out of date . . . it would appear that the provision of bomb-proof basements in factories and offices and the retention of ARP [Air Raid Precautions] and Fire Services is just futile waste . . . The answer to an atomic bomb on London is an atomic bomb on another great city.'[10] Brian Cathcart has traced how what was for Attlee in the first weeks of his premiership the imperative of establishing a 'new World Order', to prevent war by controlling through international means this dreadful new invention, gradually succumbed to reality, as did his inner group of ministers on GEN 75, the Cabinet Committee on Atomic Energy, to whose members he distributed his August 1945 paper. By the time his GEN 163 group met in January 1947 for the first and only time, it was evident to Attlee that Britain must go it alone and manufacture its own atomic weapon in a vexing world replete with continuing British global responsibilities and with the United States unwilling to sustain the wartime nuclear collaboration.[11]

The Chiefs of Staff, wishing, in Sir Michael Howard's phrase, to have 'every club in the bag'[12] including atomic weapons (and never starry-eyed about the possibility of international control of the weapon), were working in the last months of 1945, in the words of the 18 December meeting of GEN 75, on 'a report on our requirements for atomic bombs and the possibility of making consequential reductions in other forms of armament production'. At the same meeting the Cabinet committee approved the construction of a first pile to produce plutonium – indispensable to the making of a Nagasaki-type weapon.[13] Though GEN 75 heard on this occasion (and later) some ministers' concerns about the 'heavy demands' that the construction of two possible piles would make 'upon the capacity of the chemical engineering and heavy electrical industries, both of whom were of great importance to the revival of our export trade',[14] there is what might be called an atomic bias detectable in GEN 75's deliberations from this point on.

Within less than a year, the passage of the McMahon Act by the US Congress in August 1946 prohibiting collaboration with *any* other country (even the Manhattan Project partners – Britain and Canada), meant that if the UK did go ahead with its bomb, it would be a more costly and difficult business because American industrial know-how (rather than the science of the bomb, which was in the heads of the returning UK team who had worked alongside the Americans at Los Alamos), would be denied the British weaponeers. Added to this would be the cost of developing the jet bombers needed to deliver the British weapon. The RAF was already planning what became the V-force in the autumn of 1946, with its specification for an aircraft capable of carrying a single 'special bomb' of 10,000 pounds 'to a target 2000 nautical miles from a base which may be anywhere in the world'.[15]

There may have been a bias towards procuring the biggest conceivable 'club in the bag' to place at the disposal of a future British Prime Minister, but the leading economic ministers on GEN 75 – Hugh Dalton, Chancellor of the Exchequer, and Sir Stafford Cripps, President of the Board of Trade – put up a fight against acquiring it in the autumn of 1946, smoking out as they did so Ernest Bevin, the hugely powerful Foreign Secretary, who was compelled to give his unvarnished reasons for wanting a British bomb at all costs.

Dalton and Cripps took their stand when GEN 75 was informed that the Ministry of Supply (the bomb-making department) needed £30–40m over four or five years to build a gaseous diffusion plant for the production of uranium 235. According to Sir Michael Perrin (present at GEN 75 for the Ministry of Supply alongside his boss, Lord Portal, the former wartime Chief of the Air Staff, now the ministry's Controller of Production of Atomic Energy), Dalton and Cripps were doing well until Bevin waddled late into the Cabinet Room, explaining he had eaten a heavy lunch and had fallen asleep.[16]

The sparse minutes of GEN 75 capture the Dalton/Cripps line:

In discussion it was urged that we must consider seriously whether we could afford to divert from civilian consumption and the restoration of our balance of payments the economic resources required for a project on this scale. Unless present trends were reversed we might find ourselves faced with an extremely serious economic and financial situation in two to three years' time.[17]

Sir Dennis Rickett's note of Bevin's rejoinder certainly does not do justice to the Foreign Secretary's virtuoso, British bulldog performance. 'On the other hand,' the minutes record,

it was argued that we could not afford to be left behind in a field which was of such revolutionary importance from an industrial, no less than from a military point of view. Our prestige in the world, as well as our chances of securing American co-operation [i.e. by restoring the collaboration severed by the McMahon Act] would both suffer if we did not exploit to the full a discovery in which we had played a leading part at the outset.[18]

According to Perrin, Bevin's intervention in the Dalton/Cripps argument was less grammatical but much more potent. 'No, Prime Minister, that won't do at all. We've *got* to have this,' he declared. 'I don't mind for myself, but I don't want any other Foreign Secretary of this country to be talked at, or to, by the Secretary of State in the United States as I just have in my discussions with Mr Byrnes. We've got to have this thing over here, whatever it costs. We've got to have the bloody Union Jack on top of it.'[19] Bevin prevailed and, two generations on, there is still a White Ensign (to be precise) metaphorically on top of it.

On the last day of 1946 Portal circulated a minute arguing that 'a decision is required about the development of Atomic weapons in this country. The Service Departments are beginning to move in the matter . . .'[20] Attlee agreed and during the first days of 1947 convened another special Atomic Energy Cabinet Committee for the purpose. GEN 163 consisted of Attlee and five other ministers but *not* Dalton and Cripps, the GEN 75 awkward squad.[21] The nuclear quintet were Bevin, Herbert Morrison (Lord President), A. V. Alexander (Minister of Defence), Lord Addison (Dominions Secretary) and John Wilmot (Minister of Supply). When GEN 163 met at No. 10 on the afternoon of 8 January 1947, Bevin once more pursued his American-related concerns. The minutes do not record anyone specifically mentioning Russia or the Soviet threat, though Stalin *is* there by implication in Bevin's reference to 'other countries':

THE FOREIGN SECRETARY said that in his view it was important that we should press on with the study of all aspects of atomic energy. We could not afford to acquiesce in an American monopoly of this new development. Other countries also might well develop atomic weapons. Unless therefore an effective international system could be developed under which the production and use of the weapon would be prohibited, we must develop it ourselves.[22]

Attlee is not minuted as having given his views to GEN 163. But recalling the decision in later life, he took a decidedly Bevin-like line. 'We had to hold up our position *vis-à-vis* the Americans. We couldn't allow ourselves wholly to be in their hands, and their position wasn't awfully clear always,' he explained to his former press secretary, Francis Williams. 'At that time we had to bear in mind that there was always the possibility of their withdrawing and becoming isolationist once again. The manufacture of a British atom bomb was therefore at that stage essential to our defence.'[23] From the moment of atomic creation, the doctrine of unripe time fused powerfully with the importance of being nuclear. It would do so again. As Attlee told Williams, 'we had to face the world as it was'.[24]

The nastiness of the world and the unreliability of the Americans were what drove Churchill, too, in the late spring and early summer of 1954, when he had to contemplate choreographing his ministerial colleagues through the very considerable leap from atomic to hydrogen bombs. He did so in the knowledge that the most recent US test ('Bravo' in the Pacific in May 1954[25]) produced, as the Chiefs of Staff informed his nuclear-aware ministers, an explosion 'approximately 1,500 times more powerful' than the atomic bomb. To this the Chiefs appended a warning that 'There is no theoretical limit to the destructive power which can be achieved with the latest techniques.'[26]

The awesomeness of that particular piece of analysis made 1954 the pivotal year for all the nuclear-related aspects of the secret state. It forced interlocking reappraisals right across the policy spectrum, from the nature and scope of the UK nuclear weapons programme and its place within defence strategy as a whole, through civil defence and the wider concepts of 'home defence' in which it was couched, to the durability of the post-nuclear-attack British state itself. And it was unsurprisingly Sir Norman Brook, that guarantor of joined-up secret government in the UK of the high Cold War, who saw this and on 12 March 1954 summoned a super-sensitive meeting of the permanent, inner guardians of the bomb-touched realm in his room at the Cabinet Office to ponder its implications.[27]

Brook's group consisted of Edwin Plowden from the nascent Atomic Energy Authority; two scientists, Sir John Cockcroft from Harwell and Sir William Penney from Aldermaston; plus a trio of crown servants from the Ministry of Defence led by one of its deputy secretaries, Sir Richard Powell. Brook opened by saying that this was a preliminary gathering ahead of a meeting a week later at which the Chiefs of Staff would be briefed on 'the latest available information concerning the development of the hydrogen bomb' by both the United States and the Soviet Union. Brook 'believed that the development of this bomb had now reached a stage which required us to re-assess first, our foreign policy and general strategy and, thereafter, the "size and shape" of the Armed Forces, our civil defence policy and our atomic weapons pro-gramme'.[28] He asked Penney, recently returned from the United States, to brief the meeting on the latest American and Russian technology.

Penney's presentation is the reason why the minutes of Brook's gathering took so long to appear at the Public Record Office, as did the Chiefs of Staff paper which I quoted above,[29] which was circulated on 1 June after the Chiefs and their planners had absorbed the new material and pondered its implications. Penney took Brook's group through the steps the USA and the Soviet Union had taken, and were taking, to thermonuclear status. In 1952 the Americans 'had exploded a 14 megaton bomb' (the 'Mike' device) at Eniwetok in the Pacific. In August 1953 the Russians had tested a 1-megaton bomb.

Penney explained the difference between them:

There were two forms of hydrogen bomb – a 'hybrid' bomb and a 'true' hydrogen bomb. The 'hybrid' bomb was something like the earlier atomic bomb but 'boosted' with lithium deuteride. The Russians had developed a 'hybrid' bomb . . . in 1953. The 'true' hydrogen bomb was a new departure: it involved a series of chain-reactions which at the last stage produced very fast neutrons; and in theory there was no limit to the size of explosion which could be produced by a bomb of this type. Moreover, it used uranium or thorium, not plutonium, as the main explosive element; and was highly economical in its use of fissionable material. Its cost was therefore relatively low (about £1.5 to £2 millions a bomb).[30]

The Russians, Penney added, 'were likely to develop the "true" hydrogen bomb before long' and it would be possible to detect when they had done so from the magnitude of the test explosion.[31] (The Soviets reached this point in November 1955, dropping 'Joe 19' from a Tupolev bomber over the Semipalatinsk test site in Kazakhstan, which yielded 1.6 megatons[32] and was deemed a 'true' H-bomb by Western analysts.)[33]

Penney, who had a great gift for explaining the highly technical and the complicated to a lay listener,[34] painted two vivid word-pictures for Brook's group on the effect of a 'true' and a 'hybrid' bomb on the area they could see from the Cabinet Secretary's window that March morning. First a 5-megaton 'true':

A bomb dropped on London and bursting on impact would produce a crater ¾-mile across and 150ft. deep, and a fire-ball of 2¼-miles diameter. The blast from it would crush the Admiralty Citadel [a stone-clad World War II signals centre across Horse Guards Parade next to the Mall – which is still there] at a distance of 1 mile. Suburban houses would be wrecked at a distance of 3 miles from the explosion, and they would lose their roofs and be badly blasted at a distance of 7 miles. All habitations would catch fire over a circle of 2 miles radius from the burst.[35]

Next, the impact of a 'hybrid' of 1 megaton (i.e. the most lethal yet devised by the Russians):

It would produce a crater 1,000-yds across and 150-ft deep; the Admiralty Citadel would be wrecked at a distance of 1,200 yds from the point of burst, houses would be wrecked at 2 miles, and bad blast would be experienced at 4 miles.[36]

Brook's meeting felt that 'Whatever progress the Russians might make from now on in developing the hydrogen bomb, we should be justified in advising ministers now that the Russians had already developed the material for an attack on this country, the intensity of which far exceeded our previous assumptions and the plans which we had based on them.'[37]

All this had a profound effect on Churchill. He made the easement of the Cold War and the pursuit of a summit meeting to engineer this before thermonuclear destruction engulfed the world – the centrepiece of his last years in No. 10. He would regale ministers with 'Gibbonesque' (Harold Macmillan's description) soliloquies about 'the most terrible and destructive engine of mass warfare yet known to mankind'.[38] For him, a *British* H-bomb was crucial to his and his successors' capacity to shift the two superpowers towards a safer world.

At some point before Brook's meeting with the scientists and officials, Churchill had a session with Edwin Plowden, which Lord Plowden recalled many years later for the BBC radio documentary *A Bloody Union Jack On Top of It*. 'I got a minute for the Prime Minister, from Churchill,' Plowden told me,

saying to let him know what it would cost, what effort would be necessary to develop and manufacture hydrogen bombs. And under the direction of Bill Penney and [the third of the 'atomic knights', as Penney, Cockcroft and he were known in Whitehall, Hinton ran the factories making fissile material for the weapons] the collaboration of Hinton and Cockcroft, I was given the answer to his question, and I went to see Churchill in his room in the House of Commons after lunch. And when I'd explained what the effort necessary would be, he paused for a time, and nodded his head, and said in that well-known voice of his, 'We must do it. It's the price we pay to sit at the top table.' And having said that, he got up and tied a little black ribbon round his eyes, and lay down on his bed in his room, and went to sleep.[39]

Brook concluded the meeting, in his characteristically tidy and action-orientated way, with an explanation that

He had already suggested to the Prime Minister that it was necessary to re-assess, in the light of the new information about the hydrogen bomb, the following points:

(i) The likelihood of war.

(ii) The form which war was most likely to take if it came.

(iii) The changes which would need to be made in the pattern of our defence arrangements, active and passive, in order to adjust them to meet the most likely contingency.

(iv) The extent to which we should ensure [insure?] against the possibility that war might take some other form than that which now seemed most likely.[40]

Brook had also briefed Churchill that the existing atomic weapons programme had to be reassessed. The Cabinet Secretary urged that the various studies should be parcelled out to the Chiefs and the relevant departments, and that a small ministerial committee should oversee the whole swathe of activity.[41]

Churchill followed his advice and involved the full Cabinet to an unusual degree in the later stages in July 1954. Before this, the shadow of the H-bomb darkened two Cabinet committees. First, GEN 464, which met in mid-April to approve moves to acquire the raw material needed for a British H-bomb ahead of the actual decision to make one (there was a sense of urgency here as the Americans were buying-up great quantities of thorium[42]). Churchill told the five colleagues he placed on GEN 464 (Anthony Eden, Foreign Secretary; R. A. Butler, Chancellor of the Exchequer; Lord Alexander, Minister of Defence; Lord Swinton, Commonwealth Secretary; and Lord Salisbury, Lord President) 'that he would like to invite the Cabinet at an early date to decide in principle that hydrogen bombs should be made in the United Kingdom', and the meeting agreed this.[43]

Churchill took the thermonuclear question through another stage between GEN 464 and the full Cabinet which scholars have only recently been able to reconstruct. For several years I thought it was the regular, standing Defence Committee of the Cabinet which had taken the interim decision to go ahead on 16 June 1954.[44] If I had read the Cabinet minutes for 7 July 1954 more carefully, I would have realized that the ministerial group cited as having done this was a different configuration – the Defence *Policy* Committee [my emphasis].[45]*

---

* My student, Alban Webb, brought this to my attention in early 2001 when, at last, the minutes of the DPC were declassified.

DPC was essentially a fusion of Churchill's GEN 464 inner group with the Home Secretary, the junior service ministers and the Chiefs of Staff added and brought together to consider defence spending in the round (the H-bomb in particular) and to consider the substantial new study from the Chiefs and their briefers on 'United Kingdom Defence Policy'.[46] DPC confronted a dilemma. Churchill wanted both spending cuts *and* a new H-bomb (the final results of this protracted exercise were published nearly three years later in the famous Sandys Defence White Paper which so alarmed many of those who went on to form the Campaign for Nuclear Disarmament).*

Churchill concluded the DPC meeting of 20 May 1954 with a *tour de force* which blended a whole variety of other elements with the economy theme – including the 'top table' requirement and the anxiety about the Eisenhower Administration's possible inclination to a pre-emptive war. Brook allowed himself to draft a minute which did not muffle Churchillian cadence or curtail his grand sweep:

THE PRIME MINISTER, summing up the discussion, said that the difficulties of choice which lay before the Committee had been put boldly forward. The problem was to decide what practical steps could be taken to effect the saving of £200 million a year, with the least risk of weakening our influence in the world, or endangering our security. Influence depended on possession of force. If the United States were tempted to undertake a forestalling war, we could not hope to remain neutral. Even if we could, such a war would in any event determine our fate. We must avoid any action which would weaken our power to influence United States policy. We must avoid anything which might be represented as a sweeping act of disarmament. If, however, we were able to show that in a few years' time we should be possessed of great offensive power, and that we should be ready to take our part in a world struggle, he thought it would not be impossible to reconcile reductions in defence expenditure with the maintenance of our influence in world councils.[47]

Here was the bloody-Union-Jack-on-top-of-it syndrome with a vengeance. The H-bomb as the salvation for a great power seriously on the slide in terms of its finances and its armed forces relative to the superpowers; go thermonuclear and thereby both save money *and* increase

* As we shall see in the next chapter.

your relative clout in the world. The atomic knights had shown it was within budget at £1.5 to £2m per bomb. The Chiefs of Staff's memorandum for the DPC ministers a couple of weeks later pushed this notion even more forcefully than had Churchill by combining the indispensability of nuclear deterrence with the irreplaceable presence of British experience at the top table – '. . . we must maintain and strengthen our position as a world power so that Her Majesty's Government can exercise a powerful influence in the counsels of the world'. And, in a section on 'deductions' to be drawn from the new thermonuclear world which must have brought a glow to Churchill as he read on, the Chiefs (Admiral of the Fleet Sir Rhoderick McGrigor, Field Marshal Sir John Harding and Air Chief Marshal Sir William Dickson) declared:

(a) Short of sacrificing our vital interests or principles, we must do everything possible to prevent global war which would inevitably entail the exposure of the United Kingdom to a devastating nuclear bombardment.

(b) The ability to wage war with the most up-to-date nuclear weapons will be the measure of military power in the future.

(c) Our scientific skill and technological capacity to produce the hydrogen weapon puts within our grasp the ability *to be on terms* [emphasis added] with the United States and Russia.[48]

This document is one of the most significant to be produced by the Chiefs in the mid-1950s as Churchill allowed it to be circulated to the full Cabinet as a Cabinet Paper on 23 July 1954[49] (though one piece of information was deemed too sensitive to be divulged to them all – the number of H-bombs the UK was forecast to be likely to possess by 1959 (10) and 1960 (20) 'if production were started now'[50]).

The Chiefs did not spare their ministerial readers on what would await the UK if deterrence failed. If H-bombs, each one 1,000 times more powerful than the A-bomb, were dropped on ten UK cities, 'the death roll would be . . . 12 millions'. However good the developments in our defence in coming years, complete protection against these weapons was impossible. And the fear of escalation was present from the moment Churchill and his ministers pondered the thermonuclear world. Each member of the Cabinet was invited by the Chiefs of Staff to peer into the abyss:

We have given much thought to the highly speculative question whether, if global warfare should break out, there might initially be mutually acceptable restrictions on the use of nuclear weapons. We have come to the conclusion that, if war came in the next few years, the United States would insist on the immediate use of the full armoury of nuclear weapons with the object of dealing the Russians a quick knock-out blow. We must therefore plan on the assumption that, if war becomes global, nuclear bombardment will become general.[51]

The Chiefs, however, drawing avowedly on the resources of the Joint Intelligence Committee, were able to calm ministers' anxieties about the 'likelihood of war', but it was going to be a long haul:

(a) Russia is most unlikely to provoke war deliberately during the next few years, when the United States will be comparatively immune from Russian attack.

(b) The danger the United States might succumb to the temptation of precipitating a 'forestalling' war can not be disregarded. In view of the vulnerability of the United Kingdom we must use all our influence to prevent this.

(c) Careful judgement and restraint on the part of the Allies on a united basis will be needed to avoid the outbreak of a global war through accident or miscalculation resulting from an incident which precipitated or extended a local war . . .

(e) Even when the Russians are able to attack North America effectively, the ability of the United States to deliver a crippling attack on Russia will remain a powerful deterrent to the Soviet Government.

(f) It is most probable that the present state of 'cold war' will continue for a long time with periods of greater or lesser tension.[52]

For the 16 June meeting of DPC, the Chiefs appended an annex on 'Hydrogen Bomb Research and Production in the United Kingdom', based on a report from the Working Party on the Operational Use of Atomic Weapons.[53] Such was its sensitivity and detail on the number of weapons envisaged that it did not go to the full Cabinet with the main document.

Given the Chiefs' paper, Churchill's grand strategic sweep at the earlier meeting and the nuclear temptation (the H-bomb as squarer of circles), it is not surprising that the Defence Policy Committee on 16 June 1954 '[a]uthorised the Lord President [the Marquess of Salisbury] and the Minister of Supply [Duncan Sandys] to initiate a programme for the production of hydrogen bombs . . .'[54]

The full Cabinet proved more troublesome, partly because some of its members (Harry Crookshank, the Leader of the House of Commons, in particular[55]) felt that Churchill was bouncing them into a decision because 'they had had no notice that this question was to be raised', as Crookshank put it,[56] and by Churchill's introducing the item on the Cabinet agenda for 7 July 1954 with the information that 'the Defence Policy Committee had approved, on 16th June, a proposal that our atomic weapons programme should be so adjusted as to allow for the production of hydrogen bombs in this country'.[57]

Churchill had to bring the H-bomb back to Cabinet twice. On 8 July there was a substantial debate. Opting out of the nuclear race was raised (the minutes do not say by whom: 'Some of our other defence preparations were already based on the assumption that we should not engage in a major war except as an ally of the United States: could we not continue to rely on the United States to match Russia in thermonuclear weapons?'[58]).

Even a pre-echo of the Campaign for Nuclear Disarmament could be heard: 'Was it morally right that we should manufacture weapons with this vast destructive power? There was no doubt that a decision to make hydrogen bombs would offend the conscience of substantial numbers of people in this country. Evidence of this was to be found in the resolutions recently passed by the Methodist Conference in London.'[59] It would be fascinating to know which of Churchill's ministers spoke for Methody.

The 'reply' and the passage which follows it, though not attributed to Churchill, sounds like him. There was 'no difference in kind between atomic and thermo-nuclear weapons'.[60] As soon as the anxious Cabinet member received the Chiefs' paper on 22 July he or she (there was only one lady present, Florence Horsburgh, the Minister of Education) would have had their appreciation of the vastness of the difference underscored. If there was a 'moral principle' involved, the Cabinet was told 'it had already been breached by the decision of the Labour Government to make the atomic bomb'.[61]

The great power/mature-influence-at-the-top-table argument was deployed here (almost certainly by the Prime Minister himself) to quell all doubts:

No country could claim to be a leading military power unless it possessed the most up-to-date weapons; and the fact must be faced that, unless we possessed thermo-nuclear weapons, we should lose our influence and standing in world affairs. Strength in thermo-nuclear weapons would henceforth provide the most powerful deterrent to a potential aggressor; and it was our duty to make our contribution towards the building up of this deterrent influence.[62]

Churchill's anxiety about the United States, currently backing Chiang Kai-shek's Formosa in its stand-off with mainland China over the islands of Quemoy and Matsu (he would later warn Eisenhower that 'a war to keep the coastal islands for Chiang would not be defensible here'[63]), surfaced at this stage of the meeting:

It was at least possible that the development of the hydrogen bomb would have the effect of reducing the risk of major war. At present some people thought the greatest risk was that the United States might plunge the world into war, either through a misjudged intervention in Asia or in order to forestall an attack by Russia. Our best chance of preventing this was to maintain our influence with the United States Government; and they would certainly feel more respect for our views if we continued to play an effective part in building up the strength necessary to deter aggression than if we left it entirely to them to match and counter Russia's strength in thermonuclear weapons.[64]

On 16 July Churchill told the Queen that the Cabinet 'are considering whether it would be right and advantageous for this country to produce the hydrogen bomb ... There is very little doubt in my mind what it [the decision] will be.'[65] And decide to go ahead the Cabinet finally did on 26 July 1954.[66]

Listening and learning throughout the H-bomb Cabinets was Harold Macmillan. As Minister of Housing and Local Government, he did not sit on GEN 464 or the DPC. Only when he became Churchill's Minister of Defence in October 1954 did he move inside the inner nuclear circle and it fell to him to announce in the 1955 Defence White Paper the following February that Britain was making an H-bomb.[67]

Lorna Arnold has shown how the 'months following the White Paper of February 1955 were an anxious time for the Aldermaston theoreticians as they groped for solutions' on how to make a British H-bomb.[68] There was a great deal of research and development still to do. By the time British designs were put to the test (the May 1957 'Grapple' shot on Christmas Island being a 'hybrid'; the November 1957 'Grapple X' was a 'true'[69]), Macmillan was in No. 10 Downing Street and pursuing what Edwin Plowden called the 'great prize'[70] of restored nuclear collaboration with the United States. This, thanks to the November 1957 test (Edward Teller later told his British opposite numbers that it was obvious that the laws of physics operated on both sides of the Atlantic[71]), was achieved in the autumn of 1958 with the 'Agreement for Co-operation on the Uses of Atomic Energy for Mutual Defence Purposes' concluded between the Eisenhower Administration and Her Majesty's Government.[72]

With the V-bombers coming on stream in significant numbers during 1957, Macmillan can be seen as the first fully nuclear-armed British Prime Minister, especially after the first British H-bombs, the Yellow Suns Mark II, were allocated to the bombers in 1961[73] (though technically, the distinction could go to Churchill from November 1953 when the first 'Blue Danube' atomic bomb was delivered to RAF Wittering[74]). But Macmillan also saw the substantial unravelling of several of the arguments for going thermonuclear he had heard around Churchill's Cabinet table that July morning in 1954.

Before such awkward new realities had to be faced, however, Macmillan set down *his* reasons in 1957–8 for sustaining an 'independent nuclear capability' for the UK:

(a) To retain our special relation with the United States and, through it, our influence in world affairs, and, especially, our right to have a voice in the final issue of peace and war.

(b) To make a definite, though limited, contribution to the total nuclear strength of the West – while recognising that the United States must continue to play the major part in maintaining the balance of nuclear power.

(c) To enable us, by threatening to use our independent nuclear power, to secure United States co-operation in a situation in which their interests were less immediately threatened than our own.

(d) To make sure that, in a nuclear war, sufficient attention is given to certain Soviet targets which are of greater importance to us than to the United States.[75]

This quartet of justifications was very much in line with the mood of 1954 within Churchill's nuclear councils. For all his musings around the Gladwyns' table in Paris in late 1956, Macmillan was determined that he and the UK should be a serious, if second-rank, nuclear player in the world (though there is no wishful thinking here, as there was in the summer of 1954, about the H-bomb putting Britain back, in the Chiefs' words, 'on terms' with the two superpowers).

But in the mid-1950s technology and money were moving powerfully against Britain's notions of its nuclear place in the world which the restoration of US/UK collaboration on warhead know-how from the autumn of 1958 only partly mitigated. Peter Nailor, a nuclear policy civil servant before becoming an academic, has spoken graphically of the gap which opened up between the United States, the Soviet Union and the UK at the very time – 1954 – when the Chiefs' vintage thought Britain's technological skills would be narrowing it. Immediately behind the 'step change' of the thermonuclear weapon,

you got quite unexpectedly fast technical breakthroughs in reliable solid-fuel rocket motors, the development of miniaturised components, both for warheads and for guidance and instrumental systems. And the pace of change was accelerating to an extent where a country like Britain was being forced to make technical choices with bewildering rapidity. The V-bomber/free-fall [bomb] combination was a jolly good combination, but it was already becoming obsolescent almost before squadron service capability had been reached, and the question, the specific question for British defence planners was: what came next? Could we, in fact, find something that would enhance and prolong the service life of the V-bombers, or would we have to make the switch straight away to something like land or sea-based missiles? That was an option which ... as late as 1954–5 nobody thought would be an immediate problem. By 1957–8 it was already knocking on the door.[76]

The first attempts to resolve the dilemma failed very publicly and absorbed a great deal of time, energy and, senior ministers feared, substantial political capital from the Macmillan governments especially after the UK's attempt to construct its own land-based ballistic missile, Blue Streak, had to be abandoned in 1960 on grounds of both cost and vulnerability (it was liquid- rather than solid-fuelled and so took dangerously long to prepare for launch).

The huge investment in the Valiants, Victors and Vulcans of the RAF's V-force, then arriving from the factories at airfields in Lincoln-shire, on Cyprus and in Singapore, meant that the next solution had to be a system which would prolong the operational life of those aircraft in increasingly difficult circumstances given improvements in Soviet air defence. It forced another huge step-change in British thinking. Macmillan and his Cabinet had to accept a serious loss of independence in asking the Americans for the Skybolt stand-off missile (then in the process of development for the US Air Force) to be capped by a British-made warhead and fitted to the V-bombers.[77]

Philip de Zulueta, Macmillan's Private Secretary for foreign and defence matters, captured for me the difficulties and dilemmas involved when Macmillan and his team visited President Eisenhower at his Camp David retreat in 1960 to seek American help in the increasingly stretching task of keeping a Union Jack on top of it (even if much of the 'it' had to be US-provided):

> It was not at all agreeable to have to do that, but there was really no alternative, and he fortunately managed to succeed in doing it. Curiously enough, when he was asking for Skybolt at the Camp David meeting, the Americans in the background were talking about Polaris. I remember Eisenhower's naval aide, who was a charming man, had got a model of the Polaris there. Of course, he was the Navy lobby, and was trying to persuade one to go ahead with Polaris. I discussed it with Sir Norman Brook, and he said, 'For goodness sake, let's hope they don't raise that question; we must have an airborne missile, because we want to use our bombers.'[78]

Deep in Whitehall, the doomsday planners of JIGSAW, the Joint Inter-Service Group for the Study of All Out War, were preoccupied with the need for an invulnerable, second-strike system such as Polaris which would avoid the need to cobble together interim solutions to keep the V-force as the H-bomb's national carrier.

But only when Skybolt failed to perform on its test ranges in 1962 ('It was an absolute pile of junk,' Kennedy's Defense Secretary, Robert McNamara, would tell me with great force many years later[79]) was

Macmillan confronted with the need to go under water. The Americans' abandonment of Skybolt came as a terrible shock to Macmillan as, in the words of Alec Home, his Foreign Secretary: 'We'd set a lot of store by its success . . . and it was widely known that the government set a lot of store by it . . .'[80] When Macmillan, Home, Defence Secretary Peter Thorneycroft and Commonwealth Secretary Duncan Sandys set off in December 1962 for a meeting at Nassau with Kennedy hoping to salvage a serious British nuclear capacity from the wreckage, they were convinced, as Home told me later, that their personal political stakes were of the highest. Had the Nassau negotiation failed and the British team returned empty-handed, 'we would have been in a very, very nasty position politically. I think that the government would probably have been beaten. It might well have been a case for an election, I would have thought.'[81]

Macmillan did pull it off, against the advice of several in the Kennedy Administration.[82] But it was the triumph of a nuclear mendicant rather than of a serious independent contributor to the West's combined nuclear profile. The illusions of that Churchillian summer of 1954 were cruelly exposed. Such moments are highly public events in the life of the secret state. But particularly interesting are the rationales used by the key players to convince themselves, and others, in private of the need for staying a nuclear player despite the dependence on another power.

With Kennedy at Nassau, Macmillan had pulled out all his histrionic and historical stops. As de Zulueta recalled:

> He made a most moving and emotional speech, about the great losses and the great struggles for freedom and so on, and Britain was a resolute and a determined ally, who was going to stand firm, and that it was very unreasonable for the United States not to assist her to do so . . . And it was very well done indeed and very effective, and there wasn't a dry eye in the house.

Sir Philip was (and remained) well aware of Macmillan's underlying purpose – 'that we should have enough nuclear power to prevent some foolish decisions being made to our detriment on the other side of the Atlantic . . .' in de Zulueta's own words.[83] Here lay the thread linking Bevin, wheezing into GEN 75 in the autumn of 1946, with Churchill in his H-bomb summer of 1954 to Macmillan doing his 'veteran of the

Somme'[84] impression at Nassau. Nassau took place within weeks of the Cuban Missile Crisis, during which Macmillan had pointed out to Kennedy that if Khrushchev retaliated against the US blockade of Cuba with a Warsaw Pact equivalent against Berlin 'as envisaged in the various contingency plans', this 'will lead us either to an escalation to world war or to the holding of a conference'.[85] Macmillan's preference for conference over catastrophe had also been evident during the Berlin crisis of 1958–61, given his private conviction (as expressed to Norman Brook at a particularly acute phase of Berlin-related tension in July 1961) that 'any real war *must* escalate into nuclear war . . .'[86]

In the weeks between Cuba and Nassau, the JIC had prepared a bespoke paper on the theme of 'Escalation', which had been shared with the Americans.[87] The JIC defined escalation as 'the process by which any hostilities, once started, might expand in scope and intensity, with or without the consent of Governments'. Its analysts did not accept Macmillan's apocalyptic teleology, but they came close to it. Their general conclusion was that 'In any hostilities between the Soviet Union and the West, escalation to global war could only be avoided if at some stage in the process a cease-fire were agreed. When this might happen must depend primarily on the importance attributed by each side to the issues at stake and each side's appreciation of the other's determination.'[88]

But the JIC was well aware of the short timescales involved in securing a cease-fire *and* the difficulty of either side backing down:

Once any hostilities had started agreement on a cease-fire would involve one side or the other accepting a tactical defeat or both sides a stalemate on what must be a highly important issue. The chances of such an agreement would be better if the attacking side realised that it had miscalculated the importance to the other side of the interests involved or the will and ability of the other side to resist.[89]

The JIC's analysts brought some solace to their readers in the jumpy weeks following Cuba. The other side were just as anxious on this matter as the West:

The Soviet leaders have consistently affirmed in public their realisation of the grave risk of escalation in limited hostilities with the West. Indeed, at times they have even implied that the process would be virtually uncontrollable. One of the arguments on which they base this view is that nations having two such fundamentally opposed social systems could consider compromise intolerable when once [*sic*] hostilities had been joined.[90]

Without, of course, saying so (or perhaps even knowing it to be so given the small number of people who would have seen Macmillan's deeply pessimistic scribbles on Norman Brook's minutes), the JIC saw similar views prevailing in the Kremlin to those bothering the anxious old gentleman in Admiralty House (No. 10 was being rebuilt). Macmillan had confided to his diary (which nobody, not even Norman Brook, knew he was keeping) his own version of the JIC's reasoning. At a particularly fraught moment in the rolling Berlin crisis he foresaw a possible 'drift to disaster . . . a terrible diplomatic defeat or (out of sheer incompetence) a nuclear war'.[91]

In November 1962, however, in the immediate aftermath of Cuba, the JIC saw such mutual anxiety as the best hope: 'It is now the fear of global war arising through a process of escalation which constitutes the deterrent to limited aggression, rather than the fear of immediate, massive retaliation.'[92] The JIC's top customers in Whitehall that autumn may not have been so sanguine as their intelligence advisers, however. Over lunch with Iverach McDonald of *The Times* before 'the ripples of the Cuba crisis had begun to die away', the Foreign Secretary, Lord Home, warned the assembled party (which included Walter Lippmann, over from America) 'against too much cheerfulness now that the [Soviet Union's] gamble had failed. "The chief frightening thing about it all," he said, "is that Khrushchev could have miscalculated so badly. It could mean that he could blunder into war another time." '[93]

In such a mood did Home and Macmillan set off for Nassau. Any deal struck had to satisfy what the British team saw as the UK's needs – to produce a weapons system capable of destroying something approaching the 'forty largest cities' in the USSR which the JIC, based on the 'breakdown' studies made by JIGSAW, deemed 'quite unacceptable to the Russians'.[94] Macmillan also had to secure a clause in any agreement made with Kennedy whereby a British nuclear force, however dependent on the USA for its missiles, could be withdrawn from its NATO assignments and joint targeting if 'supreme national interests' were at stake. And it was this independence-of-action angle which concerned the Cabinet when it met, with Macmillan still in negotiation in Nassau, to discuss the telegrams he had sent Rab Butler, the Deputy Prime Minister, to be put before the Cabinet meeting on 21 December 1962.

Butler told the Cabinet the latest draft of the agreement

included a new provision that our strategic nuclear forces would be used for 'the international defence of the Western Alliance in all circumstances except where Her Majesty's Government may decide that the supreme national interests are at stake'. The Prime Minister had particularly directed attention [in his telegram] to those words, which had the effect of giving us the sole right of decision on the use of our strategic nuclear forces, and had asked whether the Cabinet endorsed the view, which he shared with the Foreign Secretary, the Commonwealth Secretary and the Minister of Defence, that these words could be publicly defended as maintaining an independent United Kingdom contribution to the nuclear deterrent.

Though anxious to have it clearly worded, the Cabinet went along with Macmillan's line as it 'safeguarded the essential principle of an independent United Kingdom contribution to the Western strategic nuclear deterrent', recognizing 'the value to this country of an arrangement by which we should eventually have within our own control a virtually indestructible second-strike deterrent weapon of proven capability, and with prospects of a long life . . .'[95]

Intriguingly, neither at this Cabinet meeting nor at the one on 3 January 1963 in which Macmillan gave a lengthy exposition of the Nassau negotiation, did any minister seek to discuss what kind of contingencies might qualify for the 'supreme national interests clause' to be invoked. It took a leak from a conversation Kennedy had 'on board his yacht' with the French Ambassador to the US, Herve Alphand, on 29 December for what the President had in mind to emerge. The Head of Chancery at the British Embassy in Paris was given a sight 'in strict confidence' on 2 January 1963 of Alphand's telegram reporting what Kennedy said. Philip de Zulueta passed the British Ambassador's telegram, containing the leak, to Macmillan on the day the Cabinet met to hear his report on Nassau with the words: 'Prime Minister. This is an important telegram.'

This it was for several reasons (not least because Kennedy was offering a Polaris deal to France, which did not prevent President de Gaulle within days from wrecking the Macmillan Government's application to join the EEC on the grounds that the UK lived in a dependency culture with the USA on defence and other matters). Kennedy was making available a similar arrangement on 'supreme national interests' to France too. And what he said on this to Alphand included the kind of detail the British Cabinet neither sought nor was given when Macmillan delivered his account. 'The President,' the Paris Embassy's summary of the Alphand telegram reported,

confirmed that the right of Britain or France unilaterally to decide to use their Polaris forces in the event that their supreme national interests were at stake should be assured without equivocation. Thus the crews of their submarines would be composed entirely of British and French nationals and the sub-marines would be capable of acting independently without recourse to 'foreign [i.e. US] radio-electronic systems' . . . The President then cited Suez or Kuwait [the threatened Iraqi invasion of 1961] as examples of how the 'supreme interests' formula might be invoked. If some action on the part of the British or the French, not directly affecting the United States, led to the Russians threatening either country with missiles, they would be in a position to decide to use their own Polaris missiles against say Moscow or Kiev.

British or French acceptance of the Polaris system would in no way limit their right to develop other nuclear systems which would not, therefore, come within the Nassau Agreement; but they would find it extremely costly to develop and maintain two effective long-term nuclear systems.[96]

This latter paragraph must have resonated quite powerfully with Macmillan as he had spent a broody Boxing Day worrying about whether the Nassau Agreement would hold – and, if it did not, whether (as he put it in a Top Secret minute to Thorneycroft and Home), 'if we were driven into a corner, we could either as a bluff or as a reality, make a Polaris missile perhaps of a simpler kind, ourselves from our own designs; how long would it take, etc?'[97]

Macmillan followed this up with a select, inner group meeting of ministers (Home, Thorneycroft, Ted Heath [Home's no. 2 at the Foreign Office] and officials in Admiralty House on 31 December

1962. Sir Pierson Dixon, the British Ambassador to France, was over from Paris and Macmillan suggested that the French might be told

that we did not foresee that we should have to use [the 'supreme national interests'] right in any except the most grave circumstances. If, for example, Indonesia threatened North Borneo we would not necessarily wish to pose a direct threat to President Soekarno, but if as a result of our adopting conventional methods of defending North Borneo the Russians threatened us direct as they had done in somewhat vague terms at the time of Suez,[98] then we might withdraw our Polaris force from the joint [NATO] forces to counter the threat from Khrushchev.[99]

The New Year's Eve meeting heard a revealing exchange between Heath and Thorneycroft. The 'Skybolt episode', said Heath,

had bought before the public in a very clear manner the extent of our dependence on the United States. The same difficulty would be felt to apply to Polaris and until we actually had the missiles in our possession we would be at the mercy of the United States Government. For example, if there were some strong disagreement on important policy issues they might threaten to cancel the contract.

Thorneycroft chipped in to say 'that we would not be able to afford starting from scratch to develop a reinsurance system of [sic] posing the deterrent'.[100] Indeed, in mid-January, when he received the costings and timings of home-made alternatives to Polaris in response to Macmillan's Boxing Day request, this was very apparent.[101]

Macmillan was at his consummate best before the full Cabinet on 3 January 1963. Not a trace of those private doubts about the deal – or of Nassau's vulnerabilities – was allowed to tarnish his *tour d'horizon*. How did he now define the importance of being nuclear? The old Churchillian tunes of 1954 plainly could not be reprised. But Bevin-style, there still had to be a Union Jack on it. Macmillan recognized, as Heath had, the degree of exposure made evident by the cancellation of Skybolt: 'Some sections of public opinion in the United Kingdom were disposed to take the view that this decision was intended to compel us finally to surrender any independent strategic nuclear capability. This was one indication of the current strains in the Western

Alliance.' Here he alluded to his 'veteran of the two world wars' soliloquy at Nassau: 'The present United States Administration included hardly any of the men who had been associated with this country in the Second World War; and many of President Kennedy's advisers were inclined to indulge an inflated conception of the material power at the disposal of their Government.'[102]

None the less, he and the Cabinet were 'bound to consider ... whether it was right for this country to seek to continue to make an independent contribution to the Western strategic nuclear deterrent'. Here he engaged upon a fascinating mix of the old and the new – the UK was a pioneer in work on the bomb; the world was a nasty place; the need now was for interdependence rather than independence; and there was a whiff of his own version of the indispensability of UK wisdom and restraint at the top table, the need, as he had put it nearly twenty years earlier in Algiers, to play the British Greeks to the American Romans.[103]

'The nuclear weapon,' Macmillan reminded his Cabinet,

had been invented originally by British scientists [this was something of an exaggeration; UK-based scientists had shown that such a weapon was practicable – getting there was a very different matter and depended hugely on US brains, dollars and industry] and we had made considerable progress, both before and after the amendment of the McMahon Act [in 1958], in its development. But the gradual introduction of Soviet defence systems posed new problems; and the elaboration of modern systems of guidance and delivery implied that the development of an effective deterrent would become progressively more sophisticated and expensive. There was, therefore, little attraction in a policy of complete independence in this respect.[104]

The use of the word 'attraction' is interesting. No hint here that going-it-alone was no longer a runner, that it was now a stark choice between buying a missile off-the-shelf from the United States or waiting for the effectiveness of the British nuclear force to decay as the V-bomber/free fall H-bomb combination edged deeper into obsolescence.

'Nevertheless,' the Prime Minister insisted, 'there were several compelling reasons for seeking to preserve a measure of independence as regards control over our nuclear deterrent.'[105] So what did the

Macmillan rationale (as packaged for his Cabinet) consist of in Janua 1963?

1: . . . the Western Alliance would cease to be a free association if the whol of its advanced scientific and technical capacity in this respect were vested in one member.

2: . . . we ought to ensure that we should always be able to react appropriately to a Soviet nuclear threat to this country, even if the United States for whatever reason, were disinclined to support us.

3: . . . a Soviet nuclear threat, to which there was no United Kingdom counter-threat would render all our conventional forces ineffectual.

4: . . . if this country abandoned the attempt to maintain an independent nuclear deterrent, it would be unable to exercise any effective influence in the attempts, which would eventually have to be made, to achieve some international agreement to limit nuclear armaments.

The 'supreme national interests' clause, he explained, 'represented a realistic compromise, in present circumstances, between independence and interdependence'.[106]

The Cabinet concurred. But the Labour Opposition did not. Between the Cabinet backing the Nassau 'compromise' (and, in Michael Quinlan's words, 'a Mark I level of cover', an off-the-shelf insurance policy as opposed to the much more expensive and difficult Mark II level of insurance an all-British nuclear capacity would have represented[107]) and the House of Commons debating the Nassau Agreement, Hugh Gaitskell had died and had been replaced as Leader of the Labour Party by Harold Wilson. Macmillan's party – as opposed to Civil Service – advisers were concerned that Wilson's 'election to the party leadership . . . owed much to the support of the unilateralist wing [of the Labour Party], and this may influence his position as time goes on'.[108]

In fact, as the briefing attached to this warning penned for Macmillan's eyes showed, Wilson had taken a line in the Nassau debate in the Commons on 31 January 1963 similar to that voiced by Ted Heath in the privacy of Admiralty House on New Year's Eve a month earlier. 'We on this side of the House,' Wilson told the Commons,

have not been arguing either for Polaris or for Skybolt. We support neither
... The Government have presented their case in terms of an answer to the
question of whether the missile we should have from the Americans should
be Skybolt or Polaris ... Our criticism is not of the answer, but that the
question is wrong. How can one pretend to have an independent deterrent
when one is dependent on another nation – a reluctant one at that – to supply
one with the means of delivery?[109]

Wilson sustained this argument right up to election day in October
1964. Labour's manifesto said of Polaris: 'it will not be independent
and it will not be British and it will not deter'. An unequivocal pledge
to abandon was avoided, however. The manifesto committed a new
Labour Government to 'the renegotiation of the Nassau Agreement',[110]
no more.

An impression was given, however, that Labour would begin the
process of removing the Union Jack from the bomb. The letter of 22
April 1963 from the Director of the Conservative Research Department, Michael Fraser, which Macmillan read (his initials are on it),
told John Wyndham (Macmillan's personal assistant) and his boss, in
the context of Wilson and the nuclear question, that

Perhaps the most revealing statement of his personal views was that made
during an American television interview on April 8 this year. According to
accounts in the Press, which have not been contradicted, he was asked repeat-
edly if the policy of renunciation of the nuclear deterrent would not commit
Britain to the status of a second-class military power. Wilson is reported first
to have denied it but then to have added: 'If being a first-rate military power
means being a nuclear power, that is right.'[111]

However, Alec Home, who replaced Macmillan as Prime Minister six
months later, never reckoned Wilson would abandon the bomb.

When interviewed for *A Bloody Union Jack on Top of It*, Home
told me that he

had always found, in dealing with Harold Wilson on security matters [presum-
ably on a private, privy counsellor basis[112]] that he was reliable in terms of the
national interest. And so in spite of the manifesto, in spite of what he said
during the election campaign, I didn't think he'd be able to bring himself to
cancel it [Polaris] when he understood the facts. There are quite a lot of facts

the Leader of the Opposition does not have. When he got into government I thought he would carry on the programme, so it didn't worry me unduly.[113]

Nearly seven years later I discovered one of the reasons why Alec Home had been so confident about this. When his No. 10 files for 1964 were declassified in January 1995, I came across a note from Thorneycroft of a privy counsellor-basis meeting with the shadow Defence Secretary, Denis Healey, on 3 February 1964 in which Healey had talked through the feasibility of pooling a British Polaris fleet with the Americans inside a NATO Atlantic force.[114] This, as we shall see in a moment, was the line Wilson pursued once inside No. 10. But why did he persist in public, right up to election day 16 October 1964, to create the impression that Polaris would be cancelled? In private, he told Dick Neustadt (who had prepared an autopsy on Britain and Skybolt cancellation for President Kennedy[115]) that he had little to lose by taking this line as he could not compete with Douglas-Home for the 'jingo vote'.[116]

Less than a month after taking office, Wilson, in a tiny Cabinet committee, MISC 16, consisting of himself, Patrick Gordon Walker, the Foreign Secretary, and Healey, the Defence Secretary, decided on 11 November 1964 (Armistice Day, intriguingly enough) that the construction of the Polaris fleet should continue; that when completed it should be assigned to a proposed Atlantic Nuclear Force (ANF); but its control technology 'would not mean that we could not regain independent control of our nuclear forces should, for example, the NATO Alliance dissolve'.[117] Wilson and his inner group wanted to run the idea of an ANF to thwart the creation of an American-backed multilateral force, MLF, which would involve a mixed-manned, nuclear-capable NATO surface fleet.

To increase the chances of this idea flying in Washington, MISC 16 were prepared to throw in, as it were, some V-bombers. The very paragraph in the minutes which incorporates this also gives away Wilson's *lack* of desire to remove for ever from a nuclear button the finger of a British Prime Minister:

The nuclear forces which we might offer to commit in accordance with these proposals would be part of the V-bomber force (the remainder being retained under United Kingdom control solely for us in a conventional role outside the

NATO area) together with three POLARIS submarines. The three submarines would represent the minimum force which would be acceptable to us in the event of the dissolution of the NATO Alliance.[118]

Alec Home was right. Wilson could not bring himself to do it. The pull of the nuclear was too strong. He sold this line to a larger Cabinet committee, MISC 17, and the full Cabinet before Christmas 1964.[119] Early in the new year, the Cabinet's Defence and Overseas Policy Committee decided to go for four Polaris boats.[120]

Much of this was classic Wilson smoke-and-mirrors. Denis Healey exposed one element of it in his memoirs, recalling that when he told Wilson and Gordon Walker 'it would still be possible to convert them [the UK Polaris boats] into hunter-killer submarines at no additional cost . . . they asked me not to let other members of the Cabinet know; Wilson wanted to justify continuing the Polaris programme on the grounds that it was "past the point of no return". I did not demur.'[121] The Cabinet minutes for 26 November record Wilson as saying, in the context of the proposed ANF,

we would commit irrevocably, so long as NATO existed, our V-bomber force assigned to Europe and such Polaris submarines as we might construct. The precise number of these submarines would be for further consideration; but it was relevant to a decision that the construction of some of them was already sufficiently advanced to make it unrealistic to cancel the orders. On the other hand the number to be retained would be smaller than the number [five] which the previous Government had envisaged and would be such as to make it clear that we no longer contemplated the maintenance of an independent nuclear force.[122]

But we – or rather he – did.

In January 1967, with all talk of an ANF or an MLF long past, Wilson's new Ministerial Committee on Nuclear Policy, PN (which had first met the previous September[123]), authorized Healey

to inform the authorities of the North Atlantic Treaty Organisation of our intention to assign the POLARIS submarines to NATO in terms which would retain ultimate United Kingdom control . . . As a result, SACEUR [NATO's Supreme Allied Commander Europe] has been given a firm assurance that, in accordance with the Nassau Agreement, our POLARIS missiles will be assigned to him as soon as the first submarine becomes operational ie in 1968.[124]

The moment my student Matthew Grant brought Healey's minute of 3 August 1967 into my seminar room during the spring of 2001 (having just discovered it at the PRO), it confirmed that Wilson's fingers had never been prised from the release codes. The assignment of Polaris to NATO, Healey made plain, would not change this:

Ultimate United Kingdom control of the POLARIS force will not be affected, since control of the firing chain will remain in UK hands; in particular, no submarine commander will be authorised to fire the POLARIS weapons without the Prime Minister's specific authority.[125]

So much for the 1964 manifesto and all the flimflam in Cabinet and Cabinet committee that autumn. Alec Home had read his rival perfectly.

When I asked Denis Healey nearly a quarter of a century later why he, Wilson and Gordon Walker had decided the way they did in November 1964, he replied with a mixture of pragmatism and the doctrine of unripe time:

The basic reason was that the deal which Macmillan had got out of Kennedy was a very good one. It was a very cheap system for the capability it offered. We'd already got one boat nearly complete and another was on the stocks. So the saving from cancellation would have been minimal. And, given the uncertainties – the Cuban Missile Crisis was only a year or two behind us, the memory of Hungary was still in our minds, Khrushchev had been deposed the day before the British poll, the Chinese had just exploded their bomb the same day – we felt, on the whole, it was wise to continue with it.[126]

Wilson's equivalent rationale had a resonant echo of 1954 reasoning.

MISC 16 had 'borne in mind' that the acquisition of Polaris 'would, after the end of service of the V-bomber Force, be our only means of access to United States technology in the field of nuclear missiles'.[127] Over twenty years later, a frail Lord Wilson of Rievaulx deployed this argument plus a dash of Churchill-like views on the need to watch the Americans, to justify his apparent volte-face in 1964:

I never believed we had a really independent deterrent. On the other hand, I didn't want to be in the position of having to subordinate ourselves to the

Americans when they, at a certain point, would say, 'We're going to use it,' or something of that kind – though, in fact, I doubt anyone expected it ever to be used. It wasn't that we wanted to get into a nuclear club or anything of that kind. We wanted to learn a lot about the nuclear thing, and so on. We might need to restrain the Americans, if we learnt about new things that could happen of a devastating character.[128]

Wilson's reasoning should in no way be treated as casual, the 'we-might-as-well-keep-it' attitude of a new administration faced with a vexing international scene. For, as Matthew Grant has shown, even in the teeth of a prolonged sterling crisis in 1967–8, with Wilson declaring at a meeting of PN on 5 December 1967 that 'no particular element of the defence programme could be regarded as sacrosanct',[129] he kept open the possibility of the eventual improvement of Polaris (in what during the 1970s became the 'Chevaline' programme for coping with the anti-ballistic missile screen around Moscow[130]). At that very meeting of his nuclear policy committee in the days following the devaluation of sterling, Wilson avoided reaching a decision either for or against upgrading the weapon or for or against abandoning 'the whole of our nuclear capability as quickly as possible' to save money as the Treasury and the Department of Economic Affairs and their respective ministers (including the new Chancellor, Roy Jenkins) were urging.[131]

With all these factors in mind, there are two things, on reflection, I wish I had put to Wilson that morning in 1985 in his flat just across the road from Westminster Cathedral. The first is the argument I had heard privately four years earlier for going for the very latest version of the Trident missile as a replacement for Polaris:

The key to this is for us to possess a small amount of the latest American kit. If it comes to it, the Russian radar won't be able to tell if the Trident missile which emerges from the sea off Norway has a Stars and Stripes or the White Ensign on it. All they'll known is that it's a Trident and that it's coming at them ... This is one of the ways we keep the United States locked into the defence of Europe.[132]

As we have seen, Victor Rothschild reported a similar line of argument as having been given to the Kings Norton Committee (on the future of the Atomic Weapons Research Establishment at Aldermaston) in his minority report, which Wilson would have read when it went to PN in 1968.

The second regret is that I did not put to him the question with which A. J. P. Taylor roused the foundation meeting of the Campaign for Nuclear Disarmament in the Central Hall, Westminster, on 17 February 1958.[133] After describing the catastrophic consequences of the H-bomb, Taylor cried: 'knowing all this who would press the button? Let him stand up.'[134] Would Wilson have *ever* authorized a nuclear release? I should have asked him as I have asked other (though not all) premiers since (see Chapter 5 and Conclusion).

If he ever had, one of those responsible for delivering the bomb to its target would have been Air Vice-Marshal Bobby Robson. The Cabinet committee rooms housing GEN 163, GEN 464 and MISC 16 are central to any knowledge of the British Cold War state. But what of the men crammed into the fuselage of a V-bomber atop a huge 'Blue Danube' or 'Yellow Sun' weapon to which the fuse, once lit by a Prime Minister, would pass in a matter of seconds? Bobby Robson was the navigator in a Vulcan on Quick Reaction Alert at the end of the runway at RAF Waddington in Lincolnshire during the most perilous phase of the Cuban Missile Crisis. How does he answer the A. J. P. Taylor question now?

The same way he would have answered it in 1963 had the 'scramble' klaxon gone and his Vulcan roared off towards the 'start-line' (see Chapter 4) over the Baltic: 'If the hooter had gone, we would have gone. It would not have mattered whether it was for real or an exercise. Nobody would have given it a second thought. We were doing a job. I never ever heard a conversation on the rights and wrongs of dropping a nuclear bomb.'[135]

As we shall see in Chapter 4, Bobby Robson was not alone, in the wider context of transition-to-war planning, in wondering whether 'it would really all have worked'. But he was, and is, confident that his element of it would (at least until the V-bombers encountered the Soviets' surface-to-air missiles the other side of the Baltic). 'For a nuclear strike, it was very nearly Pavlovian. You ran up the engines and went about your business.'[136] In the end, Britain's Cold War stance rested on such an approach. Alan Taylor was right to place the 'Would you? Could you?' question at the centre of CND's business. For until

Polaris took over the deterrent job in June 1969,[137] with Harold Wilson's 'specific authority' required for the release of its missiles, Bobby Robson and his fellow pilots (vulnerable as their aircraft were in comparison to the Polaris submarines) constituted the secret state's ultimate instrument of retaliatory destruction.

3

Defending the Realm: Vetting, Filing and Smashing

The tendency has persisted for Civil Servants and others in comparable positions to come to notice only from secret sources which, from their nature, are not necessarily able to provide a comprehensive picture of the situation at any given moment. The consequent difficulty of determining the extent of Communist penetration of the Civil Service is intensified by the fact that not infrequently people so employed may push their discretion to the point of avoiding any formal commitment to the Party.

MI5 report on 'The Communist Party.
Its Strengths and Activities', 1 April 1948[1]

The [Moscow] Centre calculated that since their recruitment in 1934–5, Philby, Burgess and Maclean had supplied more than 20,000 pages of 'valuable' classified documents and agent reports. The Mitrokhin Archive[2]

The Security Service has for many years made a study of subversive bodies and their adherents, both open and covert, and has built up detailed records amounting in the case of the Communist Party and its fellow travellers to some 250,000 files.

Report of the Committee on Positive Vetting,
27 October 1950[3]

Organised sabotage before war is most unlikely because the Soviet leaders will be unwilling to give away their plans to Communists in the United Kingdom. No organised sabotage will take place after the outbreak of war because, as at present

> *planned, the whole known organisation of the British*
> *Communist Party will have been smashed. Even if a secret and*
> *unknown party organisation were in existence at the time, and*
> *we consider this unlikely, it would not devote itself to the task*
> *of organising sabotage.*
>
> Joint Intelligence Committee report on the
> 'Likely Scale and Nature of Attack on the United Kingdom
> in a Global War up to 1960', 10 May 1956[4]

If World War III had come, no chances would have been taken. Special Branch, using the detailed picture pieced together by MI5, would – as the 1956 JIC document makes plain – have destroyed the known Communist Party apparatus in the United Kingdom, rounding up, no doubt, those deemed most dangerous among the membership. It is very easy to make mock of the point where the secret state would have transformed itself into the take-no-chances-state. And the transition-to-war games fully built in the 'enemy within'[5] aspect to their simulations, as we shall see in a moment, as they did the activities of the Campaign for Nuclear Disarmament and the more militant student activists of the late 1960s.

To those potentially or actually on the receiving end of the secret state's sifting and screening (the 'smashing', mercifully, never materialized), the notions on which MI5 based their work and justified it to ministers could appear overdone to the point of being ludicrous. Looking back as the century turned on the years since 1945, the Communist and historian Eric Hobsbawm said:

After 1956, my activism was transformed into something different and more detached. From that time, it was clear to me that the dream was over. The general secretary of the Communist Party of Great Britain, of which I remained a member almost up to the date of its dissolution [November 1991[6]], used to say in difficult moments that he could have done with a direct telephone line to Moscow. He thought the party was an army of messenger boys, while those who worked in the intellectual professions realised that we had to try to think things through on our own.[7]

Professor Hobsbawn later identified the man and the moment. 'It was Johnny Gollan in 1956,' he wrote (Gollan had just succeeded Harry

Pollitt). 'Whether he meant it, or was just being ironic, I don't know. Certainly he had got the job suddenly (Harry's retina gave out suddenly) and was not completely at home in the job.'[8]

MI5 definitely wanted to know who the Party's 'messenger boys' were – and, beyond them, those who might be regarded as fellow-travellers within the Party's unofficial penumbra. By the autumn of 1950 there were a quarter of a million files on these two categories combined, an awesome number (assuming that this reflected a tally of one person, one file). The Security Service's own estimate of CPGB membership at that time was 43,500.[9] Over 200,000 people on top of this were deemed to be real or possible sympathizers. So around one in 200 of the UK mid-twentieth century population was treated as being a Communist or having Communist-leaning beliefs.

This was the product of a huge enterprise over the thirty and more years after 1917 since when, in the words of the internal history of the Security Service compiled in the last phase of World War II, 'it has been recognised that the fact that the Communist Party seized power in Russia in October of that year posed a problem for MI5'.[10] John Curry, the MI5 officer charged with writing its own secret history, reflected honestly the internal view that the Security Service had never cracked the enemy within:

Since the establishment of the Comintern or Third (Communist) International in March 1919 in Moscow and of the [British] Communist Party as a section of the Comintern in August 1920, the nature of this problem has varied even more widely. It is safe to say that the machinery in MI5 – or the Security Service – has never been adequate to cope with this problem in the sense of formulating a comprehensive appreciation of developments as they occurred, and that during the greater part of the time the material for an adequate understanding of it has been lacking.[11]

Curry, who had himself headed the new MI5 F section when it was created in April 1941 to deal with internal subversion of government departments and the Armed Forces by Communists or fascists (these were the last days of the Nazi–Soviet Pact), and espionage by Soviet and Comintern agents, was graphic about the problems he and his colleagues faced after the German invasion of Russia in June 1941 with the Soviet Union now a member of the anti-Axis alliance:

The evidence available to the section soon made it clear that in spite of the Communist Party's support of the war effort its long-term policy was unchanged and the long-term policy of the section had to be adapted accordingly. It was not always easy to put this view before Government Departments which were profiting from the cessation of Communist obstruction and were in receipt of offers of positive help. It fell to members of the section to convince their opposite numbers in Government Departments that their views were soundly based on knowledge and experience. They felt that they had to make it clear that their views were 'not merely the reactionary outpourings of people who had stuck to one job so long that their opinions had become ossified'.[12]

The watchers of MI5 pressed on as hard as they could. For example, in a passage worthy of John le Carré's fictional Connie Sachs (the great expert on KGB figures operating within the UK in *Tinker Tailor Soldier Spy*[13]), Curry writes of F.2.b (the sub-group of F Branch responsible for watching former operators of the now disbanded Comintern from whom Whitehall seemed to have averted its collective gaze): 'The only palliative to this situation was that F.2.b was in the hands of Miss Bagot whose expert knowledge of the whole subject enabled her to find and make available a large variety of detailed information based on records of the past.'[14]

F Branch learned a great deal about Communist methods for penetrating the wartime Civil Service and Armed Forces when David Springhall, the National Organizer of the Communist Party, was arrested in June 1943 and convicted the following month of offences against the Official Secrets Acts for obtaining information from a young woman in the signals branch of the Air Ministry and from Captain Desmond Uren, an officer in the Special Operations Executive, for onward transmission to Moscow.[15]

As a result of the apprehension of Springhall and Uren, F Branch circulated a memo, which reached Churchill, listing fifty-seven members of the CP 'known to be engaged in the Services or in Government Departments or in the aircraft or munitions industries of some secrecy'.[16] MI5 admitted that these people had acquired sensitive posts partly because of loopholes in the vetting system and because of 'the absence of a general policy in different Government Departments towards the problem created by the existence of the Communist

Party'.[17] F Branch felt it got nowhere, and its anxieties increased when evidence procured by 'secret means' indicated that the CP was engaged upon 'a series of instructional classes . . . held in various parts of the country to train new candidates for positions of trust'.[18]

Two figures, who later forsook the affiliations of their youth and rose to prominent positions in public life, have spoken to me about what in modern management jargon might be called the 'succession planning' in which the wartime CPGB engaged. One recalled how the Party indicated which branches of the Armed Forces those with officer potential should seek to join: 'Tank regiments were among them.'[19] And we have already encountered Harry Pollitt coming to Cambridge in the last phase of the war and telling the Party's undergraduates to get the kind of degrees that could carry them high in the public service.[20]

Both the Party and MI5 were utterly serious, and the Security Service finished the war in a state of high anxiety, partly through its inability to infuse other departments with a sense of urgency and partly because of the shadow of Springhall: inquiries into his activities had 'led to the disclosure of the fact that he was in touch with an organised group of Communists among the professional and intellectual classes'.[21]

Despite the eventual accumulation of a quarter of a million files, MI5 was chiefly interested in that inner core of first-class minds in high positions within the state. Party membership had stood at 17,500 at the outbreak of the war in September 1939, fallen to some 14,000 in the period of Nazi–Soviet co-operation and surged to 56,000 at its peak in 1942 ('in part', as British intelligence recognized, 'due to an enthusiasm for the Red Army's resistance'[22]). But the rank-and-file were not regarded as the problem even when the Cold War was well under way. There is a symmetry between Curry's 1944–5 analysis (when Whitehall generally was not minded to listen) and that of the big, early Cold War MI5 assessment of the penetration threat compiled in the first months of 1948 (when it was).

For Curry,

[though] the Communist Party remained a very small affair and failed to make any effective appeal, or to obtain any important increase in influence or membership, the situation created by the fact that so many of its members

secured important positions gave it a potential importance far greater than that warranted by its numbers. The alliance with the Soviet Government and the common purpose in the war were obstacles in the way of a more drastic policy for excluding Communists from positions of trust.[23]

The Security Service analysts of 1947–8, were even more precise in their categorization of Stalin's Brits of whom, they believed, there were just over 45,000 by this stage, split into the regular Party membership of 43,500, 2,000 members of the Young Communist League; and 'the secret members of the Party, who, contrary to estimates frequently given in the Press, cannot number more than a few score at the most'.[24] They saw the Party membership as falling

into two distinct sections. By far the larger of these sections, consisting of the full-time executives and the working class members, is mainly concerned with domestic policy; wages, housing, education, taxation, unemployment, health, pensions and so on. It is not well informed about or profoundly interested in foreign affairs and it accepts the central policy on Spain, Palestine or Greece without demur.[25]

MI5 here seems to have fallen into a crude class analysis of its own, as well as exhibiting an enormous condescension towards the rank-and-file of a Party which was both unusually internationally minded and exceptionally energetic in pursuing its own notions of political education. Be that as it may, it was this larger section which led MI5 to conclude that 'The most striking feature about the British Communist Party is that it is, first and foremost, a political party like other political parties. In so far as it partakes also of the character of a subversive or conspiratorial organisation, it does so to a secondary degree.'[26]

It was the brains of the CP, carried in the heads of its professional classes, against which the realm of George VI had to be defended:

The smaller section, the intellectuals of the Party, comprising University students and graduates, civil servants and members of the professions, is on the other hand primarily concerned with international issues and this is the interest which it has in common with the amorphous body of 'communist sympathisers', who are less sympathetic to the British Communist Party than to the ideological conception of international communism. If there were any subversive activity on behalf of a foreign power carried out in peace-time, one would expect it to be carried out by individuals of the intellectual group acting on their own initiative. The working class group is unlikely to be the source of peace-time espionage.[27]

The 'if' is significant. Even as late as the spring of 1948 there is a tentative air about this MI5 assessment. The VENONA traffic was in the process of being broken, but British counter-intelligence, for all Curry's anxieties in 1944–5 and the JIC's depiction in 1946 of the Communist movement having 'an appeal of its own which cannot be disregarded without seriously under-rating its strength and resilience',[28] was still nowhere near appreciating just how successful Stalin's recruiters had been in the British universities, Cambridge in particular, a decade earlier.

The counter-penetration defences the Attlee Government set about constructing between 1947 and 1951, including GEN 183, the Cabinet Committee on Subversive Activities,[29] might well have failed to deter or catch the 'Magnificent Five' even had they been in place by 1930, but the Soviet Union's greatest ever human intelligence bonanza was long in the bag. Had the MI5 assessors, and their ministerial and Whitehall customers, known about Philby, Burgess, Maclean, Blunt and Cairncross as World War turned into Cold War, their anxieties would have multiplied several fold – not least because Kim Philby, as head of SIS's section IX (the special group formed to study Soviet and Communist activity)[30] from the end of 1944 to 1947, was almost certainly one of the chief framers of the JIC study on 'The Spread of Communism Throughout the World and the Extent of Its Direction from Moscow' of September 1946.[31] No doubt Philby directed that very document to Moscow himself.

The secret defenders of the realm may have been unaware of Philby and co.'s betrayals, but other spies and events *had* pushed counter-espionage high up the Whitehall and intelligence agenda even before the first of the VENONA intercepts had been decoded in the United States during the last months of 1946. The factor which propelled the issue upwards was the defection of Igor Gouzenko, a cypher clerk in the Soviet Embassy in Ottawa, in September 1945. Not only did Gouzenko expose a serious GRU spy ring in Canada, he also supplied the Canadian – and through them, the British and American – authorities with 'fragmentary intelligence' on KGB operations.[32]

The Gouzenko revelations were the trigger for Attlee's establishing of GEN 183 in the spring of 1947. Why the delay? MI5, as we have seen and as the first paper prepared for GEN 183 made plain, had long been 'satisfied that the Communist organisation, which has foreign support, and is subservient to a foreign power, at present constitutes the principal danger [as opposed to 'the Fascist organisations, or at the other extreme, the Revolutionary Communist Party']'.[33] But it was the 'mass of concrete evidence on this subject' contained in the account compiled by the investigatory Royal Commission set up in Canada in the wake of Gouzenko's defection and which had recently reported that led to such 'disquiet' in London, 'particularly in the light that it throws on the methods used so successfully by the Russians to recruit as agents, and to obtain information from, persons employed in the service of the Canadian Government'.[34]

British counter-intelligence, despite the best efforts of MI5's F Branch, had still much to learn about the methods of Soviet intelligence in open societies. The Gouzenko experience, too, reinforced the MI5 view that overt, rank-and-file Communists were not the problem:

It seems to be the general policy of the Communist Party not only in Canada, but elsewhere, to discourage selected sympathisers from joining the Party openly. One purpose no doubt is to allay suspicion, but a further object may be to produce a psychological atmosphere of conspiracy which would be favourable to the demands made on the individuals selected for use in this way.[35]

The Canadian lesson was read over directly to other Western societies and in their advice to ministers, the working party could not 'escape the conclusion that what was done in Canada might be attempted with comparable if not equal success in any other democratic country including our own'.[36]

In sweet innocence of the shoals of documents that had flowed, and were still flowing, from the 'Magnificent Five' to their Soviet controllers, usually but a few miles from MI5 headquarters, the working party advised Mr Attlee and the small group of ministers within his counter-subversion circle that

It is not possible to say with any authority whether or not an organisation of the size of that exposed in Canada exists here at the present time, but it is significant that over the last twenty years a number of cases of Communist and Russian-inspired espionage against this country have come to light.[37]

Ministers were give a summary of these in a special annex, with particular emphasis on the Springhall case as it had 'a number of points of similarity with the Canadian case'.

A more recent episode preoccupied the early postwar intelligence community as it both linked the UK to Canada *and* furnished real evidence that the same thing was going on here in the area of number one anxiety – atomic research. The British physicist Alan Nunn May, who had worked at the Chalk River establishment in Ontario (Canada's contribution to the Manhattan Project), had been exposed by the Gouzenko defection in the bundle of documents and signals he carried out with him. Now back at King's College, May had been arrested in London in March 1946.[38] What alarmed the threat assessors in London was the fact that

On May's arrival in Canada the Soviet Military Attaché there was instructed to approach him and was given a password. This indicates that May had already been contacted, probably in England. Elaborate arrangements for a further meeting with 'our man in London' – probably a member of the staff of the Soviet Military Attaché – were made in a series of telegrams between Ottawa and Moscow, though this meeting was never kept, presumably owing to the fact that the Russian informant [Gouzenko] came over to the Canadian authorities before May's return to this country.[39]

MI5's belief that 'secret sources' were the 'only' way to uncover spies in the public service, as they put it a year later,[40] rested, no doubt, on the Gouzenko experience and what was by the spring of 1948, thanks to the VENONA attack on the signals traffic between Moscow Centre and its American residences, a considerable and growing evidence 'of massive espionage in the wartime United States'.[41] Basing itself on its own and Gouzenko-supplied experience, the GEN 183 working party warned ministers of the swathe of information the KGB and GRU would be seeking to purloin from the UK:

First and foremost come military secrets, including scientific developments such as atomic research, radar, etc and industrial intelligence bearing upon our war potential. But this does not by any means exhaust the vulnerable field: information may be sought about Government policy or intentions in almost any field, either by the Russian Government or by the Communist Party at home, and the leakage of economic or purely industrial information may be no less serious.[42]

Counter-measures needed, therefore, to cover a wide terrain.

Here the vulnerability to penetration was plain. MI5's vetting procedure was rudimentary. It relied mainly on their own records, which 'while extensive, cannot be said to be exhaustive' – a revealing comment on that huge file mountain. For some reason, MI5 had not extended their gaze to the Young Communist League so had nothing on any CP-inclined youthful recruits to the clerical or executive classes of the Civil Service. They admitted, too, that clearance was virtually valueless: 'A "clean bill" only means that the individual concerned has not come to notice; it is no *proof* of his trustworthiness. This limitation is of importance, since it means that some "undercover" members of the Party, and those who are instructed not to join it (potentially the most dangerous category), may not come under notice at all.'[43] A plaintive echo of Curry's wartime cry was heard at this point. MI5 could only advise government departments on some cases of who not to employ, and anyway the 'field over which enquiries are made' about an individual depended on their department rather than the Security Service.

The Canadian Royal Commission report had persuaded the GEN 183 group that 'existing arrangements must be considerably tightened up'. There were difficulties, however, the first being the question of civil and personal liberties. Should membership of the CPGB, open or covert, of itself be 'a bar to employment in the Public Service on *secret work*, or whether other facts beyond mere membership must be advanced, e.g. friendship with fellow-Communists suspected of contact with the Russian services in this country'. Attlee's security advisers came down in favour of a hard line as it was impossible to separate those British Communists who would spy for Russia from those who would not until the damage had been done.

In effect, GEN 183 constructed a revised definition of loyalty to what was already by the spring of 1947 becoming a new notion of the state shaped by the Cold War – a definition devised by its most secret element, the security and intelligence community. 'We appreciate,' they told Attlee and his ministers,

the objections to the adoption, in times of peace, of a procedure under which candidates for or members of the Public Service might be penalised simply because they are – as they have a legal right to be – members of the Communist Party. On the other hand, the first duty of every Civil Servant is to give his individual allegiance to the State, and the State has a right – indeed the duty – to protect itself by ensuring that its interests are not endangered by the employment of persons who may not accept this view of their obligations. The ideology of the Communist involves, at the least, a divided loyalty, which might in certain contingencies become active disloyalty: the Canadian case has amply demonstrated the reality of this danger.[44]

It may be that the framers of the first paper to go to the Cabinet Committee on Subversive Activities were aware that several Labour ministers would have known and liked, and have very likely worked with, members of the Communist Party of Great Britain quite recently during the Grand Alliance years between June 1941 and August 1945. Demonizing decent people might have been counter-productive.

Whether sensitive to this possibility or not, they penned a section which appeared to take account of it:

This is not to say that all Communists would be prepared, even after long exposure to Communist indoctrination, to betray their country by consenting to work for Russian espionage agents; but there is no way of separating the sheep from the goats, at least until the damage has been done or suspicion is aroused, and even if a Communist Party member conceives himself to be entirely loyal to this country, he may not be averse from furthering what he regards as the constitutional aims of the Party by supplying information which may be of use in their political manoeuvres. Such an individual may easily become an unconscious espionage agent by supplying information which he thinks will be used for political purposes only, but which is being passed to the Russian agents by intermediaries.[45]

The conclusion, therefore, was the absolutist one 'that the only safe course is to decide that a member of the Communist Party is not to be employed on work where he may have access to secret information'.[46]

Within three weeks of the report being circulated, ministers had accepted it. Under the chairmanship of the Minister of Defence, A. V. Alexander, a mixed committee of ministers and officials including the Foreign Secretary, Ernest Bevin; the Home Secretary, James Chuter Ede; and the Minister of Labour, George Isaacs with the Director-General of MI5, Sir Percy Sillitoe, and the Head of the Civil Service, Sir Edward Bridges met on 16 June 1947. There was swift 'general agreement' on this core recommendation from the working party 'and the discussion turned mainly' on the areas to which the no-Communists rule should apply and how the new arrangements should be presented to the Civil Service unions.[47] The formal conclusion of the first meeting of GEN 183 placed fascists within the ban, too. The committee

agreed that members of all subversive organisations of the Right or Left should continue to be subject to security scrutiny and should not be employed on work involving access to secret information, and that, in particular, Communists should not be employed in the public service on such work.[48]

Built in at the start – and maintained throughout the Cold War and since – was a 'no martyrs' policy, whereby officials already in post 'in respect of whom adverse advice had been received from the Security Service', should be redeployed where possible in other branches of the public service which did not involve 'contact with secret matters'.[49] Only in cases where this was not possible would they be sacked.[50]

So here, in the realms of vetting, as in the British intelligence community's perception of the wider Soviet threat, the mould was set by the summer of 1947. The enemy within and the enemy without had been assessed and integrated. But, as with the JIC's sweeps of the world, the internal security picture was not static. For the 'tightening up' which the GEN 183 working party sought was refined several times in the 1940s, 1950s and 1960s and never seemed foolproof to the defenders of the realm – as it could not be, given the openness of British society and the weight of the GRU and KGB operations against the UK which the Mitrokhin Archive has substantiated in great detail.

The first efforts at raising the level of defence now appear truly feeble. The GEN 183 working party identified certain departments and areas of Civil Service work which, by their very nature, generated

material whose disclosure 'would be definitely prejudicial to the normal national interest' – the Cabinet, Foreign Office and Home Office
were included, as was the Ministry of Supply as the home of atomic
research and general weapons work. The private offices of ministers
and senior civil servants would be no-go areas for Communists. No
under-21-year-olds were to be employed on secret work as MI5 had
not investigated the YCL. What is mystifying about the GEN 183
report, which ministers accepted, with the resultant measures being
announced in the House of Commons by Attlee on 15 March 1948,[51]
was that it allowed for the *existing* procedures for vetting to be applied
more widely and integrated with the new ban on Communists and
fascists. Despite MI5's candour about the inadequacy of the contents
of its files, there was no suggestion that steps should be taken to
improve the quality of the information apart from the stricture that
'Departments should continue to exercise care even as regards staff
who have been cleared by the Security Service.'[52]

When MI5 produced its next big survey of the Communist problem
in the public service in the spring of 1948, the working party felt able
to reassure itself and its ministerial customers (this time on GEN 226,
Attlee's Cabinet Committee on European Policy – a strange body to
be considering such matters)

that Communism in the Civil Service does not at present constitute any serious
threat to the loyalty of the Service as a whole. The problem in relation to the
Civil Service is, therefore, entirely one of security in its narrow sense i.e. of
ensuring that individual civil servants are not given access to secret information. This risk has been dealt with and there is, therefore, nothing more
we need to say.[53]

What makes this so surprising is that the MI5 paper on which it was
based, on the face of it, gave no grounds for such complacency. As we
have seen, the Security Service stated in this assessment that usually it
was only 'secret sources' which threw up the names of Stalin's UK civil
servants and, in a paragraph devoted specifically to the senior ranks,
Sillitoe's people declared:

The number of known cases of people in the Administrative Grade of the
Civil Service who are members of the Communist Party, or who can be

regarded as virtually committed to it, does not exceed a score. None is of higher rank than Assistant Secretary and a number are unestablished. They form, however, a valuable reservoir of expert knowledge on which the Party can draw as required and as individuals they present security problems of real difficulty.[54]

Within two years, such complacency (however caveat-laden) was brutally exposed and a proper examination of vetting procedures was commissioned by Clement Attlee.

It has long been realized that the arrest of Klaus Fuchs, '[t]he most important of the British atom spies',[55] in January 1950 administered a profound shock to the guardians of British national security. Painstaking work on the VENONA intercepts the year before had revealed that the wartime atomic spy codenamed 'Charles' at Los Alamos in New Mexico had been Fuchs.[56] Only when the VENONA secret was fully divulged by the declassifications in Washington and London in the mid-1990s was it appreciated just how important the flow of its decrypts had been for those charged with gauging the degree of Soviet intelligence penetration of the Western allies. Though the documentation surrounding GEN 183, GEN 226 and the Committee on Positive Vetting (PV) naturally does not allude directly to the VENONA material, it can be deduced that it was a powerful factor driving Attlee's decision in 1950 to commission yet another review.

The question was whether the secret state needed a change in kind in its defences – from what became known as 'negative vetting' (the checks on the files which continued as the basis of security screening even after the 1947 review and the 1948 announcement of the restrictions on employment of Communists and fascists in the public service) to a more intrusive and focused system of investigation known as 'positive vetting'. After a meeting of GEN 183 which he chaired on 5 April 1950, Attlee appointed a Committee on Positive Vetting 'to consider the possibility of listing a limited number of posts in regard to which positive vetting could be undertaken and to assess the risks and advantages of embarking upon any such system of positive enquiry'.[57]

The PV Committee was chaired by John Winnifrith, the senior Treasury official who almost certainly invented the phrase 'positive vetting' and who did much of the Civil Service personnel work for Sir Edward Bridges, and two MI5 men, Roger Hollis and Graham Mitchell (both suspected later of having been secret agents themselves and accused of trying to delay and thwart the attack on the VENONA intercepts[58]). Continuity with the 1947 and 1948 working parties was provided in the person of S. J. (Joseph) Baker, the senior Home Office official who had signed both the earlier reports.

Winnifrith and his colleagues deliberated at a time of considerable hysteria in the United States. The House Committee on Un-American Activities had been in full swing for several years. Loyalty oaths were being imposed on public servants. And in February 1950 Senator Joe McCarthy made his famous speech in Wheeling, West Virginia, claiming to have in his possession a list of 205 known Communists in the US State Department.[59] The United States was very much in Attlee's and Bevin's minds; for great efforts were under way to reconstitute the World War II collaboration between the Manhattan Project partners broken by the 1946 McMahon Act and only partially restored by the so-called 1948 'Modus Vivendi' compromise between the US and UK governments (which allowed, for example, continued intelligence pooling on Soviet atomic activities).[60] The exposure of Fuchs had intensified American concerns about British security arrangements, especially on matters nuclear. The PV Committee inquiry was fuelled by the need to find a way of reassuring the United States without imitating its excesses – hence the emphasis on the risks as well as the advantages of more vigorous procedures, not least because the UK had, so far, avoided any naming and shaming of suspected security risks. Attlee, like Churchill after him, regularly rebuffed requests from the Conservative backbencher Sir Waldron Smithers to set up a House of Commons Select Committee on Un-British Activities.[61]

The question Winnifrith and his team posed to themselves was: 'Is there an inner circle of special secret posts and can such a category be confined within reasonable limits?'[62] From the outset they seem to have excluded the secret agencies from their reach, presumably because it was assumed that extra, special screening measures were already applied to them. MI5, through its Director-General, had been insisting for some time, as Sillitoe told GEN 183 in June 1947, 'that it was important that the number of names submitted to the Security Service should be kept to an absolute minimum if the process of vetting was to work efficiently and smoothly, and from his point of view any arrangement which, by narrowing the definition of "secret work", reduced the area over which vetting would be applied'.[63]

Hollis and Mitchell succeeded in ensuring that the MI5 line suffused the work of the Winnifrith Committee which produced a 'formula for defining such posts':

Posts to be included on the special list must make the holder privy to the whole of a vital secret process, equipment, policy or broad strategic plan, or to the whole of an important section of that process, equipment, policy or plan, where disclosure would be of crucial value to an enemy or potential enemy strategically or politically.[64]

Driven by this desire to avoid cost and the overloading of MI5, the committee convinced itself that the senior military could be excluded from any new vetting procedure as 'the need for special enquiries in the case of such officers is less, because in general more is known of the private background of serving officers than civil servants so that any undesirable associations are more likely to be known to their personnel branches'.[65] Added to this touching faith in the 'good chap' theory of crown service was the view that 'subordinate staff' should, with a few exceptions, remain outside the inner PV circle 'regardless of the admitted security risk involved' as their inclusion would be 'unmanageable'. The Treasury were to be brought in to ensure that departmental lists of sensitive posts did not get out of hand. By these means, the total of vettees 'would not contain more than 1000 posts' across the whole public service.[66]

What of the enhanced procedures to which the secret thousand would be subjected? The committee began with existing British practice before turning to the latest US methods:

Under present procedure the names of officers to be employed in connection with work the nature of which is vital to the security of the State (a category which is loosely defined and covers in present practice a very wide area of the Civil Service) are submitted by Departments to the Security Authorities. The Security Service has for many years made a study of subversive bodies and their adherents, both open and covert, and has built up detailed records amounting in the case of the Communist Party and its fellow travellers to some 250,000 files. Names submitted by Departments are checked against these records of persons of doubtful associations. In certain cases this some-times is supplemented by a further check of the Central Criminal Records at New Scotland Yard. These procedures do not, unless the man concerned is on the list of known suspects, reveal any facts about his wife, let alone his other relations, friends or associates.[67]

In the main, Whitehall departments did no more than 'rely completely on the check provided by the Security Service . . . without making any conscious effort to determine whether the candidate has the required degree of trustworthiness'. The Foreign Office *did* go further with staff to be posted behind the Iron Curtain, undertaking 'a very careful check based on an examination of their personal file'.

The America of J. Edgar Hoover's Federal Bureau of Investigation and the Washington of loyalty oaths are given short shrift in a single paragraph:

We understand that the FBI system is extremely elaborate. Before any person is appointed to any Government post in which he would have access to classified information, his name is checked over FBI records and he has to fill in a detailed and lengthy form listing his ancestry and the whole of his previous career, education etc. He is then subject to intensive overt police enquiries based on this form. We consider that any such procedure would be repugnant to British thinking.[68]

So with the UK status quo inadequate and the American way intolerable, what was the middle course devised by the Winnifrith Committee?

Driven powerfully by the need to clear any individual with 'access to cosmic documents' ('cosmic' being the special nuclear classification), they came up with a five-point plan to protect the state generally and its atomic segment in particular:

1: Existing screening methods should in the case of posts on the proposed vital list be supplemented by positive enquiries, the Department in all cases making a conscious effort to confirm the officer's reliability before appointing him to a post on the vital list.

2: Positive enquiries should normally take the simple form of a careful study of his records . . . combined with enquiries within or without the Department.

3: Personal records of officers likely to be appointed to vital posts should be maintained more fully than at present.

4: Where the study of an officer's record supplemented by departmental enquiry discloses that the Department knows nothing whatever about him, further enquiries should be made through the Security Authorities.

5: Where an officer has been appointed to a vital post, the Department should maintain as full a record as practicable of his background and associates. They should from time to time review his case and ensure, so far as possible, that nothing has occurred since his appointment to cast doubt on the initial presumption as to reliability.[69]

Herein lay a significant move, but a reluctant one. Winnifrith and his team loaded it with caveats, some of which had a touching, Ealing comedy air to them.

They were terribly concerned that word would get out that a civil servant was being vetted and suspicion would be aroused about 'men of blameless life and unblemished reputation' within their own departments and the neighbourhoods where they lived. Chief Constables should be involved to make sure that inquiries were by experienced police officers. Such policemen would need to ask questions of the civil servants' associates, tradesmen and 'domestic servants'. However discreet the policework, word might get out.

Perhaps most significant of all was the combination of reluctance *and* scepticism about the value of positive vetting which overlay the Winnifrith Report. At least two of the committee's members – Hollis and Mitchell – would by mid-1950, have begun to appreciate the magnitude of the 1930s and 1940s penetrations thanks to the VENONA decrypts, and the failure of MI5's efforts to break into them (which would probably have continued if GRU cypher security had not briefly turned sloppy, with the reuse of one-time encoding pads in the late World War II and early postwar years, that gave the VENONA codebreakers their chance).[70]

Compared to the rich counter-intelligence VENONA revealed, positive vetting was, and would always be, nowhere. And without, of course, mentioning signals intelligence, the Winnifrith Report said:

We do not suggest that this procedure will yield substantial results by way of disclosure of unreliable civil servants. It is reasonable to assume that the small total percentage (about 1%) of unreliables in the community at large is reflected in the Civil Service, though the percentage may be higher in the Scientific Civil Service. Moreover, the great majority of unreliable persons will already be known to the Security Authorities and their presence disclosed by current methods. Hence the chances of detecting the occasional individual who may have escaped the notice of the Security Authorities are very slight.

In line with earlier analyses of the internal threat, Winnifrith knew full well it was a small number of carefully camouflaged Soviet agents-in-place who comprised the real threat to security and whose existence would be detected only if they made a mistake themselves or they were exposed by a defector or a SIGINT breakthrough.

The additional enquiries which we propose will, moreover be open enquiries which will only produce the open information likely to be known to a man's neighbours and acquaintances. Whilst, therefore, these enquiries may reveal open association with Communists, they will fail to detect the really dangerous crypto-Communist. The latter's true nature will not be revealed by his accomplices and is unlikely to be known to his ordinary acquaintances. The detection of such persons can only be secured by the scientifically planned study of Communist activities which it is the task of the Security Authorities to carry out.[71]

None the less, the report, prepared for a meeting of the Cabinet Committee on Subversive Activities (with Attlee in the chair on this occasion), reached the firm conclusion that

The case for positive enquiries, which we recommend, is that it is the duty of the public service to take all reasonable steps to check the reliability of persons holding vital posts, that they would bring home to Departments their duty to consider security when making such appointments and that the detection of even a very small number of unreliable persons in such posts would counterbalance any disadvantages in the system.[72]

In the chill climate following the arrest of Fuchs, with the Korean War in an acute phase, Attlee and his colleagues had no difficulty in accepting the Winnifrith proposals when GEN 183 met on 13 November 1950.

Manny Shinwell, the Minister of Defence, said exactly this once Winnifrith had finished his presentation of the report: 'In present circumstances the country could not afford to take the risk of neglecting any practicable measure for increasing security.'[73] There was no dissent around the table, though the junior minister from the Air Ministry, Aidan Crawley, warned that American experience showed that FBI methods could impair scientific vitality. Attlee, a great believer in discretion and the self-disciplining concept of public service and personal duty, added a very British tone to this extension of the reach of the secret state that afternoon in the Prime Minister's room at the House of Commons. For him,

the chief point arising from the report was the need to change the attitude of Departments to one of conscious endeavour to confirm the reliability of holders of key posts, and to ensure that all in positions of responsibility become security-minded. It followed that Departments should not too easily accept the results of routine enquiry when deciding on the fitness of an individual to hold a key post, and should be prepared to go further if necessary. This was not likely to apply to most regular civil servants: the difficulties would be greatest in Departments of recent growth employing staff who had not absorbed the traditions of the public service. Special enquiries through the Security Service and the local police should, however, be quite exceptional and should be undertaken only with the approval of the Minister concerned.[74]

This was Attlee the public school headmaster, as Patrick O'Donovan characterized him a year of so later[75] – decency blended with a touch of naivety about the goodness of others.

For positive vetting took on a life of its own and became far from 'quite exceptional'. Two middle-ranking ministers present at GEN 183 that day, John Strachey, the former Marxist now Secretary of State for War, and Arthur Henderson, Secretary of State for Air, thought the lists of PV posts in their departments 'were not full enough'.[76] How right they proved. PVing, as it became known in Whitehall, spread mightily.

Figures are hard to come by both for the full reach of positive vetting or of those transferred or dismissed on the basis of its inquiries. But, in the early 1980s, I managed to acquire privately a set of figures for the Home Civil Service and published them in *The Economist*, where

I then worked. Since the adoption of the first 'purge procedure' in 1948, twenty-five British officials had been dismissed for security reasons, twenty-five resigned, eighty-eight people were transferred to non-sensitive work and thirty-three officials were later reinstated. None was named. In the United States, by contrast, security purges had led to the sacking of 9,500 federal civil servants. A further 15,000 resigned while under investigation for suspected Communist affiliations. All were named.[77]

Positive vetting was swiftly extended to the Armed Forces and, in 1955, to 'senior staff of firms handling top secret Government contracts'.[78] The Ministry of Supply, which contained the largest number of posts to be vetted from the start, became responsible for running a team of investigating officers, instead of the police, to carry out the inquiries across Whitehall. The Ministry of Defence took over responsibility for this on the demise of the Ministry of Supply.

From 1955, following inquests into the defection to the Soviet Union of Guy Burgess and Donald Maclean in 1951, what today would be called the sexual preferences of those within the reach of PVing were added to the scope of inquiry, on the grounds that certain activities could, if concealed or illegal, leave an official liable to blackmail by a hostile intelligence service.[79] A glance at Air Ministry files for the early 1960s shows just how unexceptional positive vetting had now become in what was then the key department for the nuclear deterrent. An internal notice to divisional heads explained that

A special procedure, known as positive vetting (PV) is used to determine the reliability of civilian staff who are to be employed on particularly secret work. This procedure is to be applied to any member of the staff who is required to have

(a) regular and constant access to top secret defence information; or

(b) any access to top secret atomic or cosmic information.[80]

The 'Security Questionnaire' attached to the file covers standard curriculum vitae matters plus relatives living abroad, foreign travel, offences against the law and fascist or Communist affiliations, sympathizers or associates ('the word "Communists" embraces Trotskyists for the purposes of this form' adds a nice, definitional touch). The

97

vettee is warned that 'enquiries which will be made will not necessarily be confined to the former or present employers and character referees named in your answers . . .'[81]

Serious vetting of a different kind was extended to senior officials of Civil Service trade unions who were involved in pay and conditions negotiations on behalf of public servants within the secret state following the Radcliffe Report of 1962 which examined the implications of, among others, the case of John Vassall, the homosexual Admiralty clerk who had been blackmailed into spying for Russia.[82] As a result the government decided not to allow some very senior trade unionists to negotiate on behalf of their members in the Cabinet Office, the Ministry of Defence, the Service Departments, the Foreign Office and the Atomic Energy Authority.[83] The vetting of senior politicians has never been admitted. But throughout the Cold War years it was the practice of the head of MI5 on a change of government to leave a dossier containing things the new Prime Minister needed to know when first back from the Palace before making his or her ministerial appointments.[84] A small number of journalists, too, had inquiries made about them if their reporting took them some way into the workings of the secret state.[85]

Was PVing worth it? A former Special Branch policeman, now an investigating officer, asked me this in the late 1980s after I had helped him renew a senior civil servant's clearance which was required every five years. He plainly thought the effort and expense was very much open to question. I was not so sure for two reasons: one, pure Winnifrith, was that such steps were necessary even if only a few genuine security risks were either deterred from trying to move into sensitive posts or discovered if they did so; and, secondly, the process of PVing, including the completion of the questionnaire, made those concerned directly and personally aware that they were shifting into the inner circle of the state where security really mattered. This was particularly important, I thought, as Section 2 of the 1911 Official Secrets Act (not repealed until 1989) was so crudely and widely drawn as to be discredited and 'signing' it – as new civil servants were required to do – was largely meaningless.

What of the wider 'Communist problem'? Apart from deeply concealed agents-in-place, the main concern from the late 1940s on was with the influence the CPGB wielded among the senior officers of trade unions, which was out of all proportion to overall numbers (30,000 out of 8.7m UK trade unionists, MI5 reckoned in 1948[86]), the personal qualities of some Communist union leaders such as Arthur Horner of the Mineworkers[87] and with the 'central discipline and co-ordination' the Party brought to the trade unionists within its ranks.[88] In 1955 MI5 briefed the Prime Minister (Sir Anthony Eden being alarmed by the current level of industrial unrest) that, as Cabinet Secretary Sir Norman Brook's summary put it, the CPGB believed that 'the advocacy of strike action would more often hinder than help it in its primary objective of penetrating and eventually controlling the trade union movement . . . while its members account for less than one in 500 of the national trade union membership, the Party now controls the Executive Committees of three trade unions; and thirteen General Secretaries and at least one in eight of all full-time officials are Communists'.[89]

Reading the files, including those dealing with the internal threat posed by the CPGB and the Party's dealings with Moscow which reached the JIC, it is striking to see the detail with which inner-Party matters are displayed. One gets the unmistakable impression that MI5 had the inside of 16 King Street (the Party's headquarters in Covent Garden) very well covered in terms of both human agents and technical surveillance.[90] When the CPGB, in severe financial difficulties, sold 16 King Street to Lloyds Bank for over £1m in 1980, 'a hidden microphone was found embedded in the wall'.[91] It is plain from Curry's internal history that MI5 were monitoring throughout World War II 'a steady flow of secret information about weapons and about operations to Party Headquarters' provided by the 'Forces Organisation' of the CP, some of the most important of which Curry listed.[92] And the huge haul of KGB archive material copied by its archivist, Vasili Mitrokhin, and removed (along with Mitrokhin and his family) to the UK by MI6 in 1992[93] demonstrated the unsurprising fact that Soviet intelligence knew King Street was bugged, thanks to Anthony Blunt's presence in MI5. Blunt told his controller, Boris Krotenschield (whom he shared with Philby), that James Klugmann, a leading British Communist intellectual who later wrote two volumes of the Party's official history,[94] had boasted within the walls of 16 King Street of passing to

Yugoslav Communists classified information gleaned in the course of his work in the Yugoslav Section of the Special Operations Executive in Cairo.[95] King Street's telephones were tapped continually.[96]

If war had come, MI5 and Special Branch, in organization-smashing mode, would have known quite well who and where most overt Party members were. The detailed contingency plans for the round-up are not yet declassified. But we do know from fragments of the Defence Transition Committee archive that, by early 1949, plans were in place to reopen, if necessary, internment camps on the Isle of Man which had been used to house so-called 'enemy aliens' during World War II.[97]

In a strange way, both MI5 and the CPGB knew where they were with each other. Their tussle had been continuous, as Curry indicated,[98] since 31 July 1920 when 160 'revolutionary socialists with new hope in their hearts' strode in to the Cannon Street Hotel near St Paul's Cathedral in the City of London to set about founding a Communist Party of Great Britain with Lenin's encouragement.[99] From the very earliest years Party members knew they were under surveillance, some of which went ludicrously awry. In 1924 the speaker at a CP meeting opened a trapdoor beneath the stage 'to discover two men taking shorthand notes. The police were called and they arrested the men, only discovering later that they had arrested fellow policemen.'[100]

By 1957, however, both Party and Security Service had to face a new phenomenon which left both, initially, somewhat surprised and baffled. This was the sudden revival of the peace movement, in the run-up to what became the foundation of the Campaign for Nuclear Disarmament. For historians of these movements the bigger surprise is that a serious anti-nuclear weapons movement did not form earlier. Attlee's Defence Minister, A. V. Alexander, had announced in the House of Commons on 12 May 1948, in reply to a planted Parliamentary question, that 'all types of modern weapon, including atomic weapons, are being developed',[101] and the press and the political nation had hardly taken any notice.[102] A month before, there had been a meeting on atomic weapons at Caxton Hall in Westminster addressed by such peace-movement stalwarts as Vera Brittain and Ritchie Calder,[103] but it took another nine years before a coalescence of radical and pacifist groups came together with a degree of force and verve that enabled them to catch and ride a mood which left both the Labour Party and the CPGB somewhat baffled.

It is intriguing to compare the histories of CND Mark I (1958–64, as distinct from its 1980s revival) written in the early 1960s by Christopher Driver, a sympathetic observer, for a public audience[104] and the much shorter MI5 one prepared for a very select audience of one – the Prime Minister, Harold Macmillan.[105] In the spring of 1963 Macmillan held a meeting on 'Security', partly prompted by the so-called 'Spies for Peace'. During the Easter 1963 CND Aldermaston March (Aldermaston being the site of the government's Atomic Weapons Research Establishment) the direct-action offshoot of CND, the Committee of 100, began distributing a pamphlet of six sheets of duplicated foolscap as the march passed through the Berkshire woods on its way to Reading.[106]

The timing and location were perfect. The pamphlet's authors, the 'Spies for Peace', knew that one of the government's new underground regional seats of government (which we will examine more fully in Chapter 4), RSG-6, lay nearby, close to the village of Warren Row. The flimsy document carried a dramatic title, 'Danger! Official Secret: RSG-6', and it went on to inform its avid readers 'about a small group of people who have accepted thermo-nuclear war as a probability, and are consciously and carefully planning for it . . . They are based in fourteen secret headquarters, each ruled by a Regional Commissioner with absolute power over millions of people.'[107]

This disclosure represented a substantial breach of official secrecy. The 'Spies for Peace', who have never been identified, but who 'emerged' from the London Committee of 100 over the winter of 1962–3,[108] had actually managed to break in to the Warren Row installation in February 1963 and left after photographing several classified files and removing a suitcase-full of material.[109] As a result, on Easter Saturday 1963, hundreds of marchers left the main column to demonstrate outside Warren Row '[m]uch to the annoyance of the CND leadership'.[110]

Within a few days, Macmillan held his 'Security' meeting (the minutes of which have not been declassified) and asked for information on 'the development of the Nuclear Disarmament Movement'. Within a day, Sir Charles Cunningham, Permanent Secretary to the Home Office, forwarded to No. 10 'a memorandum which has been prepared summarising the information available to us'.[111] It is plainly an MI5 brief as it deals with the degree to which CND had been penetrated by Communists.[112]

The MI5 paper opened with a very succinct history of the faltering early, pre-CND days. The nuclear disarmament movement, the Security Service told the PM,

grew from small beginnings in the early and middle 1950s. Two small demonstrations, one at Aldermaston, took place in 1952 [organized as a one-off by Hugh Brock, then editor of *Peace News*[113]]. In 1954, the year of the American Pacific test with its effects on the crew of the Japanese fishing smack 'Lucky Dragon', Canon Collins [of St Paul's Cathedral], Fenner Brockway, MP and Dr Donald Soper [a leading Methodist minister] tried to mount an anti H-bomb campaign.[114]

The huge US thermonuclear explosion at Bikini Atoll on 1 March 1954 (at 15 megatons the 'Bravo' shot was the largest the Americans ever mounted[115]) covered the Japanese fishermen and their ship eighty-five miles away and outside the exclusion zone, with fall-out. The vessel returned to Japan with nearly the whole crew ill 'with classic symptoms of radiation sickness'.[116] The Japanese Government protested. The outside world, for the first time, began to appreciate fully what these weapons could do and debate was widespread, including in the House of Commons on 5 April 1954, which led to the foundations of the Hydrogen Bomb National Campaign two days later,[117] to which the short MI5 history of CND and its precursors referred.[118]

It still surprises me that this pressure group resonated so feebly. As Christopher Driver wrote less than ten years after Soper, Collins and Brockway made their initial attempt to mobilize opinion: 'The Hydrogen Bomb National Campaign is little remembered and it is an index of its obscurity that a year or two later, when anti-nuclear agitation sprang up spontaneously in various parts of the country, most people felt that they were starting something fresh . . .'[119]

There were a few mid-1950s sputterings which the MI5 analyst felt worth summarizing:

In 1956, the year when the British Government announced its intention to test a thermo-nuclear bomb at Christmas Island, a National Council for the

Abolition of Nuclear Weapons Tests was set up with Peggy Duff as Organiser and Secretary and Lord Russell as one of its sponsors. Small independent demonstrations occurred from time to time; for instance, shortly before the Christmas Island test in May 1957, a procession of women in black sashes marched from Hyde Park to Trafalgar Square.[120]

But what led to the welling up of spontaneous anti-nuclear agitation in 1957? The Driver and MI5 analyses overlap to a considerable degree. For the Security Service, 'an organised Nuclear Disarmament Movement can perhaps be said to have begun with the formation of the Direct Action Committee in November 1957 and the Campaign for Nuclear Disarmament in February 1958'.[121]

MI5's dating of the origins of the DAC is a little awry. The Emergency Committee for Direct Action against Nuclear War, as it was first called, was created in April 1957 to help get Harold and Sheila Steele to the Pacific, where they wished to mount a floating protest against the Christmas Island Test (in the event, they arrived too late to protest against the May explosion). MI5 were up against an unusually eclectic group in the DAC, as Driver neatly illustrated: 'Its sponsors included several Quakers (Horace Alexander, Ruth Fry, Laurence Hansman), an Earl (Russell), a Goon (Spike Milligan), and an Anarchist biologist (Alex Comfort).'[122] The 23 November 1957 meeting, which the Security Service analysts rightly saw as significant to the wider history of the revived peace movement, was held 'to welcome Harold Steele, who had returned from Japan, and to discuss further projects'.[123]

It was at this meeting, too, that the possibility of an Aldermaston March emerged. It was proposed by Hugh Brock, a veteran pacifist who had been imprisoned during World War II as a conscientious objector. It had been suggested to him by Laurence Brown in May 1957 as they watched the procession in the pouring rain of 2,000 women in black sashes from Hyde Park to Trafalgar Square organized by the National Committee for the Abolition of Nuclear Weapons Tests,[124] the demonstration MI5 had thought worthy of inclusion in its paper for the Prime Minister.[125] The DAC recruited Pat Arrowsmith, a social worker and an NCANWT activist, who put off finding a new job to organize the first Aldermaston March instead[126] – an event central to CND's image which, along with other aspects of the Campaign changed the face of protest and pressure in postwar Britain and paved the way for Greenpeace and a host of single-issue organizations whose vitality and, in some cases, membership figures came to eclipse those of the mainstream political parties.[127]

MI5's dating system was a little astray too, on the foundation of CND. The key meeting took place on the evening of 15 January 1958 in Canon Collins's study at 2 Amen Court in the shadow of St Paul's Cathedral. The intention to proceed was announced at a press conference on 30 January and the inaugural meeting took place in Central Hall, Westminster, on 17 February (clearly the founding moment MI5 had in mind). The packed, 5,000-strong gathering was roused to passion by the political and diplomatic historian, A. J. P. Taylor in particular as we have seen.[128] The cause of unilateral British nuclear disarmament took wing.

It took many by surprise. What retrospectively, did MI5 believe gave it life? 'The factors,' they told Macmillan over five years later,

that prompted their formation at this time were increasing anxiety about testing; the public discovery that American planes carrying H-bombs were patrolling over Britain; inferences drawn from the Defence White Paper that nuclear forces would be used to reply even to conventionally armed enemy attack; the Anglo-American agreement on missile bases in Britain; and increasing publicity for the view that Britain could offer no realistic defence to nuclear attack.[129]

Driver's analysis is remarkably similar to MI5's, though he (unlike the Security Service, which may have felt constrained in addressing its Downing Street customer), filled in the wider picture of post-Suez and Hungary disillusionment, 'which at one stroke turned the most sensitive minds of [this] . . . generation [of the intellectual left] equally away from Communist leanings and from all forms of political bipartisanship . . .'[130]

Both MI5 and Driver placed great emphasis on the contribution of Macmillan's first Minister of Defence, Duncan Sandys, to the mix of causes which led towards the road to Aldermaston (the first march over Easter 1958 went from Trafalgar Square to the Atomic Weapons Research Establishment; subsequent ones went in the reverse direction). The 1957 White Paper containing the results of the Sandys defence review, with its promise both to reduce spending and to abolish conscription thanks to a central reliance on nuclear deterrence with the H-bomb-equipped V-force on the horizon, spared the Queen's subjects very little:

It must be frankly recognised that there is at present no means of providing adequate protection for the people of this country against the consequences of an attack with nuclear weapons. Though in the event of war, the fighter aircraft of the RAF would unquestionably take a heavy toll of enemy bombers, a proportion would inevitably get through. Even if it were only a dozen, they could with megaton [i.e. hydrogen] bombs inflict widespread devastation.[131]

The argument of the Macmillan Government, as expressed in the Sandys White Paper, was that, in the absence of international agreement, 'the only existing safeguard against major aggression is the power to threaten retaliation with nuclear weapons'.[132] Sandys went on to declare that

While Britain cannot by comparison [with the United States] make more than a modest contribution, there is a wide measure of agreement that she must possess an appreciable element of nuclear deterrent power of her own. British atomic bombs are already in steady production and the RAF holds a substantial number of them. A British megaton weapon has now been developed. This will shortly be tested and thereafter a stock will be manufactured.[133]

It was Sandys's claim that there was 'a wide measure of agreement' on Britain as a nuclear deterrent nation that CND set out to disprove.

The Labour Party declined to make itself the vehicle for this during the famous debate at its Brighton Conference in October 1957 when the shadow Foreign Secretary, Aneurin Bevan, horrified many of his followers by denouncing unilateralism as an 'emotional spasm' and deriding the notion that a British Foreign Secretary should have to stride 'naked into the international conference chamber'.[134] Though unilateral nuclear disarmament never did prevail as the numerically dominant strand of thought in the UK (the opinion polls suggest it peaked in April 1960 when 33 per cent indicated a belief that Britain should '[g]ive up nuclear weapons entirely'[135]), it exerted a huge appeal across a spectrum of opinion in the late 1950s before, briefly, capturing the Labour Party (though not the Labour leadership) at the 1960 Scarborough Conference.[136]

A future Chief of the Secret Intelligence Service, David Spedding, went on the 1959 Aldermaston March and wrote it up as part of an anti-nuclear article in his school magazine at Sherborne, 'which caused some merriment when it was resuscitated by his MI6 colleagues many years later'.[137] A young grammar schoolboy, who within a few years would be one of MOD's nuclear retaliation planners, was a keen CND member in its early days (a fact which gave his positive vetters pause – but they passed him).[138] Among the right-wingers there was a reaction too. Some, true to form, tried to convert future nuclear anxiety into present laughter. Noël Coward, on a flight to California to meet (among others) Marlene Dietrich in the summer of 1957, read Neville Shute's *On the Beach* on the plane. It is, he wrote,

a grisly description of a group of people left alive in Australia when the rest of the world has been annihilated by H-bombs. They are waiting for the spreading radioactivity to spread to them and wipe them out which, eventually, it does. It's written with his usual fluency and is a good idea, but all the characters are so sickeningly decent and 'ordinary' and such good sorts that personally I longed for the slowly approaching 'fall-out' to get a move on.[139]

Even P. G. Wodehouse managed to weave CND into his extraordinary world with 'Bingo Bans the Bomb' when Bingo Little finds himself pulled to the pavement in Trafalgar Square by a beautiful young spriguette of the aristocracy, Mabel Murgatroyd, his subsequent arrest and a photograph of it in the *Mirror* newspaper causing him no end of bother with 'Mrs Bingo'.[140]

One set of imaginations, however, which the anti-nuclear movement did not capture in 1957–8 was that of Moscow's 'messenger boys' in King Street, but a few hundred yards from Trafalgar Square. Unlike several of those who quit the CPGB in horror at Hungary to create the early 'New Left', and who found in CND 'the cause and the comradeship'[141] they had lost by leaving the Party, the Gollan-led CP 'hesitated before lending its support to CND'.[142] Francis Beckett sees this as a crucial moment in the long decline of the British Communist Party 'allowing its enemies on the left to claim that it had betrayed the one movement which offered hope for the world. Its instinctive radicalism had deserted it. Its leaders did not seem to understand that 1956 had broken the Party's near monopoly on the left.'[143]

In Driver's words:

Despite extensive early coverage by the *Daily Worker* the Communist Party as such did not begin to support CND systematically till 1959, and at the 1957 Labour Party Conference Communist-controlled [trade union] votes were actually cast against the unilateralist motion. By 1960 the position was reversed, and Communist activity in unions on behalf of unilateralism, though probably not decisive in terms of votes, did give plausibility to Mr Gaitskell's [the Labour Party Leader's] outburst at Scarborough against 'pacifists, unilateralists and fellow-travellers'.[144]

Driver noted that during the Scarborough conference, 'Communists were unusually conspicuous among the CND claque. But the more popular CND's own brand of protest became, the less point there was in the Communist Party crying up what it had failed to control.'[145]

The rather shambolic structure – or lack of structure – on which CND rested made the standard CPGB skills at taking over trade union branches inoperable.[146] And MI5 reported this accurately to Harold Macmillan:

Since 1959 the Communist Party have participated in the Aldermaston marches and other demonstrations organised by the C.N.D., Direct Action Committee and the Committee of 100. This is not from the belief in the unilateralist cause but because the Communists see in these movements a chance to embarrass the Government and weaken the NATO alliance. At the same time there is little evidence that the Communists have succeeded in penetrating the movements to any great extent.[147]

In a strange way, Macmillan and CND deserved each other. The critic and writer Anthony Hartley was among the first to notice the symmetry between the veteran of the Somme and the young veterans of the Aldermaston marches. Writing of CND in 1963, he pointed out that there existed a 'gulf between undirected idealism and political possibility which has been opened by the decline of Great Britain's world power'. Looking back twenty years later, A. J. P. Taylor agreed that 'we made one great mistake which ultimately doomed CND to futility. We thought that Great Britain was still a great power whose example would affect the rest of the world. Ironically we were the last Imperialists.'[148] In other words, the ministers round the Cabinet table in 1954 and 1962–3, so keen (with Churchill) to go thermonuclear as a way of keeping a place at the 'top table' and (with Macmillan) to purchase Polaris for an updated version of the same impulse, shared with CND a belief in Britain as a big player in the world's game and a powerful shaper of the behaviour of others.

Such speculations were not for MI5's analysts, however. They may not have seen reds under every CND banner, but the real question for them was what kind of a threat did a non-CP-penetrated CND represent? And here they were particularly concerned with the direct activists on the DAC and, later, the Committee of 100. Indeed these were the trigger for Macmillan's request for his spring 1963 briefing. This element of CND, the image of the aged and distinguished Bertrand Russell sitting down outside the MOD in Whitehall, or demonstrators being carted away, very roughly in some cases, and placed in police 'Black Marias' after the Committee of 100's sit-down in Trafalgar Square on 17 September 1961,[149] is the one that chiefly remains in the popular memory – partly because it was imitated endlessly by the student protest movement, powerfully driven from 1965 by the escalation of the Vietnam War, into which much of CND-style activist politics mutated.

As Driver put it: 'From 1957 until 1961 (when it was merged into the Committee of 100) the DAC was the heart and soul, or the thorn in the flesh – according to taste – of CND.'[150] MI5 stressed the importance of direct action developments in 1960–61:

The Committee of 100 was launched in October 1960, under the leadership of Lord Russell and Rev. Michael Scott as a breakaway from CND. The Committee felt that more directness and urgency were needed to change national policy; they planned to do it by organising acts of civil disobedience involving at least 2000 people at a time. The Direct Action Committee soon became absorbed into the Committee of 100.[151]

MI5 listed for Macmillan the 'progressively more numerous and stubborn encounters with the police and the courts' in which the Committee of 100 engaged during 1961, culminating 'in Trafalgar Square in

September 1961 where crowds, including sightseers, at one time reached 8,000; 1,297 arrests were made'.[152]

CND had a penchant for taking on nuclear-related defence installations from its early days when the DAC lobbied workers building a missile site at North Pickenham near Swaffham in Norfolk in December 1958, enraging sections of those they sought to influence by sitting down in a cement-mixer.[153] It was the Committee of 100's spreading of this practice which concerned the authorities and, later, in the weeks following the Cuban Missile Crisis, attracted the attention of the Joint Intelligence Committee.

In fact, two direct action veterans, arrested after National Disobedience Day, 9 December 1961, when three air bases (Wethersfield, Ruislip and Brize Norton) were among the demonstrators' targets, have entered British intelligence history. MI5 reckoned the subsequent imprisonment of Michael Randle, Pat Pottle and four other members of the Committee of 100 'and the failure of the "National Civil Disobedience Day" demonstrations marked the beginning of a decline in the Committee of 100's influence'.[154] Pottle and Randle, however, MI5 would hear of again nearly thirty years later when their names came up in the memoirs of George Blake, the MI6 officer who spied for the KGB and was sentenced to forty-two years for it in 1961.

In the spring of 1962 Blake found himself a member of the same musical appreciation class in Wormwood Scrubs as Pottle and Randle, who were serving eighteen months for conspiring to incite others to commit a breach of section one of the 1911 Official Secrets Act in and around RAF Wethersfield in Essex, on which US Air Force planes were parked.[155] As Blake explained much later:

From the very beginning there was a good rapport between us. We all three considered ourselves political prisoners, had all three been sentenced under the Official Secrets Act . . . It is true, that they in no way approved of what I had done – they condemned spying in general – and made no secret of this. But they thought the sentence I had been given vicious and inhuman . . . and had a great deal of sympathy for me.[156]

They were able to demonstrate this four years later when they helped shelter Blake after his escape from Wormwood Scrubs and then helped smuggle him out of the country to where he presented himself to surprised East German border guards.[157]

In 1963 MI5 reckoned that with Pottle, Randle and others at its heart in prison, 'increasing disagreement among the leaders, increasing debts and decreasing support by the public', the Committee of 100 had been on the slide throughout 1962:

Plans to promote ideas of nuclear disarmament and disobedience tactics in the armed forces and in industry met with little success. The Committee aimed at getting a minimum of 7,000 pledges of support for a demonstration outside the Air Ministry in September 1962, but only 1,000 supporters turned up.[158]

Within weeks the Cuban Missile Crisis had come from nowhere and concentrated minds – including those of British intelligence – on CND's big theme to a degree quite unlike any other crisis before or since.

As MI5 reminded Macmillan six months later:

During the Cuban Crisis in October 1962, the CND and the Committee of 100 took part in a number of demonstrations which were largely spontaneous and fairly well supported. After the crisis, public support, which some of the leaders hoped would increase, appears to have dwindled; and in recent months, partly no doubt because of the weather [the 1962–3 winter was the worst since 1947], there has been little public activity until this Easter's Aldermaston march.[159]

None the less, Cuba (as we will see in Chapter 4) concentrated the minds of Whitehall's nuclear and home defence contingency planners and the JIC, too, who commissioned a report on 'Anti-Nuclear Demonstrations at RAF Airfields in a Period of Tension'. And here elements within CND and the CPGB were treated as separate contributors to an identical problem. The report noted that since 'the Wethersfield demonstration support for the Committee of 100 has continuously declined, partly as a result of intrigues and partly because its more idealistic followers are shocked at the way it is being exploited for political purposes'.[160]

Consistent with its long-standing theme that CP membership does not itself indicate disloyalty, the JIC offered some reassurance (on this front, at least) to the Prime Minister and its other regular readers about a possible future transition to war:

If hostilities are imminent, natural loyalties will come into play and only a minority [of CND and Committee of 100 people] will be prepared to take active steps to impede the operation of the bases. A similar state of affairs will obtain in the Communist Party, which will lose much rank and file support. Those who continue to accept the party's discipline, however, can be expected to be particularly militant, stimulated not only by a desire to help Russia but by a belief that, when it comes to a real crisis, provided everything has to be done to undermine their position, the imperialists will give in without a fight. It is reasonable to conclude, therefore, that while the number of nuclear disarmers and Communists will be considerably reduced in a period of tension, there will be a militant rump which will try to be as obstructive as possible.[161]

From the time of Cuba onwards, Whitehall's intelligence and war-planning circles do appear to have shifted permanently from the late 1940s notion of internal danger, to a wider one that incorporated assessments of the problems which the more militant end of the student movement might impose, as well as some nuclear disarmers, during a transition to war.

The historian of 'the sixties', Arthur Marwick, cautions against too blithe a fusion of first-wave CND and mid- to late 1960s youth movements but sees some connection. Noting that after the 1963 Aldermaston March enthusiasm for CND 'greatly waned', Marwick (perhaps wrongly) says the campaign 'was not really a part of youth subculture' (as a grammar schoolboy, though a non-CND one, it struck me as very much a part of what then passed as a 'youth sub-culture' in Stroud in Gloucestershire). But Marwick does see CND as providing 'a link between the New Left revival of the mid-1950s, and the radical student movements of the middle and later sixties; it also provided a symbol, the upturned "Y",[162] and a badge, which many young protesters sported for the rest of the decade, even if not directly associated with CND'.[163]

In the aftermath of the Grosvenor Square demonstration of 17 March 1968, when 25,000 people (mainly young) took part in an anti-Vietnam War protest outside the US Embassy organized by the Vietnam Solidarity Campaign, the student demo factor was firmly built into transition-to-war planning. At and after Grosvenor Square, nearly 250 people were charged with offences and forty-five demonstrators and 117 police officers received medical treatment following scenes which 'were the most violent yet seen on British television'.[164] MI5 carried out a new subversion threat assessment over the summer of 1968, which fed that autumn into a study for the Chiefs of Staff on the 'Security of the United Kingdom Base in the Pre-Attack Phase of General War',[165] which included protest movements as well as the CPGB and the smaller Trotskyist parties.

This MI5 report has not been declassified,[166] but its gist can be derived from the document compiled for the Chiefs by their Defence Policy Staff. Its overall conclusion, in the words of the DPS summary, was 'that it is doubtful whether the subversive threat as currently seen would be beyond the normal capacity of the police, though there could be interference with movement on a scale large enough to have a significant cumulative effect on a complex timetable' for moving military 'reinforcements to the Continent in a period of tension'.[167]

The MI5 report concentrated 'on activity involving the Communist Party of Great Britain and known Trotskyist or anarchist groups . . . since the SS [Security Service] regards as remote the likelihood that other protest movements or the like could reach the point of posing a significant subversive threat without members of these groups taking an active part in organising them, if only on a "bandwagon" basis'. MI5, however, appears to have been a touch uneasy about its generally reassuring assessment. This report, its policy staff told the Chiefs, 'relates to the position as it is known today. It is impossible in this field to make long-term forecasts with any confidence, though the SS is disposed to think that in general movements of a Trotskyist or anarchist [k]ind will tend to grow in strength. The SS has it in mind to review the assessment annually.'[168]

At the same time MI5 was preparing its subversion assessment for the military, the Cabinet Office's transition-to-war planners and the JIC were drawing up the scenarios that would be used to test the entire secret state's procedures in 'INVALUABLE', the UK's specific 'War Book Exercise', which would run in parallel to NATO's 'FALLEX 68' during the autumn of that year[169] – an event provided with an extra *frisson* by the Soviet-led Warsaw Pact invasion of Czechoslovakia overnight on 20 August 1968. It is intriguing to winnow out assumptions about the subversive threat (though it always has to be borne in mind that in such exercises verisimilitude has to give way to the need to test all capacities and plans).

INVALUABLE ran from late September 1968 when, according to the JIC scenario, 'hawks' had supplanted the 'doves' in the leadership of the Soviet Union (codenamed 'ORANGE' in the JIC's fictional 'sitreps'),[170] through to late October, by which time 'ORANGE bloc' forces are well into West Germany, biological and chemical weapons have been used against NATO forces[171] and the UK Prime Minister and his War Cabinet have the full Cabinet's approval for authorizing NATO's top command to release nuclear weapons if circumstances require it.[172]* According to the scenario-writers, domestic protest swiftly flares, followed later in the sequence by touches of subversion:

*2 October 1968: A large-scale student demonstration took place in Oxford . . . calling for a complete and immediate break with NATO and the dismantling of all nuclear bases in this country. The students attempted to enter various public buildings and the police had some difficulty in ejecting them. The students also succeeded in halting a convoy of six Infantry Brigade vehicles bound for [RAF] Brize Norton and [RAF] Lyneham. After some hours, order was restored by the police and the convoy was able to proceed. Many arrests were made and a number of people were treated in hospital for injuries. No further large scale demonstrations have been reported since then, although there have been isolated incidents at RAF and USAF bases and at Southampton where students held up an army convoy before they were dispersed by the police.[173]

*10 October 1968: At a dockers' rally addressed by Jack Dash [a legendary Communist and leader of unofficial strikes in the Port of London[174]] . . . a resolution was carried calling for a ban on the handling of arms and other cargo bound for BAOR [British Army of the Rhine]. This resolution appears to have been largely ignored, but some incidents have been reported of dockers refusing to handle cargoes. A pirate radio station calling itself the 'Voice of Peace' has been heard in the London area calling for the neutrality of the United

---

* Though the Prime Minister did not need such Cabinet approval before authorizing a nuclear strike, as we shall see in Chapter 4.

Kingdom, and the War Resisters' International Organisation has continued its pamphlet and poster campaign.[175]

*14–15 October 1968: ... petrol bomb incidents damaged a total of four aircraft at five RAF bomber stations.[176]

*17 October 1968: Communist inspired propaganda and strikes are on the increase. Half the London docks are out and Liverpool, Hull and Bristol are affected. One-day strike tactics have brought chaos on road and rail. Extensive fire damage, possible sabotage, has been done to an SSN [a Royal Navy Strategic Nuclear Submarine] at Birkenhead [presumably at the Camell Laird Shipyard].[177] ... No mass demonstrations have been reported, but numbers of individuals are carrying placards or attempting to speak at street corners. The poster campaign for the withdrawal of the United Kingdom from NATO continues unabated.[178]

*18 October 1968: The Forward Scatter [radar] station at Cold Blow Lane ... has been damaged, but there is no proof that the few sabotage incidents in this country were centrally directed.[179] ... No mass demonstrations have been reported, but parties of students from the University of Kent demonstrated outside Shorncliff transit camp, and marched to Dover where they attempted to occupy the Dover Ferry terminal building in an apparent effort to delay the departure of reservists bound for BAOR. They were eventually dispersed by the police and a number of arrests were made ... Small crowds have gathered in Downing Street and outside the Houses of Parliament, but no incidents have been reported.[180]

*19 October 1968: Apart from minor incidents at one or two RAF stations, no demonstrations have been reported during the past twenty-four hours. Anti-war rallies have been called tomorrow in London, Liverpool and Manchester. Police leave has been stopped and arrangements are being made to deal with any disorder that may occur. Dockers at Felixstowe, engaged on loading military stores for BAOR, have struck in support of a demand for extra pay for shift work. There has been some response by train and lorry drivers to the call for unofficial strike action. Some passenger trains have had to be cancelled and the oil companies report that deliveries to garages are being hampered by the fact that only about 80 per cent of tanker drivers are at work. There has, however, been little interference with the movement of essential food and other supplies.[181]

*20 October 1068: The invasion of BROWNLAND [Austria] was reported in BBC news broadcasts and in special late editions of this morning's newspapers. Radio programmes are to be interrupted for news reports at hourly intervals throughout the day and the Prime Minister is to make a radio and television broadcast this evening . . . The demand for petrol has increased and shortages have been reported in some areas as a result of the continued absence from work of a number of tanker drivers . . . The dockers at Felixstowe have returned to work following agreement by the employers to 'productivity' payments. It seems likely that this settlement will encourage similar industrial action elsewhere. It is too early to judge the reaction of the population to the events of the past twelve hours, but crowds are beginning to form in Downing Street and Whitehall. They are mostly silent, but there are isolated calls for the neutrality of the United Kingdom. So far there have been no disturbances and the crowds are well under control.[182] . . . Reported plans to kidnap the UK Prime Minister are probably not inspired by ORANGE [the Soviet Union].[183]

*21 October 1968: In his television and radio broadcast last night the Prime Minister said it was quite wrong to think war was inevitable and appealed to the people to remain calm . . . Church services of all denominations yesterday attracted exceptionally large congregations in response to church leaders' appeal for a national day of prayer. Small demonstrations took place outside Westminster Abbey, Westminster Cathedral and a number of churches in University towns. No arrests were made. Large crowds attended the anti-war rallies in London, Liverpool and Manchester yesterday. The addresses, which were given by well-known unilateralists and pacifists, were all on the theme of the warlike intentions of the United States of America and demanded a complete and immediate break with NATO and the neutrality of the United Kingdom. This was not received favourably by the large anti-ORANGE [Soviet] elements in the crowds and fighting broke out. These [sic] developed to large proportions and it was some hours before the police were able to restore order in the areas where the meetings were held. In London, attempts were made to storm both the American and the ORANGE Embassies, but the police managed to hold the crowds in check, though they had considerable trouble at the ORANGE Embassy. In Liverpool and Manchester there was a 'sit-down' of students to attempt to block troop movements and train services were interrupted to some extent in consequence. An unofficial strike of ground staff in support of demands for a 'productivity' bonus has delayed the departure of aircraft from London Airport.[184]

The international and intelligence backdrop to this domestic section of the JIC's transition-to-war diary was now very grave. In addition to Warsaw Pact (Czech and Hungarian) forces invading Austria, Greece and Turkey were under attack too. Soviet forces were mounting repeated border incidents against West Germany and violating its airspace. There was 'widespread and systematic sabotage throughout NATO' directed at communications, public utilities and radar sites. Soviet air defences were being brought to high alert and a Soviet attack on Norway appeared imminent. There were indications that 'dormant agents' had been activated by Soviet intelligence in NATO countries.[185] That morning – 21 October 1968 – MISC 222, simulating the Cabinet: 'took note with approval that the Prime Minister, in consultation with the Foreign Secretary, if available, would examine and if necessary authorise any requests from NATO for the use of nuclear weapons without further reference to the Cabinet'.[186]

The following day Soviet and Warsaw Pact forces attacked NATO 'in what amounts to a general offensive against Central Region'.[187] From 8.00 a.m. frequent news bulletins report heavy fighting in West Germany.[188] The JIC simulated one last bit of human subversive activity on 22 October: 'A United Kingdom communist, after visiting ORANGE Embassy, has remarked "We shall be engaged in nuclear war before we know where we are." '[189] In its final FALLEX 68 assessment, the JIC concluded that

ORANGE, by a combination of military and psychological pressure is trying to achieve its political objectives quickly, presumably before the West can resolve to resort to nuclear war. We believe ORANGE hoped to defeat the Allies without using nuclear weapons and is probably still relying on its much publicised nuclear retaliatory capability to deter the West from resorting to nuclear war.

The document is rounded off beneath this paragraph with 'EXERCISE EXERCISE EXERCISE'[190] which, of course, is all it was, rather than an attempt to paint a picture of a possible real-time transition to war between NATO and the Warsaw Pact. The JIC's scenario-writers even allowed themselves an occasional grim, insider joke as in their noon assessment on 17 October 1962 for FALLEX, when they opened its 'Political' section with an unadorned, unexplained sentence to the effect that 'ORANGE astronauts have landed on the moon.'[191]

In terms of domestic security – the world of Whitehall's vetters, filers and smashers – what is and is not included in INVALUABLE is intriguing. Of course, without the Government War Book we cannot decode exactly which of its measures MISC 222 activated and when. But the scenario-painters do not carry any newspaper reports of or responses to the 'smashing' of the CPGB organization or the transportation of real, suspected or alleged subversives to the Isle of Man. The transition-to-war gamers sitting in the Cabinet Office's first-floor Conference Room 'B' overlooking Horse Guards Parade that autumn *did* spend more time pondering the problems posed by a combination of the CPGB, CND and student radicals than the September 1968 MI5 report for the Chiefs of Staff seemed to think they would if it happened for real.

But what of the people the guardians of national security had been most concerned about since the very first report had been presented to GEN 183 over twenty years before – the sleepers, the concealed Communist agents described as the 'dormant agents' by the JIC in its FALLEX/INVALUABLE mode? In 1968 they continued to regard the threat of saboteurs (rather than providers of information) as limited. In the Defence Policy Staff's report to the Chiefs that autumn, the MI5 view is recorded like this:

This SS [Security Service] concludes . . . that the USSR probably still has some capability for sabotage in the United Kingdom, though the likelihood of its being used in a period of tension is questionable; and that there is no evidence that any other organisations have sabotage plans on a substantial scale, though the possibility of isolated acts by individuals cannot be ruled out.[192]

The Defence planners evidently thought MI5 a tad complacent here and let their bosses, the Chiefs of Staff, know this:

We deduce that while the currently assessed threat of interference which existing police capability could not contain is low, it is not so plainly negligible that it can be dismissed out of hand. It is important to note against the background of the difficulties of long-term prediction in this field, that a new or increased threat could develop faster than a counter-capability could be built from scratch to offset it.[193]

The military turned out to be nearer the mark than MI5, as became apparent three years later when Oleg Lyalin, a Soviet sabotage expert working under diplomatic cover in London, came over to British intelligence.

And we know from the Mitrokhin Archive that in 1967, a year before the MI5 assessment and EXERCISE INVALUABLE, Yuri Andropov, on taking over the KGB, revitalized its sabotage capacity in the form of a new Department V.[194]

Lyalin, 'an expert in hand-to-hand combat as well as a highly proficient marksman and parachutist',[195] was not on the list of intelligence officers operating out of the Soviet Embassy and Trade Delegation in London with which MI5, via the Foreign Secretary, Michael Stewart, provided the Prime Minister, Harold Wilson, when INVALUABLE was getting into its stride in September 1968.[196] When MI5 recruited him as a defector-in-place in the spring of 1971 (the following September he came over in person[197]), Lyalin produced an alarming list of contingencies for which Andropov's saboteurs were planning in a transition to war. It was partly due to Lyalin's information that Edward Heath, Wilson's successor in No. 10, and Stewart's successor at the FCO, Sir Alec Douglas-Home, authorized the dramatic expulsion of 105 KGB and GRU officers operating undercover in the UK in 1971.[198]

George Walden, the FCO official who had much to do with devising the expulsion and coined its title – 'Operation FOOT (my none-too-clever code-name for giving the KGB the boot)'[199] – has a vividly written portrait of Lyalin in his memoir, *Lucky George*:

Lyalin was a good example of the problem we faced. He did legitimate work as an importer of clothes, travelling widely in the North of England and buying nothing more security-sensitive than knitwear and woollen socks. In his spare moments he made sabotage plans for use in time of war, including maps for landing sites for Soviet submarines. His efforts, which I saw, appeared a little fantastical (park the sub, come up the beach, and turn right at the Bill and Duck), but he was the sort of person who, given the choice, you would prefer not to have running around.[200]

But Andrew and Mitrokhin's account suggests the planning went much further than this, from destroying the V-bombers on their airbases in Lincolnshire and blowing up the Ballistic Missile Early Warning Station on Fylingdales Moor in Yorkshire to flooding the London Underground and infiltrating KGB agents as messengers or delivery men into Whitehall's corridors, where they would scatter poison capsules designed to kill those who trod on them.[201] There were some small caches of explosives secreted in the British countryside which British counter-intelligence uncovered thanks to Lyalin's information.[202]

It is impossible to know how much of this really *was* fantasy – fairy-story possibilities spun to impress line managers in the KGB, the GRU and their customers in the Kremlin. Yet, at every stage of the British vetters', filers' and smashers' efforts to penetrate and thwart the 'enemy within', either in the form of KGB and GRU officers or that of the Queen's subjects they ran as agents, one gets the feeling that John Curry experienced when compiling his secret internal history of MI5 in the last stages of World War II – that the UK's security apparatus had never quite reached the level of adequacy needed to cope with the problem. The only way Curry or the anonymous senior Whitehall official quoted at the end of Chapter 2 could have known whether it was or not (assuming they had lived) was if deterrence had failed and a real, deadly transition to nuclear war really had occurred. Just as several of the best minds of post-1945 Whitehall were deployed on the nuclear weapons policies and programmes, they had their counterparts in the 'what if?' branches of the secret state who had to think through the steps to destruction of much of the Queen's kingdom and what could be done with the remnants – human and physical – that might survive.

4

'Breakdown': Preparing for the Worst

It was . . . essential to avoid a situation in which the Government would be driven to devote resources to civil defence on a scale which would cripple the national economy, detract from our power of offence and alienate our allies in Europe . . . the Government were not prepared to devote resources to passive defence at the expense of weakening our striking force or impeding our economic recovery.

Clement Attlee addressing GEN 253, the Cabinet
Committee on Civil Defence, 1 October 1948[1]

To render the UK useless as a base for any form of military operations the simplest and most effective form of attack would be by surface bursts effected in suitable meteorological conditions. These, besides causing local damage, would cause very considerable areas of the country to be affected by fall-out. We are advised that something like ten 'H' Bombs, each of a yield of about 10 megatons, delivered on the western half of the UK or in the waters close in off the Western seaboard, with the normal prevailing winds, would effectively disrupt the life of the country and make normal activity completely impossible.

Joint Intelligence Committee report on 'The "H" Bomb
Threat to the UK in the Event of a General War',
January 1955[2]

. . . breakdown might be defined as occurring 'when the government of a country is no longer able to ensure that its orders are carried out.' This state of affairs could come about through breakdown of the machinery of control . . . or through

the mass of people becoming preoccupied with their own survival rather than the country's war effort and prepared to run the risk of being shot rather than to obey orders which would seem to them to involve unreasonable personal risk, in a word, through breakdown of morale.

Dr Edgar Anstey of JIGSAW on 'Note on the Concept and Definitions of Breakdown', June 1960[3]

I still believe that what we've got to hang on to as administrators is the paramount need to keep in existence a machine of central control which can take hold of the situation as soon as that initial period of agony is passed in order to provide, as smoothly as may be, for a period of recovery thereafter.

Sir Norman Brook, Secretary of the Cabinet, on 'The Cabinet System in War', June 1959[4]

Norman Brook was the last man in Whitehall to underestimate what a nuclear attack on the UK might mean. Throughout the high Cold War, he briefed his four premiers – Attlee, Churchill, Eden and Macmillan – on the catastrophe that awaited the UK if global war came. As we have seen, he was the human fulcrum around which the 1954–5 rethinks took place in the shadow of the H-bomb. He drove through the plans for pre- and post-attack always bearing in mind, as he told his private audience of Home Office civil servants in 1959, that '[e]ven taking the most extreme forecast or appreciation of the nature of a future global war, we would have to hold on to political control [by which he meant Cabinet government] for as long as possible and aim to recover it as soon as possible thereafter'.[5] Elaborating his theme, Brook explained to his fellow insiders:

We plan to maintain central direction . . . even in the most rudimentary form, for as long as possible in the intensive period of nuclear attack and – and this is the point I want to stress – the capacity to re-assert civil control, and, as soon as possible, central political control, for the period of recovery after the initial nuclear phase.[6]

In a moment, we will examine the elaborate plans, which, by the turn of the 1950s, gave flesh to the Brook philosophy.

But for anyone involved in the actual business of UK war planning in those decades – as for any of the scholars (myself and my students included) attempting to reconstruct this grim enterprise whereby the British state looked into the abyss – reality, ghastliness and *un*reality mix constantly. This appears to have been true at all levels (and must have been so for Brook in his more anxious, private moments when contemplating that 'period of agony'[7] (where he might have spent it and with whom is the subject of Chapter 5). In my own generation, we did not have to wait until Peter Watkins's 1965 film *The War Game* (which Brook, by this time Lord Normanbrook and Chairman of the BBC, had much to do with keeping off the television screen in the 1960s[8]), to brood on our last moments or think what we might do if the old World War II air-raid sirens whined into action telling us we had but four minutes to go.

Philip Allen, the Home Office under secretary responsible for home defence, was the Home Office representative on the 1955 Strath Committee, which was instructed to convert the JIC's appraisal of what but a few Soviet A-bombs could do to the UK, and the scientific forecasts of Bill Penney's people on the details of the practical effects of blast, heat and thermonuclear destruction, into advice for ministers on home and civil defence and how the government somehow might be carried on from the ruins. Many years later he recalled for me the ambiguities this aroused in his mind:

I can remember sitting on a committee working out the horrors of the H-bomb as distinct from the much more modest A-bomb. And, although it seemed like Never-Never Land at the time, we did work out these theoretical methods of keeping on the government – setting up organisations. One had a feeling that, if it came to it, nothing would quite work out the way one was planning. But, nevertheless, one simply had to plan.[9]

At around the time Norman Brook was lecturing the Home Office about the post-attack plans for 'a maximum degree of devolution to regions; a very small nucleus at the centre . . .' to maintain 'contacts with allies and liaison between civil and military power – and the maintenance for as long as possible of the civil power'[10] (Brook clearly thought the military could well be dominant for a period), a young military figure, Bobby Robson, was beginning his navigator training for the RAF's V-force. As his career in the cockpit of the deterrent progressed, he acquired similar views to Philip Allen's and to Harold Macmillan's private thinking along the lines that 'any real war *must* escalate into nuclear war'.[11] Though confident that his Vulcan would have got airborne, 'I wonder if it would really have all worked. I'm pretty sure that if you got to the last resort, the whole thing has gone anyway. We all were cynical about it.'[12]

But the most vividly effective antidote I have encountered against becoming overelaborate and distracted by the detail of the transition to World War III was provided in the spring of 1962, between the Berlin and Cuba crises, by Norman Brook's deputy, Michael Cary. It leaps out at the reader in the Cabinet Office's working file on nuclear retaliation procedures.[13] Cary was responding to a minute from Nigel Abercrombie, the Cabinet Office under secretary responsible for transition-to-war planning, about the efforts then under way to simplify the communication procedures for consultation between the US President and the British Prime Minister right up 'to the last possible moment' and the taking of 'a final decision to launch a nuclear attack'.[14] After much toing and froing between the Foreign Office, the Ministry of Defence and the Cabinet Office, a draft was prepared for putting before Macmillan and Kennedy which, Abercrombie briefed Cary, the Cabinet Office should leave in the hands of the two other Whitehall departments until the Americans had had their say.[15]

Cary's reply is a classic. Suddenly, humanity and reality trump bureaucratic fine-tuning;

Mr Abercrombie

I agree that this should go ahead as you propose, and that we should look at it again on the next round.

2. But it is really conceivable that the President & the Prime Minister, on the brink of Armageddon, will solemnly go through this nightmarish gavotte? Will they not simply ask themselves whether to use nuclears <u>at all</u> and leave the rest to the experts? In any case, if the answer is yes, we should worry.

21/5   <u>MC</u>[16]

This surely would have been close to the dreadful reality if the moment of the last resort had to be faced.

By the time Cary, son of the novelist Joyce Cary, old Etonian and classical scholar whose private passion was the building and restoration of harpsichords,[17] pondered Armageddon, the secret state had been engaged in dancing one or other version of a 'nightmarish gavotte' for nearly fourteen years – ever since the severing of the land and water routes to Berlin in 1948. It may have taken Stalin's first direct action against the Western allies to pep up civil defence and transition-to-war planning in Whitehall, but the Prime Minister, Attlee, as we have seen, had been acutely aware from the moment he wrote his think-piece on the atomic bomb at the end of August 1945 that much of the recent history of his country's domestic mobilization for war had, at a stroke, passed into near irrelevance. The dispersal of industry and airfields, World War II bomb shelters and air-raid precautions would henceforth be 'just futile waste'.[18]

The big planning paper prepared for the Cabinet's Ministerial Committee on Civil Defence during the first weeks of the Berlin Crisis reached the same conclusion as the Prime Minister almost three years before:

There is no single solution to the problem of Civil Defence. The provision of atom bomb proof shelters for the whole nation would not in itself solve the problem; nor would the dispersion of the population and industry at an even density all over the country. In any event neither solution would be an economic or practical possibility. The solution lies in making the maximum use of a large number of expedients for minimising the effects of damage.[19]

A solution was never found. Expediency prevailed. In the trade-off between active and passive defence, the former won each time at the A-bomb and the H-bomb stages. On every occasion that the policy was reviewed until, following the 1965 rethink, substantial cost savings were made by the reduction of what limited cover there was[20] with the scaling-down of the Civil Defence Corps (which had been established by the Civil Defence Act 1948) and a concentration on 'only those measures which are likely to make a contribution to national survival'.[21] In other words, from the days of Attlee's GEN 163 to Wilson's PN Committee, the bomb was always put before shelters.

Exactly what was meant by civil defence and home defence was a problem from the start, not least because Cabinet committees so labelled ran in parallel for much of the high Cold War. As late as

October 1968 the UK Commanders-in-Chief Committee were so fret-
ful about the lack of official definitions of the two that they produced
their own:

a. <u>Home Defence</u>

The measures necessary to defend the United Kingdom against internal or
external threat. In the case of a nuclear, biological or chemical attack, where
no adequate defence may be possible, the measures necessary within the
United Kingdom to minimise the effects of such an attack and to enable the
nation to survive.

b. <u>Civil Defence</u>

That element of home defence involving the actions of Civil Government and
Local Authorities in the control and administration of the nation in the setting
of general war.[22]

The C-in-C's version reflects very much the military angle on the two
concepts. A fuller, better definition, which brings out the distinctions
between the two, has been produced by Nicola Bliss:

Civil defence was concerned with the protection of the British people during
and after an attack on the UK. Measures . . . included: evacuation, shelter,
food provision and emergency hospitals.

Home defence covered a much wider area of both civil and military preparations which aimed to ensure national survival during and after air attack.
Areas . . . included: the machinery of government in war, strategic location of
industry, town planning and stockpiling.[23]

In the Berlin summer of 1948 when 'Ministers agreed that paper plans
for war should be brought to a high state of readiness but ruled that
any steps taken should be kept within official circles since any overt
action taken . . . might . . . aggravate international tension',[24] the planning process was conducted in such a rush that such niceties of definition and distinction appear (and probably were) surplus to
requirements. That summer the priorities of the civil defence and war
planners were the production of 'paper plans . . . for a crash emergency'
(in the case of civil defence)[25] and a new 'Government War Book
designed to meet essential needs in the event of a possible emergency
in the near future' for the Defence Transition Committee.[26]

The archives for both areas, the DTC especially, are far from fully declassified even now. But it is possible to reconstruct the chief anxiety of the summer and autumn of 1948 as it was simple and obvious. The civil defence planners, influenced no doubt by the unlikelihood of the Soviet Union being capable of sustaining a major war 'before 1957', as the big July 1948 JIC assessment put it,[27] took January 1957 as the target date for 'all our preparations for Civil Defence' to be completed.[28] War, however, might come 'from some unforeseen incident or from a miscalculation of the enemy situation and intentions'. An emergency plan, therefore, had to be prepared for implementation at short notice. But, '[a]t the present time it will probably be found that the measures which could be taken in an emergency would be quite inadequate'.[29]

There was no 'probably' about it. As we have seen, the planners in 1948 'assumed that our enemy will be in possession of the atom bomb in limited numbers by 1957'. Ministers were briefed in a special appendix on the damage a Nagasaki-type plutonium bomb bursting between 500 and 1,000 feet up would do:

It is estimated that in London a crater 450 yards in diameter and 40 to 50 yards deep would be produced. Damage to underground services will be severe . . . Total collapse of all buildings including multi-storey framed structures is to be expected up to a distance of about 600 yards from ground-zero . . . and heavy internal damage, probably resulting in fires, up to at least 1,500 yards . . . Suburban houses of the type common in England . . . would be destroyed or would require demolition . . . to a distance of about 1,400 yards from ground-zero and would be rendered uninhabitable . . . to about 2,000 . . . Severe flash burns will occur on the unprotected parts of the bodies of people in the open at a distance of up to 2,000 or 3,000 yards from ground-zero . . . Gamma radiation from an airburst will cause death to people caught in the open to a distance of about 1,400 yards from ground-zero.[30]

The civil defence planners reckoned 'the enemy's primary objective is the immediate elimination of this country. It is believed that, to achieve this end, the enemy will adopt all-out air attacks with all the power at his command and for as long as he can maintain them. It will be assumed for planning purposes that these attacks will coincide with the outbreak of hostilities and will last for not less than four months.'[31]

The emergency plan drawn up on the basis of this analysis did not convince ministers. The Home Secretary, Chuter Ede, admitted to Attlee that it contained 'a large element of improvisation'.[32] In essence, it amounted to World War II-style provision plus evacuation from areas deemed most vulnerable, with shelters built, if the steel could be found, in such areas.[33] (Ministers agreed to halt all demolition of surviving World War II ones.[34]) The RAF would provide fifteen minutes' warning of attack if the Russian planes were coming in above 20,000 feet; less than five minutes if they flew below 3,000 feet.[35] Casualties were expressed in terms of the still vivid Great War folk-memory: '(cf, Somme, 1916, where 55,000 casualties were evacuated in the first three days). No system designed for peace purposes can cope with the evacuation, treatment and reception problems that this involves . . .'[36]

Nye Bevan, the Minister of Health (whose responsibilities at that time also included local government), was hugely sceptical when this first substantial report reached the Cabinet Committee on Civil Defence. He did not believe that the 'potential enemy' had the capability to launch attacks on this scale, but if the Russians did, 'this emergency plan was, in his view, quite inadequate'.[37] And Bevan carried his scepticism into the Cabinet Room the following month when Attlee himself convened an ad hoc Cabinet Committee on the subject adding, for good measure, that even if the Chiefs of Staff [i.e. the JIC] were to produce a new assessment indicating a lower level of threat, it 'would probably show a scale of attack against which any civil defence preparations that were possible at the present time would be ineffective'.[38] Attlee, as we have seen, shared his scepticism about the degree to which civil defence could provide serious protection at an affordable cost. Though the committee authorized Ede to make a public statement about the 'emergency civil defence measures' such as they were.[39]

By the time Attlee left office in the autumn of 1951, the British secret state – its pace and preparations quickened by the outbreak of the Korean War in June 1950 – had made considerable strides in other, non-civil defence areas. For example, Berlin had stimulated the Prime Minister and the Cabinet Secretary to draw up plans for a World War III War Cabinet should all the JIC's reassurances suddenly be exposed as misplaced.[40] Attlee agreed with Brook's suggestion that a War

Cabinet Secretariat, fusing the Cabinet Secretariat with the Chiefs of Staff Secretariat, should be created if hostilities broke out.[41] In the spring of 1951 Attlee approved a plan whereby in a third world war, he or one of his successors would merge the job of Prime Minister and Minister of Defence as the conduct of 'strategy is indivisible'.[42]

The Chiefs themselves had had ready since May 1950 (just before Korea) an elaborate plan for their part in the transition to World War III. Broken down into three phases,

(a) Stage I – When there is a Threat of War
(b) Stage II – Precautionary Stage
(c) Stage III – War Stage,

it covered not just general strategy and allied 'Higher Direction of War' plus strategic deception plans, but subversive operations, psychological warfare, biological and chemical warfare, strategic air offensive and (though the fruits of GEN 163 were not to reach the RAF in the form of a bomb for another three and a half years) the 'Initiation of atomic warfare'.[43]

Once one has acquired a sense of the destructive power of a 'true' H-bomb, it is perhaps somewhat easy to forget just how dreadful the earlier atomic bombs were as the potential 'destroyer of worlds' in the phrase Robert Oppenheimer, the physicist who led the scientific side of the Manhattan Project, borrowed from the *Bhagavad Gita* on witnessing the first atomic test in the New Mexico desert on 16 July 1945.[44] As the UK readied itself for the Coronation of the young Queen in the spring of 1953 (amid a great deal of nonsense being spoken and written about a new Elizabethan Age[45]), the home defence planners, as they must henceforth be described, were circulating to ministers and officials within their world a picture of the kind of kingdom Her Majesty might have left if the Soviet Union, by then in its fourth year as a nuclear weapons power, dropped 132 atomic bombs 'of the Nagasaki type' on the major population centres of her realm.

Allowing for the evacuation policy having worked,[46] (5.2m women, children and elderly plus 4m who might evacuate themselves[47]), a body-count of 1,378,000 dead and 785,000 seriously injured was compiled.

Casualties and house damage from 132 atomic bombs

Area	Bomb ref Nos.	Casualties		House damage. No. of people whose houses are:–	
		Killed	Seriously injured	Destroyed or irreparably damaged	Temporarily uninhabitable by last war standards[1]
Greater London	1–35	422,000	241,000	663,000	3,273,000
Birmingham conurbation	36–47	127,000	72,000	199,000	927,000
Merseyside	48–58	106,000	59,000	165,000	723,000
Clyde	59–68	98,000	57,000	155,000	824,000
Manchester conurbation	69–76	98,000	57,000	155,000	742,000
Tyneside	77–82	45,000	26,000	71,000	394,000
Sheffield	83–87	53,000	30,000	83,000	304,000
Teesside	88–91	20,000	11,000	31,000	166,000
Bristol	92–94	25,000	14,000	39,000	203,000
Coventry	95–97	9,000	6,000	15,000	134,000
Hull	98–100	21,000	11,000	32,000	121,000
Belfast	101–102	14,000	7,000	21,000	149,000
Edinburgh	103–104	52,000	30,000	82,000	248,000
Southampton	105–106	3,000	2,000	5,000	48,000
Swansea	107–108	4,000	2,000	6,000	43,000
Aberdeen	109	9,000	5,000	14,000	98,000
Barrow	110	11,000	7,000	18,000	50,000
Bolton	111	16,000	9,000	25,000	79,000
Bradford	112	11,000	7,000	18,000	94,000
Cardiff	113	6,000	3,000	9,000	57,000
Chatham	114	8,000	4,000	12,000	56,000
Derby	115	18,000	11,000	29,000	80,000
Dundee	116	17,000	10,000	27,000	101,000
Grangemouth	117	1,000	1,000	2,000	12,000
Huddersfield	118	15,000	8,000	23,000	88,000
Leeds	119	11,000	7,000	18,000	143,000
Leicester	120	21,000	12,000	33,000	102,000
Luton	121	6,000	3,000	9,000	66,000
Nottingham	122	18,000	11,000	29,000	112,000
Newport	123	16,000	3,000	24,000	60,000
Plymouth	124	2,000	1,000	3,000	20,000
Portsmouth	125	9,000	5,000	14,000	97,000
Preston	126	17,000	10,000	27,000	100,000
St. Helens	127	11,000	7,000	18,000	90,000
Stoke	128	16,000	9,000	25,000	116,000
Sunderland	129	11,000	6,000	17,000	88,000
Warrington	130	6,000	3,000	9,000	60,000
Carlisle	131	14,000	7,000	21,000	54,000
Londonderry	132	11,000	6,000	17,000	41,000
Total		1,378,000	785,000	2,163,000	10,163,000

1 The figures given in this column are inclusive of the destroyed and irreparably damaged houses.[48]

Of course, the home defence planners did not know how many bombs the Soviet Union had in 1953 or what their targeting plans were (though they had to make assumptions about both for planning purposes). But the awesomeness of those figures to early 1950s eyes can be compared to the body-counts incorporated in their own still recent memories of World War II. Over the six years of that conflict the tally was as follows:

Deaths (Military and Merchant Navy)	380,000
Deaths (Civilian)	60,000
Houses Destroyed	500,000
Houses Severely Damaged	250,000[49]

Yet less than a year after the home defence planners more than tripled, in their minds, the combined military and civilian death toll of World War II, Norman Brook was convening his meeting of nuclear insiders as the hydrogen bomb created possibilities of a magnitude and a grimness that surpassed by far the threat to country, society and state posed by the atom bomb.

The first result during what might be called Britain's thermonuclear year from the spring of 1954 (when Brook's inner group first met) to the spring of 1955 (when the Strath Committee reported on the home defence implications of the H-bomb) was, revealingly enough, the decision to upgrade the UK nuclear weapons programme from fission to fusion. Brook, however, had established a Central War Plans Secretariat in the Cabinet Office to pull all the aspects together, reporting directly to him. Its head, William Strath, was chosen in the last days of 1954 to lead a small interdepartmental group charged with examining the impact of not only the huge and immediate destructive force of an H-bomb attack on the UK but also the lethal and protracted effects of 'fall-out' on all aspects of life, not just governmental activity. The Strath Committee had to ponder, quite simply, the survivability of the nation.

In December 1954 Brook minuted the new Minister of Defence, Harold Macmillan, on the purposes of Strath;[50] in turn, Macmillan briefed Churchill.[51] Brook attached his minute to a brief from Strath covering what the Cabinet Office's chief war planner regarded as the essentials, much of which, unsurprisingly, reflected the thinking of both the JIC and the 'atomic knights':

1. The grim effects of 'fall-out,' added to the destructive power of the thermo-nuclear weapon, make global war less likely. The possibility of mutual annihilation is too great.

2. In the next three or four years it is even less likely that Russia will provoke war, while she is unable to strike decisively against the USA.

3. But in a war the United Kingdom – the nerve centre of European resistance – would be extremely vulnerable to nuclear attack. There is not in sight any air defence system which could protect us effectively.

4. In short, possession by the West of the nuclear weapon is at present a real deterrent. Overwhelming and immediate retaliation with it is our only reliable defence.[52]

Nowhere in the files is the importance of being nuclear – the bias that trumps all other considerations including civil defence – more graphically and directly expressed.

Strath then reprised for Macmillan and other inner group ministers (Brook talked in his minute of a meeting in the Foreign Secretary's room on 9 December 1954, the minutes of which have yet to reach the Public Record office[53]) the danger that, as 'major adventures became more imponderable' for the Soviet Union, other Cold War activities, such as 'limited and local aggressions' might become a greater temptation. Part of countering the Communist bloc was the need to demonstrate the economic superiority of the Western nations.

Severe strain could be put on resources by this combination of purposes, Strath warned. But he was convinced before his committee's three-month inquiry had fully begun that it was 'evident that civil defence in the broadest sense of the term must command a higher priority in defence planning than it has so far received'.[54] The paragraphs in which Strath explains his reasons for this resound to the noise of existing plans from the 1948–53 period being torn up:

Under nuclear bombardment we can no longer count on the United Kingdom being able to function as a main supply base . . . The widespread damage and immobilisation caused by 'fall-out' call for a radical reshaping of our plans for the defence of the home front. New problems of an unprecedented kind are created for the protection of the population – for shelter and evacuation plans. The role and organisation of the Civil Defence Services need radical overhaul. How far should they be geared to their normal tasks of fire fighting and rescue and how far to relief and decontamination measures? The part which the military forces may have to play in support of the Civil Authorities needs to be determined. The effects of radioactive contamination create vast and novel problems for the medical services and for agriculture. And finally there are the problems of the survival period.[55]

Within days Strath had been given Churchill's go-ahead for his study, the Prime Minister minuting on 14 December 1954: 'Keep me informed please.'[56]

Strath had begun his official life in the Inland Revenue, but had spent the bulk of it in military or military-related ministries before joining the Central Economic Planning Staff in 1947. He was seconded from the Treasury by Brook to set up the new War Plans Secretariat. His liaison with the Chiefs of Staff was General Sir Nevil Brownjohn. Sir Richard Powell and Sir Frederic Brundrett represented the administrative and the scientific sides respectively of the Ministry of Defence. Philip Allen and General Sir Sidney Kirkman, the Home Office Director General of Civil Defence, completed the team.

Within a month, at the Strath Committee's request, the JIC had produced a special report for them on 'The H-Bomb Threat to the UK in the Event of a General War'.[57] The JIC gave the Strath group its planning period of five years as the intelligence analysts thought it inconceivable that the Soviet Union would launch a nuclear attack against the UK until they could deliver a devastating one on North America which, the British intelligence world believed, would be unlikely before 1960.

Sir Patrick Dean, Chairman of the JIC, and his colleagues felt able to be precise in their attempt to penetrate what the 'Soviet objectives' for the UK would be in the event of war, if or when it should break out:

(a) to knock out as quickly as possible those airfields from which nuclear attacks could be launched against the Soviet Union.

(b) to destroy the organisation of government and control.

(c) to render the UK useless as a base for any form of military operations.[58]

The JIC rounded this grim picture of ultimate possibility with a bone-chilling addendum:

We believe that the Russians will regard the UK as such a threat that they will aim to render it unusable for a long period, and will not hesitate to destroy great parts of the UK to achieve this aim.[59]

If this assessment had leaked, it is very possible, to put it no higher, that CND would have sprung into vibrant and vociferous existence three years sooner than it did.

Intriguingly, the JIC in those first days of 1955 did not think the Soviet Union would be in a position to attack the UK with H-bombs 'before 1958' given the difficulty of producing them in a size and weight that an aircraft could carry – though reductions here were anticipated. Russian submarines could do it sooner; and ballistic missiles would be in a position to do it during the 1960s.

Where the Russians needed military results immediately in World War III, they would burst their H-bombs at 20,000 feet over London, for example, to achieve maximum blast effect. Atomic bombs, the JIC thought, 'should be adequate for airfield targets'. The effects of fall-out, however, would be 'somewhat delayed'.[60] Then came their terrifying passage, quoted at the head of this chapter, about a mere ten 10-megaton H-bombs dropped on the western side of the UK having sufficient capacity to effectively wreck the Queen's realm.

How soon would she, her ministers and her subjects know this was about to happen?

Assuming that we shall be able at least to maintain the present state of our intelligence, and in view of the intense Russian security awareness, this is by no means certain . . .[61]

Here lay an implicit admission of the lack of human agents inside the inner core of the Soviet state apparatus – the indispensable requirement for serious intelligence on intentions as opposed to capabilities. But, the JIC continued, 'we

(a) expect to be able to say when the Soviet leaders are making preparations for war;

and (b) should be able to estimate when those preparations are reaching various stages of readiness and the weight of attack which could be launched at each stage.[62]

Full mobilization of the Soviet Union should be detectable at least a month ahead unless it were done gradually over a very long period. Only with 'the detection of enemy aircraft on Allied radar screens' could a warning of 'actual attack' be given. As we have seen, a Russian bomber targeted for a 20,000-foot air burst could be detected 200 miles from the radars, giving a warning-time 'of the order of 20 minutes. If we can use radars based in Northern Europe, the total time of warning from the UK may be as much as sixty minutes. But if the Russians are prepared to risk low level approach and delivery, we may get as little as 3 minutes warning of crossing the coast, but this technique is unlikely.'[63]

In a perverse way, the slim warning-times became a sort of comfort to some at the centre of the British nuclear capacity in the Cold War years. It was unlike anything else they ever had to do as senior civil servants. One who had a variety of jobs on the economic and industrial side as well as with defence planning, once told me how 'policy failure' was knowable in these earlier areas. By contrast 'I would have only known for four minutes if all the advice I had given on deterrence turned out to be wrong!'[64]

Strath and his committee worked very quickly. They reported in March 1955 and their findings were discussed by the Home Defence and Defence committees of the Cabinet.[65] Several scholars – including myself and my 'Secret State' students – spent a good part of turn-of-the-century Britain attempting to get Strath declassified. A great many interested departments had to reach agreement on it. And it had still not been released at the time of writing. We were, however, able to reconstruct its essence from the briefings which surrounded it and from the minutes (which were declassified) of the ad hoc Cabinet committee Macmillan chaired on it, GEN 491, on 24 March 1955.[66] On Macmillan's recommendation, a copy of the Strath Report was sent to all Cabinet ministers 'for their personal information', by the end of March.[67]

Brook prepared a brief on Strath for the new Prime Minister, Sir Anthony Eden, who had succeeded Churchill on 6 April 1955. (Eden sent Macmillan to the Foreign Office and put Selwyn Lloyd at Defence in his place.) In the third week of his premiership Eden was invited by his Cabinet Secretary to contemplate the Strath Committee's 'broad conclusion ... that although a determined hydrogen bomb attack against this country would cause human and material destruction on an appalling scale, it would be possible to contain its effects and enable the nation to survive if adequate preparations had been made in advance'.[68] Strath, however, had done no more than outline possible solutions to the problems posed by the H-bomb; 'much more work must be done before it can be firmly decided how far these are practicable and financially acceptable'.[69]

Strath had, the new PM was told, ruptured important strategic assumptions of the atomic age. Because the Chiefs of Staff reckoned any future war in which the UK suffered attack would involve the H-bomb, 'we should discontinue any home defence preparations which are relevant only to war fought with nothing but conventional or atomic weapons'. Following on from this Strath, as reported by Brook, had concluded that

Because of the widespread devastation which would inevitably be caused by a hydrogen bomb attack on this country, we should discontinue any plans (eg for the building up of industrial war potential) which rest on the assumption that the United Kingdom would be available as a main supply base after the attack.[70]

Macmillan and his colleagues on GEN 491 had heard at their meeting on 24 March 1955 that 'The earlier conception of a period of broken-backed warfare following the initial attack, in which this country would take part, had been abandoned.' After a thermonuclear exchange, '[f]ighting would go on in other parts of the world but the main supply areas would be outside this country, possibly Australia, South Africa or even the United States'.[71] GEN 491 also faced the reality that preparations against an H-bomb attack 'were at present virtually non-existent'.[72]

Brook warned Eden that

The two most difficult and politically sensitive questions of policy are those concerning evacuation and shelter. Dispersal of the population would inevitably cause social and economic dislocation and the report rejects anything like total abandonment of the highly vulnerable areas on that account; it concludes nevertheless that some measure of evacuation would have to be undertaken if casualties on a disastrous scale were to be avoided. The proposal is that priority classes, such as mothers and young children, should be removed to safer areas but that other people should remain at work on a shift system in the high risk areas, moving out at other times to the periphery of the large towns.[73]

There was an air of unreality about some of the Strath elements which later planners did not share (as we shall see). But one hard reality, money, was a constant attender in the councils of those who pondered the cindering of the realm. As Brook reminded Eden: 'War planning is in itself an exercise in choosing between various risks: as the resources available for home defence are so limited.'[74]

Within a few years, another of the post-Strath assumptions would come to look hugely optimistic. Even before the Cuban Missile Crisis erupted with startling suddenness, the intelligence and war-planning committees had become more and more preoccupied by what the 1952 Ministry of Defence War Book called the '"Bolt From the Blue" Emergency'.[75] GEN 491, however, carried on stressing post-Strath that 'for planning purposes, Departments should continue to proceed on the assumption that the Government would be able to detect a deterioration in the international situation some six months before war came and would know, say, seven days in advance that an attack on this country was to be expected'. For good measure GEN 491 added a Pollyanna-like statement of the obvious: 'The importance of a period of warning for the carrying out of home defence plans, for example on evacuation, emphasised the high value of good intelligence work in discovering the enemy's intentions.'[76]

The shadow of Strath reached through the 1950s and into the mid-1960s (and beyond, in the sense that the geographically small and densely populated UK will for ever remain vulnerable as long as thermonuclear weapons exist). It reached into the War Cabinet's bunker when that secret shelter first came into existence under the codename STOCKWELL, then BURLINGTON and later TURNSTILE from about 1960, five years after the committee reported.[77] For, after Strath, 'Ministers . . . accept[ed] the view that it would be extremely unlikely that central control would continue to operate from London after attack and that the government of the United Kingdom would be conducted by a central nucleus in protected accommodation in the country.'[78]

Bunkerdom for ministers was one thing and easily agreed; shelter for the rest of the Queen's subjects quite another. Strath stimulated what Alban Webb has called the mid-1950s 'battle for Home Defence Policy',[79] which, at root, reflected not just the limited resources to which Brook referred but also the arguments for the primacy of active (i.e. nuclear) over passive (i.e. civil) defence. The tussle took place in a new Ministerial Committee on Home Defence which Eden set up in August 1955 under the chairmanship of the Minister of Defence.

Building on the grim picture most of the ministers round the table had absorbed when it was presented to them by the Chiefs of Staff a year before, Strath warned that 'If no preparations of any kind had been made in advance, a successful night attack on the main centres of population in this country with 10 hydrogen bombs would, we estimate, kill about 12 million people and seriously injure or disable 4 million others ... they would mean the loss of nearly one third of the population.' Blast and heat would kill nine million and fall-out radiation would eventually carry off nearly three million more people.[80] Strath estimated that a single H-bomb on London could cause four million casualties. A serious evacuation policy might reduce it by three quarters; a shelter policy still further.

The essence of the Strath recommendations was that the government could seek to mitigate the consequences of a thermonuclear attack by evacuation from target areas, local dispersal of those remaining from the places at greatest risk, and the construction of shelters: 'These are not alternatives. In practice a combination of all three would be required.'[81]

The full Strath, as it might be termed, had one unequivocal champion in the Cabinet committee when it began work in earnest during autumn 1955 – the Home Secretary, Gwilym Lloyd George.* His

---

* Son of the Great War leader, who deserves to be remembered for more than his wonderful aphorism, delivered a year before at an undergraduate meeting in Cambridge, that 'Politicians are like monkeys. The higher they climb up the tree, the more revolting are the parts they expose.'[82]

memo to the Home Defence Committee of 25 October 1955 showed him to be both high-minded and humane, as well as a vigorous pursuer of a policy, civil defence, for which his ministry was lead department. 'It is in my view the duty of the Government, by planning evacuation and the gradual provision of shelter, to reduce the possibilities of casualties on this scale,' he told his colleagues, adding, 'it is no use keeping any forces for the "hot war" if the morale of this country is to collapse and we lose the will to fight. I suggest that with no shelter, morale would collapse.'[83]

Lloyd George's paper contained a self-collapsing element – costings. Finance trumped humanity. Morale cannot be measured nor, therefore, priced. Buildings can. A 6-foot by 6-foot by 5-foot shelter beneath a living room would cost £100 if constructed as part of each new house (i.e. £30m a year at then current building rates). The price would double for existing housing stock and would come out at £1.25 billion.[84]

As soon as the committee met, the Home Secretary's paper was savaged. General Brownjohn noted that the sum involved was comparable to that required to sustain the nuclear deterrent, adding that the 'Chiefs of Staff would be seriously alarmed at a proposal that £1,250m should be spent on what was purely a "passive measure"'.[85] From the chair, the Minister of Defence, by this time Sir Walter Monckton, backed the Chiefs, arguing that 'the primary objective was to prevent war and a sum of this order could be spent on medium bombers [i.e. the V-force] and would be more likely to influence the decision of an aggressor than the same sum spent on shelter'.[86] Lloyd George lost again when the question rose a notch in the hierarchy of decision-taking and reached the Cabinet's Defence Committee on 7 December 1955. Research on shelters could go ahead. Surveys of existing housing stock could proceed. But the committee 'agreed that the financial and economic situation precluded a programme for the construction of domestic shelter at public expense'.[87]

Despite Berlin 1961, Cuba 1962 and a host of other lesser alarms, it always did. And Britain was not unique here. As David Miller has shown:

In most countries, policies seemed to follow a seven-to-ten-year cycle, varying from, at worst, almost total uninterest to, at best, a grudging and lukewarm enthusiasm. The figures speak for themselves: as a proportion of the defence budget, the USSR spent just under 1 per cent on civil defence, while the USA spent approximately 0.1 per cent, and the figure in most other countries was even less.[88]

Miller noted that the 'difficulty was that, if it was to be taken seriously, the scale of the problem was huge and the costs were enormous ... Very few countries proved willing to undertake such measures on the necessary scale, particularly if they were achievable only at the expense of cuts in the more active part of the national defence budget.'[89]

West Germany passed a law requiring all new housing to include a cellar built to state requirements. But only Norway (62 per cent cover for the population), Sweden (70 per cent) and Switzerland (90 per cent)[90] ran really serious shelter programmes, suggesting that you had to be both financially rich and demographically small to be adequately civilly defended. Britain did keep a substantial Civil Defence Corps costing £10m a year[91] in being until the mid-1960s, when it fell victim to Labour's 1965 Home Defence Review. And successive economic crises saw the Wilson Government putting HD on a 'care and maintenance' basis by the end of their term, spending falling from £22m a year to between £7m and £8m.[92]

Yet, despite the no-shelter policy, home defence spending did rise as part of post-Strath decision-taking, from £69.6m in 1955–6 to a projected £150m by 1960–61.[93] On which activities were resources concentrated? In essence, four:

1: Pre-attack evacuation (priority classes being schoolchildren; mothers; expectant mothers; the aged; the infirm – just over 11m people in all).[94]

2: Stockpiling for post-attack needs (food, oil, medical supplies).[95]

3: Public utilities (fire services, gas, electricity, water, ports, railways, communications, BBC Wartime Broadcasting Service).[96]

4: Post-attack government ('TURNSTILE,' regional seats of government, integration of military and civil authorities).[97]

In effect, there were twin biases at work; the deterrent and, should it fail, command and control of the survivors, and supply of the basic rudiments of continued survival.

After Strath, the secret state thought in three phases:

*A 'Precautionary Stage'[98] of about seven days between a period of international tension reaching a point which indicated it could trigger 'global war'.[99]

*A 'Destructive Phase' in which 'the devastation caused by the nuclear attack on the United Kingdom would be very great' during a 'period which might last from 48 hours to 7 days'.[100]

*A 'Survival Phase'.[101] Planning for it would be aimed 'solely at tackling the problems of <u>survival</u>' with a high degree of devolution, initially at least, to Civil Defence Regions, each with its own mini-government (as we have seen) of ministers, officials, police and military.[102]

The 'machinery of control' had been a priority from the moment Strath reported, with Macmillan's group, GEN 491, picking up strongly on Strath's recommendation 'that the regional organisation of government should be strengthened now'.[103]

The Commanders-in-Chief Committee swiftly did the spadework for the Chiefs of Staff on the integration of the civil and military branches of government under a Cabinet minister outside the War Cabinet, based in one of the twelve regional seats of government. Reporting to the Chiefs of Staff in June 1956, the Commanders explained that

Because of the tremendous dislocation which nuclear attack will cause, and the complexity of the problem arising from the possibility [odd word to use given the state of knowledge following the US H-bomb tests in the Pacific] of fall-out, plans are being made for the maximum decentralisation of Government. For this purpose, joint Civil and Military Headquarters are being planned at which the Army District Commander and Regional Director of Civil Defence together with representatives of the other Services and of the Civil departments will be available to support the Regional Commissioner [the Cabinet minister] . . .

The degree to which Regional Commissioners will have to assume control within their Regions will depend upon the nature of the attack. Broadly, the functions of the Regional Commissioners will be: –

(a) Co-ordinating the Civil Defence measures of the various local authorities, Government departments and the Services within the Region.

(b) Taking control of the civil administration in the Region in the event of a breakdown of communications with the Central Government.[104]

'Breakdown' is a word that lives in many a text of the Cold War secret state. As some of the post-Strath policies worked their way through into practical form in the late 1950s and early 1960s, the word came to acquire a very wide meaning as that special JIGSAW group we have already briefly encountered of military, scientists and civilians were brought together in great secrecy in a couple of rooms in the Old Admiralty Building on Horse Guards Parade, right next to the Citadel that Penney had used in 1954 as the focus of his pictures of the destruction a 'hybrid' and a 'true' H-bomb could bring. The Joint Inter-Service Group for the Study of All-Out Warfare for six years of the high Cold War between 1958 and 1964, were the secret state's 'what if' team. Set up by the Chief of the Defence Staff, Lord Mountbatten, in 1958, their brief was to ponder the nature, duration and likely outcome of a global war around the late 1960s and early 1970s. They were to range widely and report to Mountbatten and the MOD's Chief Scientific Adviser, Sir Solly Zuckerman.[105] In January 2001 a shoal of their papers (on which a forty-year retention had been imposed) reached the Public Record Office.[106]

Some of JIGSAW's output does strike an early twenty-first century reader as being in the realms of Strangelovian fantasy. In May 1960, just as the Paris Summit fell apart after the Russians shot down the CIA's reconnaissance/spy plane carrying Gary Powers over the Urals,[107] E. A. (Ted) Lovell, a scientist seconded from the Air Ministry, placed a scenario before his JIGSAW colleagues as part of 'Some Thoughts on Deterrence or the Lack of It', which he admitted 'perhaps sounds fantastic and unreal' but needed contemplating none the less. In brief, the Russians 'put into effect their threat to shoot at any bases from which a reconnaissance flight originates and the Americans retaliate with the weight of attack which they have calculated will cause "breakdown" and this consumes all their nuclear weapons'.

Khrushchev and the Soviet leadership 'have prepared for this eventuality by retiring to a deep shelter in the Urals where they have radio transmitters capable of communicating with the West and of talking to the survivors of the Russian people who have their radio sets intact'.[108] The Russians then fire missiles at heavily populated and industrial areas and ports in America, but hold back about half of their nuclear armoury. Khrushchev and the 'Russian leaders now instruct the West to pay tribute in the form of a massive aid to them and threaten any nation which offers aid to the USA.' The Soviet Union will, therefore, recover and the United States will not.[109]

JIGSAW seems to have been a wonderfully disputatious group. As Dr Ian Shaw, who was one of the pioneers of using computers to model fall-out[110] and was the War Office's scientist in the group, expressed it: 'One would need to be an incurable optimist to hope that any general statement would receive unanimous agreement in this group.'[111] Nevertheless, JIGSAW does eventually seem to have reached agreement both on the notion of 'breakdown' (the point at which survivors turn inwards, and cease to be assets to a state which has lost the capacity to govern and the means of waging war, leading both industry and whatever society helplessly continues to slow down of its own accord[112]) *and* on the number of thermonuclear warheads required to bring it about (the figures cited by Shaw were 300 cities in Russia; 200 in the West, twenty of which were in the UK).[113]

It is plain from Shaw's paper that, in the last months of 1960, the group were still at odds on the criteria and the numbers. But Dr Edgar Anstey, a psychologist by profession, says that eventually the group did agree on three hypotheses (the last of which took care of Lovell's 'Russia wins' scenario):

1: About 30% destruction of a city renders the whole city population 'Ineffect-ive' – ie wholly preoccupied with their own survival. The survivors would become a liability rather than an asset to the country.[114]

2: A megaton delivery on a city such as Birmingham would also render 'ineffective' 50% of the population within a radius of about 20 miles, including eg Coventry, where the people would see, hear and smell what happened to Birmingham, and would either take to their cellars or get into their cars and drive to where they think they might be safe.[115]

3: Our third hypothesis, confirmed by studies of the effect of intensive bombing of Germany during the last months of WW 2,[116] was that a general collapse of the national structure of a country, which we call 'Breakdown,' occurs when about 50% of the population have been rendered ineffective.[117]

Dr Anstey, who with Dr Alan McDonald, a fellow Principal Scientific Officer from the Home Office, did a good deal of the work which read across the experiences of destruction of German and Japanese cities (and of Clydebank in Scotland), into post-nuclear attack possibilities, felt able to brief me on the JIGSAW 'breakdown' notions once the files arrived at the PRO:[118]

Combining these hypotheses, we calculated that the number of megaton deliveries required to cause breakdown was about 25 for the UK, and about 450 for the USA or Soviet Union. Moreover, and this was the really important finding, this scale of delivery was well within the capacity of either the USA or the Soviet Union, even <u>after</u> it had been subjected to a pre-emptive attack by its major adversary.[119]

Intriguingly enough, the eight senior members of the JIGSAW team were in Washington pooling analysis with their American counterparts in the first week of October 1962, the month of the Cuban Missile Crisis. In his May 1963 'Summary of JIGSAW "Breakdown Studies"', Anstey noted the impact of their conversations with the US Weapons Supply Evaluation Group in their Washington discussions in April 1960 and October 1962:

... WSEG and other US organisations still tend to use number of (immediate) deaths as almost the sole criterion of the effects of attack. In 1960 and again in 1962 JIGSAW maintained that deaths greatly underestimated the effects of nuclear attack and that there is little point in saving people from immediate death without securing the means of keeping them, and the nation, alive during the following months. These arguments made some impression.

The US agencies have not yet fully accepted the doctrine that breakdown could occur in the USA (this doctrine is highly objectionable for political reasons), but the exchange of views with JIGSAW has resulted in their devoting some attention to the likely consequences of deliveries of some hundreds of megaton weapons, whereas previously their studies had been confined solely to the effects of many thousands of deliveries.[120]

The effect of JIGSAW thinking can be detected (along with many other factors) in the acquisition of an invulnerable, second-strike nuclear capability in Polaris (remember Group Captain Shelfoon's elegy in praise of a 'secure' and 'quietly unobtrusive' system which is 'in every way compatible with the British character'[121]).

Many of its arguments found an echo in the justifications for the run-down of home defence following the 1965 review, much of which was based on the acceptance that the risk of nuclear war was 'very greatly reduced' as 'a consequence of the development of a second strike capability on each side, and of each side's awareness of this . . . In view of this there is stability since an aggressor who struck first would nevertheless suffer unacceptable damage in return.'[122] There are touches of JIGSAW, too, in the emphasis on concentrating resources on 'survival measures, including the control system' (by which the Home Office meant the post-attack civil administration of the UK) rather than rescue (i.e. life-saving of those trapped in the ruins).[123] The decision to 'emphasise survival measures rather than life-saving operations' had been part of the 1960 Home Defence Review which had led to a fall in the Civil Defence Corps from 360,000 in 1960 to about 140,000 by 1965.[124]

No shelters. Slimlime Civil Defence Corps tasked to concentrate on survival and recovery rather than rescue. Increasing role for deterrence – the power to retaliate in time and with sufficient force to wreak unacceptable damage. The ministers, the military and the civil servants whom JIGSAW briefed at, for example, their session in the Admiralty Cinema on 16 November 1961 (Harold Watkinson, the Minister of Defence, Mountbatten and Brook leading their respective professions)[125] on what an H-bomb would do to Birmingham, as well as on a general nuclear exchange between the Soviet Union and the United States, can have been left in no doubt that, in Dr Anstey's words, 'There would be complete breakdown in both of the great powers. Neither the USA nor the Soviet Union stood the slightest chance of "winning" a global nuclear war in any meaningful sense.'[126] This conviction alongside the British calculations of eight million dead and eight million injured at the hands of the Royal Air Force,[127] should retaliation be ordered, would be enough to deter any likely Soviet leadership in most foreseeable circumstances from seeking a British version of 'breakdown'.

But the restless Mountbatten became anxious at the turn of 1960–61 about the speed and reliability of exactly those retaliation drills available to Harold Macmillan.[128] As he put it to Norman Brook in February 1961, he was not convinced that Whitehall was making full use of the 'speed, capacity and presentation facilities afforded by new techniques' should the brink be reached.[129]

Mountbatten was right. Given the cost, infrastructure and regular exercising required to keep the V-bombers on their Lincolnshire air-fields capable of getting airborne within one and a half minutes of the order to scramble – not to mention the scientific effort and finance required to design and produce the nuclear weapons for their bomb-bays – it is amazing to discover from the files just how rudimentary, almost casual, were the arrangements as late as 1960–61 for the Prime Minister to authorize the ultimate retaliation.

As he later made plain to Brook, Mountbatten was well aware that the President of the United States had with him at all times an officer bearing the codes that would unleash his B-52 bombers and the US's intercontinental ballistic missiles against Soviet bloc targets.[130] What, by comparison, was available to Macmillan? The Cabinet Office, prodded by the CDS's concern, produced a brief on present practices for a meeting between Mountbatten and Brook on 5 February 1961.

The JIC's view was that a pre-emptive strike by the Russians was 'unlikely' unless they felt 'unacceptably threatened', as a paper by Freddie Bishop (at that time Brook's deputy) for the Cabinet Secretary and the Chief of Defence Staff put it. This had been so fully taken to heart that no prime ministerial drill was deemed necessary to cope with such a contingency. Should it happen, Bishop explained that

Radar might give about ninety minutes warning of the moment of a Soviet attack on this country by manned bombers, but there would be no warning of a ballistic missile attack until the completion of the Ballistic Missile Early Warning System [on Fylingdales Moor in North Yorkshire] in 1963. This system when operational, would give only a few minutes warning of attack by ballistic missiles.

In the event, therefore, of a 'bolt out of the blue' attack . . . there might be only short radar warning, or even virtually no warning. It is hardly practicable to provide means whereby instant contact can be made with the Prime Minis-ter, and in these circumstances it must be accepted that it may not be possible to establish contact with him before the impact of the attack.[131]

Bishop gave no reason for the impossibility of arranging constant contact or why it simply had to be accepted as given. His next sentence, on first reading, is even more alarming:

But in these circumstances, authority exists for the despatch of our nuclear bombers under 'positive control' procedures designed to prevent the launching of an attack except with specific authority from this country. It is contemplated that, if after a massive nuclear attack had been received here, it had proved impossible to establish contact with the Prime Minister, authority for our nuclear retaliatory forces to complete their mission would be provided by somebody else.[132]

Bishop did not specify who that 'somebody' would be, presumably because he knew that Brook and Mountbatten already knew.

In fact, that 'somebody' was Air Marshal Sir Kenneth Cross, Commander-in-Chief of Bomber Command. In a letter to Cross on his appointment to the post in 1959, the Vice Chief of the Air Staff, Air Chief Marshal Sir Edmund Hudleston, had informed him in the penultimate sentence (in the grandly casual tradition) that 'It is also appreciated that circumstances could exist, such as a total breakdown in communications, under which you would have to assume responsibility for launching the attack.'[133] It was plain from Hudleston's letter that an attempt at greater precision was under way as the 'Air Ministry now have under urgent consideration the steps which are required to bring the political machinery into line with the readiness of the weapon.'[134]

Cross had the power to order his bombers airborne as the tolerances were so fine. The planes had one and a half minutes from being given the order to get off the airfields before Soviet missiles would start to fall on the runways[135] and a further one and a half minutes 'for the aircraft to be certain of getting clear of the danger area from bursts of nuclear bombs aimed at their airfields'.[136] 'Positive control' was the procedure whereby the V-force 'would take off but would not complete their mission unless they received orders to do so. Without such orders they would return to base after being airborne for a given period.'[137]

Deep within the retaliatory loop, not everyone was at ease with these arrangements whereby in a few fraught minutes, with the Prime Minister already killed by a pre-emptive strike on London or out of reach, the Chief of Bomber Command, from his bunker under the Chilterns at High Wycombe, could get his planes aloft and, if Soviet bombs had burst over the UK, give them the order to fly on to their targets in Russia. Not for nothing did some civil servants privately refer to this as the 'decapitation' or 'headless chickens' scenario.[138]

In 1961, as part of the rethink of nuclear retaliation procedures, Frank Mottershead, the MOD Deputy Secretary responsible for nuclear and War Book matters, drafted an amazingly candid brief for his Permanent Secretary, Sir Eddie Playfair. It was intriguing for a number of reasons, not least because it indicated that Macmillan was not pushing for the officer-with-the-briefcase solution.

Mottershead reminded Playfair that the existing, 'relatively simple' procedures for launching nuclear retaliation had been 'exercised in skeleton form' in 1959:

the thing the exercise did throw up, which was perhaps clear to most of us before, was that we are not organised to cope with a 'bolt from the blue' attack. This is perhaps in accord with out [our] belief that there will be no such thing.[139]

To cope with such a cataclysm, Mottershead contended, 'the Prime Minister must . . . always be accompanied by a mobile secure communications set and an operator day or night', or be prepared to hand over the responsibility to a deputy whenever he is away from his desk.

Even if we do not really believe that a 'bolt from the blue' is possible, it may well be advisable to take the small insurance step of attaching to the Downing Street Secretariat and telephone system a Ministerial Deputy for nuclear retaliation purposes. There are really three possibilities, to do nothing, to lay on a full 'operational' system or to set upon an easy going insurance system. Previous forms [form?] suggest that the present Prime Minister [Macmillan] would refuse a full blown system.[140]

The section of Mottershead's brief for Playfair dealing with the powers of the C-in-C of RAF Bomber Command to authorize retaliation contains a strong echo. It was written in March 1961 – the year Neville Shute had chosen in *On the Beach* for the nuclear war that was eventually to kill every human being on the planet thanks to 'the Russo–Chinese war that had flared up out of the Russo–NATO war, that had been born of the Israeli–Arab war, initiated by Albania'.[141] Mottershead expressed concern to Playfair, in a Shute-like way, about

the classical 'destruction of Russia by mistake' situation: eg Egypt acquires a nuclear bomb somehow drops it on London and C. in C. Bomber Command then ensures that Russia, the United Kingdom and the USA are all destroyed by bombing Russia.[142]

Quite apart from this little gloss on Colonel Nasser, it is intriguing to note how a top civilian in the MOD had his worries about the men-in-uniform:

There is a lot to be said for internal consumption only for being very careful to tie down C in C Bomber Command and give him very precise instructions eg. About getting in touch with the Americans and doing his best, by contact with any surviving authorities eg. in NATO, to discover whether Russia launched the nuclear bomb that destroyed Whitehall, before he has a go at Russia.[143]

How CND would have loved to get their hands on the Mottershead memorandum as they prepared for the 1961 Aldermaston March the following month.

Certain passages in Freddie Bishop's memorandum on the same subject were a parody of the alleged British genius for improvisation:

The arrangements for recalling the Prime Minister when he is travelling out of London depend at present on communicating with known points on his route. It has been suggested that these arrangements might be supplemented in this country by installing a radio in the Prime Minister's car which would permit messages to be relayed in plain language through the Automobile Association's radio network.[144]

The file contains a diagram of immense complexity describing the various communication links that would be needed in a transition to war, including in its top-right corner the little graphical gem opposite.

Out of the Mountbatten–Brook correspondence and meetings a full-blown review of nuclear retaliation procedures emerged conducted by an official Cabinet committee, GEN 743, chaired first by William Geraghty, an under secretary in the Cabinet Office's Oversea and Defence Secretariat, and, after he returned to MOD, by Nigel Aber-

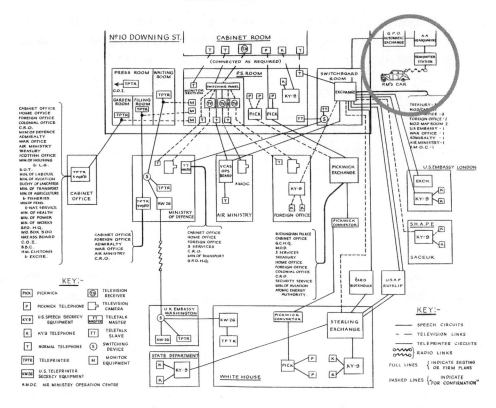

crombie (Bishop having been succeeded by Cary in the meantime in his watching role). Macmillan approved the establishment of the 'Working Group on Nuclear Retaliation Procedures', as GEN 743 was known, in July 1961. It reported in February 1962.

Before commissioning Geraghty and his team to 'undertake a comprehensive review of:

(i) the procedure best adopted to meet the operational requirements involved in the decision to authorise nuclear retaliation; and

(ii) the communications which the Prime Minister will need for this and other purposes in a period of tension,'[146]

Brook wrote one of his mind-clearing papers on 'alternative means' for authorizing 'the release of nuclear forces from this country'.[147] It should be remembered that all this work was initially carried out against the backdrop of the Berlin Crisis of 1958–61 in its most acute phase. In

October 1961 Macmillan actually reached the point of designating by name which ministers, if the crisis tipped into war, would have gone with him to the alternative seat of government and which would become Regional Commissioners in the twelve Civil Defence regions (the file detailing the names and their locations has not been declassified).[148]

In his March 1961 paper, and in a subsequent letter to Mountbatten, Brook revealed his assumptions about the pattern and location of decision-taking in a period of acute international tension. He divided his paper into pre- and post-attack sections (TURNSTILE was known at this stage as STOCKWELL):

(a) Before Attack

The appointment of a Prime Minister's deputy for nuclear retaliation purposes would ensure a greater certainty and speed of retaliation if the Prime Minister were not available, since decisions could be taken before the arrival of bombs and missiles on this country affected Government control, disrupted communications and possibly neutralised some of our own nuclear forces or their weapons. The Prime Minister's deputy would be able to consult the President, thus facilitating the process of retaliation by procuring the release of United States weapons and warheads in this country before attack. The deputy would presumably be a senior Minister, who would be required to remain within easy call of Whitehall in any absence of the Prime Minister.

(i) If there were only a radar warning of attack without a previous period of political tension (which is not considered likely), the Prime Minister's deputy would try to contact the Prime Minister immediately. If he were unable to do so, then he would consult the President and authorise nuclear retaliation on the Prime Minister's behalf.

(ii) If, as is more likely, there were a period of political tension, the Prime Minister's deputy would still act as above in the event of a radar warning of attack in the Prime Minister's absence. However, in this case the Government might have decided to man STOCKWELL, and it may therefore be advisable to plan to send a senior Minister to STOCKWELL as early as possible in a period of tension. This Minister should not be the Minister deputed to act on the Prime Minister's behalf in Whitehall, and would only assume responsibility for nuclear retaliation if the Government in Whitehall were destroyed by attack before the Prime Minister or his deputy had authorised a counter-attack.[149]

It was Brook's next paragraph that provoked Mottershead into placing his doubts before Playfair about the fall-back position:

(b) After Attack

If this country were hit by nuclear weapons before Bomber Command had received instructions to retaliate, it is envisaged that the Commander-in-Chief should have discretion to despatch his bomber forces under 'positive control,' and should try to seek instructions from the Government, either in Whitehall or elsewhere. If his efforts to communicate with the Government by all reasonable means should fail, then he should assume responsibility for releasing nuclear retaliatory forces on offensive missions.[150]

Brook was not convinced of the need to have a nuclear command-and-control capacity by the Prime Minister at all times. As he told Mountbatten (who disagreed[151]), it was 'hardly practicable to make communications plans which would ensure immediate contact with the Prime Minister at all times . . . If there were to be a "bolt from the blue," we must accept that it may not be possible to contact the Prime Minister before the impact of the attack.'[152]

Brook's letter is revealing, too, of his reasons for wishing the seat of government to remain in London for as long as possible at a time of acute and rising international tension even though

STOCKWELL might have been manned and although some Ministers might have been directed there, the Prime Minister, with some of his principal colleagues and his main advisers, would remain in Whitehall until a warning of nuclear attack on this country had been received and nuclear retaliation had been authorised – but that planning for the Prime Minister's survival of attack should be confined to the arrangements already made for his speedy removal from London in an emergency.[153]

What could these be? An RAF helicopter waiting on Horse Guards Parade? Road? Or even rail? (See Chapter 5.) No file on this has yet emerged.

Brook went on to tell Mountbatten why he wanted to leave the resort to the last redoubt in STOCKWELL until the last minute. The Cabinet Secretary believed that

in a period of developing international tension it would be best for the Prime

Minister, and indeed his colleagues and advisers, to continue to use their normal methods and machinery of work as far as possible. The period in question might be quite protracted, and the Prime Minister's main preoccupation would be to assess the intentions of the enemy from political at least as much as military intelligence, and to supervise the conduct of political negotiations. We are more likely to secure the best setting and atmosphere for this by maintaining normal arrangements as far as possible.[154]

Brook recognized, however, that in this pre-bunker phase, 'arrangements would need to be streamlined, accelerated and supplemented . . .'[155]

Five months later, anxiety over Berlin led him to draw up in detail just such a plan to 'be prepared for a lengthy period of fluctuating political tension' to 'allow vital decisions to be taken in an orderly and speedy way'.[156] Ministers and their advisers would 'not go underground [i.e. to the bunker] . . . [b]ut the normal methods must be accelerated'.[157] For this purpose he suggested a Ministerial Committee on Berlin which would consist of the PM, the Home Secretary, the Chancellor of the Exchequer, the Foreign Secretary, the Commonwealth Secretary and the Minister of Defence.[158]

Meanwhile, the Geraghty/Abercrombie group worked on. Macmillan accepted their report and recommendations when Brook presented it to him in early March 1962[159] and it reflected the Cabinet Secretary's thinking rather than that of the Chief of the Defence Staff. No nuclear officer would be with the Prime Minister night and day. Should he need to be rushed back to London:

Normal communications would suffice in most circumstances except for periods when the Prime Minister is travelling by car or rail. In either case it should be possible to intercept him through police or railway channels, but the Working Group recommend that consideration should be given to providing a radio link in the Prime Minister's car.[160]

Brook's thinking on staying put until the last minute was there, too, as was the appointment of two ministerial deputies, one of whom 'would be available to act as the Prime Minister's deputy for purposes of nuclear retaliation during any period, however short, when the Prime Minister was not immediately available'.[161]

Annex B to the Geraghty/Abercrombie report dealt with the powers of Air Marshal Cross and his successors (though not in a way that addressed the Mottershead anxiety):

The Prime Minister has agreed, as a basis for future planning, certain powers for C-in-C Bomber Command to cover the following situations.

(i) A 'bolt from the blue' – that is, a tactical warning, with no preceding period of strategic warning, that a nuclear attack is imminent;

(ii) A nuclear attack actually having been received (ie nuclear bombs having burst) in this country before any authority has been given to a nuclear force to retaliate.

2. These powers are as follows –

(a) To order all his bombers airborne under positive control;

(b) To seek contact with the Prime Minister or his deputy in London or at BURLINGTON [as STOCKWELL was now known], and if possible the United States authority responsible for launching United States strategic nuclear weapons from this country.[162]

(c) In the last resort, when he has confirmed that a nuclear attack has actually landed on this country, to order on his own responsibility nuclear retaliation by all means at his disposal.[163]

This annex was reflected fully in the directive to Cross from the Chief of the Air Staff, Sir Thomas Pike, in September 1962, a few days before the Cuban Missile Crisis began.[164]

I have reconstructed the secret state and states of readiness aspects during the Cuban Missile Crisis in my volume on *The Prime Minister*.[165] On the instructions of Macmillan, Pike, through Cross, put the V-force on alert condition 3 at 1.00 p.m. on Saturday 27 October 1962.[166] This meant that

[t]he maximum number of aircraft are to be made Combat Ready. At Main Bases, aircraft planned to operate from those bases are to be prepared for operational take-off; the remainder are to be armed and prepared for dispersal.[167]

In 'Exercise Micky Finn II' the month before, Cross had 112 V-bombers at his disposal as they moved through all five of the alert stages until being stood down on 22 September 1962.[168] They held the for-real alert condition 3 from 27 October to 5 November 1962.[169]

Norman Brook was ill and unable to be at Macmillan's side during Cuba. His place was taken by Michael Cary who had had that memorable outburst about the 'nightmarish gavotte' on the 'brink of Armageddon' as he and Abercrombie wrestled with simplifying the nuclear release consultation procedures between Macmillan and Kennedy as part of the unfinished business of GEN 743.[170] Macmillan's group of ministers stayed in London as Brook would have wished. BURLINGTON was not manned. Nor was a half-way house committee formally established along the lines Brook had sketched the previous September for Berlin purposes. But an informal Cuba group of ministers did exist, with Macmillan and his Foreign Secretary, Lord Home, at its heart.[171]

Cuba, however, did stimulate the secret state to new refinements of the drills for the 'brink of Armageddon'. The October 1962 crisis was no 'bolt from the blue' involving a sudden indication of danger on the radar screens with but a few minutes to decide what to do. Nor, as we have seen, was it the endgame of a long, slow, carefully monitored build-up of international political tension. As a result, the secret state looked again at its procedures and plans.

There were two significant outcomes of the 'Post-Cuba Review of War Book Planning' which Macmillan ordered from the Ministerial Committee on Home Defence 'in order to ensure', as the new Cabinet Secretary, Sir Burke Trend, put it, 'that it was sufficiently flexible to enable us to react quickly and appropriately to a sudden emergency, in which we might have no more than two or three days warning of the outbreak of war'.[172] The Prime Minister henceforth could institute a Precautionary Stage without recourse to the Cabinet.[173] The other result was the drafting of a ferocious Emergency Powers (Defence) Bill to be rushed through Lords and Commons in the last days of peace, granting to the Regional Commissioners such huge powers over life, property, food and finance 'as to amount to a voluntary abdication by Parliament of the whole of their functions for the period of the emergency'.[174]

Not only did this draft measure reflect the planners' belief that 'the powers now required are more extensive than those which were envisaged' as recently as 1959,[175] but the defence regulations contained in the proposed bill 'would have to be more drastic than the Regulations in the Second World War . . .'[176] A mere glance at clause one of the Emergency Powers (Defence) Bill for World War III makes it difficult to think of *any* powers left over life, liberty and property with which the Regional Commissioners could have been invested:

1 – (i) Her Majesty may by Order in Council make such regulations (to be known as 'Defence Regulations') as appear to Her Majesty to be necessary or expedient for any of the following purposes . . . that is to say –

(a) the public safety;

(b) the defence of the realm;

(c) the maintenance of public order;

(d) the meeting of special circumstances arising or likely to arise out of any war in which Her Majesty may be engaged or out of the threat of such a war;

(e) the efficient prosecution of any such war;

(f) the maintenance of supplies and services essential to the life of the community.[177]

The 'special circumstances' catch-all sub-section (d) would mean anything the Regional Commissioners wished it to mean once the Bill had been converted into an Act by Parliament in the last days of peace.*

What might the civil libertarians in Parliament, had they seen the Emergency Powers (Defence) Bill, have made of its section 4, for example? This covered the 'administration of justice' whereby the courts, acting under its Defence Regulations delivered 'a sentence of death . . . (whether for an offence against Defence Regulations or for any other offence) shall provide that any proceedings in which such a sentence is so imposed shall be reviewed by not less than three persons

---

* The Bill was deemed too fierce to put to Parliament in peacetime proper. Instead it would go before both Houses 'early in the precautionary Stage . . . The point that Parliament is likely to raise fewer objections to such legislation under threat of war than it would do in peacetime is a formidable one . . .'[178] For these reasons no one outside the war planning community had a sight of the measure until it appeared in an MOD file at the Public Record Office in the late 1990s.

who hold or have held high judicial office within the meaning of the Appellate Jurisdiction Act 1876'.[179]

The Armed Forces, as well as what remained of the senior judiciary, were central to the planning. Whether or not, as Sir Frank Cooper suggested, for a time post-attack, 'you would probably have had to have had a military government . . .',[180] the Defence Policy Staff in the autumn of 1968 spelt out, in some detail, for the Chiefs of Staff just how involved those under their command would be with the police and the civil authorities generally during the transition to war and after – what they called 'the total Threat'.[181] It is an especially intriguing portrait for, not only did it draw on JIC and MI5 material,[182] but its production coincided with the INVALUABLE war game.

This was a period of some anxiety for the Chiefs not because they feared Brezhnev was about to do something rash, but because the Labour Government's post-devaluation defence review was eating into those troops that would be needed to assist the civil authorities, protect 'key points' and military installations generally, as well as to fulfil the 'special tasks' laid upon them by the Government War Book. These last were very interesting in themselves, including as they did:

a. Special duties toward Royal Family
– One Infantry Battalion [i.e. about 400 men]

b. Special duties for Central Government
– One Infantry Battalion

c. The security of gold reserves and art treasures
– One Infantry Battalion

d. Aid to HM Customs and to the Police in the seizing of potentially hostile ships and aircraft; possibly manned by armed crews.[183]
– Difficult to assess but probably one Infantry Battalion.

From the military perspective, this was the late-1960s image of a Britain engulfed by a third world war:

a. <u>Period of Serious International Tension</u>. The threat within the United Kingdom during this period might be limited to individual acts of sabotage against military installations particularly those with a connection with NBC

[Nuclear, biological, chemical] warfare. At the same time subversive groups might endeavour to create disturbances in large urban areas in order to stretch the police forces and to weaken the resolution of the Government.

b. Period of Mobilisation and Initial Deployment of Armed Forces. During this period the now much increased earmarked forces ... would move from the United Kingdom to their NATO tasks, and a greater sense of the proximity of nuclear war would spread through the civil population. The enormous potential of mass media debate would leave nobody in any doubt of the possible outcome. In that atmosphere a more widespread public antagonism to military moves could develop. The previously small-scale demonstrations inspired by anarchist and communist groups could be increased by the co-operation, perhaps unwittingly given, of ordinary citizens. The attitude of the trades unions would be crucial to the quickening tempo of our military preparations. The possibility of widespread strikes including a breakdown in our public transport and shipping systems could seriously affect our delicately programmed mobilisation and movement plans. Military installations, ports and airfields, essential to our military movements, could become targets of action by anti-war groups. If only, say, 5% of our working population became actively anti-war minded, this would present a very serious security problem.[184]

We see here once more the military analysts being noticeably less sanguine than their MI5 counterparts about the possibility of counter-ing the possible threats to military efficiency or law and order. True pessimism – or realism, as it strikes me – afflicted them at the next stage on the road to 'breakdown':

c. Period of Direct Defence. Once our forces were engaged, even in limited conflict, either in Europe or on the flanks of NATO, the importance of the United Kingdom as a military base could be crucial to our ability to support them. The public would by now be even more aware that the nation was possibly on the threshold of nuclear attack. Evacuation of likely target areas might already have started spontaneously if not officially. Anti-war action might spread and involve considerable numbers of normally stable and law-abiding people. [Huge value judgements were about (a) what would be 'nor-mal' or rational in such circumstances, and (b) a lack of discrimination between protest and law-breaking, though there is a touch of this in what follows.] The Soviet bloc could bring to bear the full weight of their subversive activities, sabotage and psychological warfare. Key points, military head-quarters, logistic installations, movement facilities and training depots could now become targets for more widespread protest action and action aimed at paralysing our military ability. The civil problems of maintaining law and order, of protecting VIPs and centres of Government, of keeping open essential routes and services, the distribution of supplies, all these would present very serious problems for the police and other agencies of government.[185]

A Vietnam factor intrudes at this point. The war in Indochina was at its height as the defence planners were drafting, and the impact of its GI body counts and the direct depiction on television screens of the effects of napalm on Vietnamese villages and villagers was a nightly influencer of US domestic opinion to a degree not experienced in any previous conflict.

d. Period of Deliberate Escalation. Once tactical nuclear weapons were used on the battle front, the horror of nuclear war would be seen in practically every home. Truly democratic countries with very limited news censorship, would be at a disadvantage over their tightly controlled enemies. All the possible reactions which might already have started in the period of direct defence would now become greatly increased. The will of the free nations would be under its greatest test and the Soviet bloc would be likely to exploit every opportunity to break it and gain a victory short of a general nuclear response.[186]

One of the paradoxes of the Cold War once both sides had acquired a thermonuclear capability was what – if anything – would be left worth having that once belonged to the vanquished even if a 'victor', in any sense, were conceivable. The British planners side-stepped this in 1968 (though their sketch of post-attack Britain bore the imprint of the JIGSAW assumptions on 'breakdown'):

e. Period of Nuclear Exchange and its Immediate Aftermath. We do not envisage any Soviet or other externally inspired military threat in the short term. We believe the threat facing those endeavouring to save lives and restore some vestage [sic] of control would derive from basic law and order problems. Millions of homeless, bewildered people would need rudimentary shelter and sustenance. Looting of food stocks and other essential supplies, the blocking of essential routes by refugees, the seizing of property, all these problems on a mammoth scale could overwhelm the surviving police resources.[187]

Intriguingly, the Chiefs of Staff's thinkers reckoned the threat in the protracted post-attack phase would be the enemy within rather than what might be left of the enemy without – which itself implies doubts about the efficacy of 'smashing' the CPGB or any wider round-up of those individuals MI5 thought it desirable to place within the internment camps on the Isle of Man:

f. <u>The Long Term Post-Attack Period</u>. As the long term battle for survival progresses, crucial struggles are likely to arise over securing sources of food and other essential commodities together with the means of transporting them by sea and air. We foresee the possibility of new threats developing affecting both our overseas activities and our home base. Subversive organisations are likely to survive and the general chaos of the post-attack struggle could provide a better opportunity for them to succeed than anything which obtained pre-attack.[188]

The planners reached the obvious conclusion that the government's post-nuclear attack plans 'to enable those who remain to survive would be largely dependant [*sic*] on the presence of organised and disciplined manpower'.[189] They reckoned the police would need and would ask for 36,000 members of the Armed Forces to assist them during the 'escalation to general war', rising to 196,000 post-attack.[190]

Like all else to do with nuclear war, the degradation of the United Kingdom into twelve shrivelled irradiated little fiefdoms filled with wretched and desperate survivors theoretically governed by men in bunkers and probably ruled, in reality, by armed soldiers and policemen with ultimate powers over life and death (give or take the occasional surviving judge to interpose himself or herself) is too ghastly to contemplate. But contemplate it, in secret, the planners were regularly required to do. How long, once a period of tension began to turn into the run-up to a nuclear exchange, would it take for an ancient, settled kingdom like the UK to become an irreversibly broken and perpetually indefensible realm? No one could say.

But, for exercise purposes, the transition to war – sensibly enough – had to be a relatively protracted affair. INVALUABLE 1968, as we

Barents Sea

hite Sea

● Archangelsk

O r a n g e

Moscow ●

● Kiev

Sea of Azov

Caspian Sea

Black Sea

Bosporus
● nbul

● Ankara

T u r k e y

F o u l P l a y

Tehran ●

Sandland

Bagdhad ●

I r a q

Cyprus

Lebanon
Beirut ●

● Damascus

Israel
● Tel Aviv
● Amman

Jordan

● Kuwait

Persian Gulf

Egypt

S a u d i A r a b i a

have seen, begins with the shift to a hard-line regime in Moscow, effectively negating the overriding assumption of all the big JIC assessments of Russian intentions since the protean productions of 1947–8. It rested heavily, however, on JIC thinking about 'Escalation' (which is hardly surprising given that the compilers of its fictional 'sitreps' were exactly the same Cabinet Office analysts). Take the opening INVALUABLE 'sitrep' of 27 September 1968:

In an article in the 'Guardian,' Victor Zorza [a real and much respected commentator] said that it was clear that the struggle between the 'hawks' and the 'doves' in ORANGE [the Soviet Union – see the map on pages 160–61 for this and other country codenames] had resulted in a victory for the 'hawks' and that the immediate prospect was for a return to the coldest of Cold War conditions. In a leading article, the 'Daily Telegraph' warned that the greatest danger in the world today was that of miscalculation by the new ORANGE leaders, it was difficult to believe that they wanted war but there was a very real risk that they would set off a train of events that they could not control.[191]

This, again unsurprisingly, is roughly what happens.

According to the INVALUABLE scenario, by mid-October the new hard-line leadership in the Kremlin 'has coupled threats with its call for a revision of the status of the Baltic. OLD STAFF [Bulgaria] has raised tension on her border with Turkey. Turkey has protested at "excessive" ORANGE military supplies to SANDLAND [Syria]. Increased BAD BED [Chinese] hostility to its policies is putting ORANGE on the political defensive.'[192]

The 16 October 1968 'sitrep' paints a desperate picture which has plainly lit up a host of JIC Watch Book indicators and is to lead in a downward spiral to a Warsaw Pact invasion of West Germany five days later, by which time those officials and military officers simulating the Cabinet as MISC 222, had agreed to the Prime Minister, the Foreign Secretary and the Defence Secretary authorizing 'any requests from NATO for the use of nuclear weapons without further reference to the Cabinet'.[193]

What was the simulated mid-October 1968 scene which led to MISC 222 dancing a Michael Cary-style 'nightmarish gavotte'?

*ORANGE forces have deployed along the ORANGE-Norwegian border and are in positions from which an attack could be launched at any time. Several violations of the Norwegian border by ORANGE aircraft have occurred.

*A large concentration of ORANGE Bloc shipping including landing craft is building up in the Baltic. Although there is good evidence of an impending amphibious exercise in the Gulf of Danzig, this does not adequately account for the number of ships reported.

*Mobilisation of DEEP WATER [East German] and BROAD TERM [Czechoslovak] ground forces is taking place, and intense troop movement is reported in Bohemia. Troop movement on a large scale is also reported from Western ORANGE, BLUE EXPRESS [Poland] and DEEP WATER, predominantly in a westward direction.

*Heavy troop movements are reported through OLD STAFF towards Thrace. A clash occurred yesterday between OLD STAFF and Turkish frontier units.

*There are reliable reports of an offer to ORANGE by the new SANDLAND government of naval and air bases.

*In the Atlantic ORANGE naval and merchant shipping is deploying as if for war. Merchant shipping appears to be withdrawing to neutral or friendly ports. Intense air surveillance of the [NATO] Strike Fleet is being main-tained.[194]

And what did the JIC make of the darkening scene?

The internal pressures which are behind ORANGE's widespread diplomatic, military and subversive activity have not abated. ORANGE still claims that her troop movements are connected only with Warsaw Pact exercises. But this may be to give herself a pretext for retracting should she achieve her political objectives without war. Nevertheless, the high state of readiness in Central Europe is being maintained and certain military indicators are consistent with readiness to attack . . .[195]

Such was the secret state's simulated mental geography of the world on the brink.

If global war and general nuclear release *had* come for real in the late 1960s, the JIC had its views, too, on where the missiles would land in the UK. This list (pp. 164–8) is full of intriguing pointers.

PROBABLE NUCLEAR TARGETS IN THE UNITED KINGDOM: ASSUMPTIONS FOR PLANNING

Notes: (i) Figures in brackets denote total targets in each category: (ii) (A) denotes Air Burst; (iii) (S) denotes Surface Burst

		Missile Weapon yield per target	Aircraft Weapon yield per target
TARGETS RELATED TO ALLIED NUCLEAR STRIKE CAPABILITY (65)			
CENTRES OF CONTROL ETC. (22)			
(i) Government – Central (2)	London	8 × 1 MT(A)	2 × 500 KT(A)
	Cheltenham	2 × ½–1 MT(A)	2 × 500 KT(A)
–ex-Regional (12)	Catterick	2 × ½–3 MT(S)	2 × 1 MT(S)
	York	"	"
	Preston	"	"
	Cambridge	"	"
	Dover	"	"
	Reading	"	"
	Salcombe	"	"
	Brecon	"	"
	Kidderminster	"	"
	Armagh	"	"
	Edinburgh	"	"
	Nottingham	"	"
(ii) Military – Maritime (4)	Northwood (HQ, CINCHAN/CINCEASTLANT)	2 × ½–1 MT(A)	2 × 1 MT(S)
	Plymouth (HQ, COMCENTLANT)	"	"
	Pitreavie (HQ, COMNOPLANT)	"	"
	Fort Southwick (HQ, C-IN-C, UK Home Station)	"	"

Catterick to Nottingham: } former RSG sites

These are considered to be possible, rather than probable targets

See also paragraph 2

– Air (3)	High Wycombe (HQ, Bomber Command)	2 × ½–3 MT(S)	2 × 1 MT(S)
	Ruislip (HQ, 3rd US Air Force)	"	"
	Bawtry (HQ, 1 Gp. Bomber Command)	"	"

BOMBER BASES (including dispersal recovery and flight-refuelling bases) (32)

(i) RAF (26)	Scampton	2 × 500 KT(A)	2 × 1 MT(S)
	Wittering	"	"
	Waddington	"	"
	Honington	"	"
	Cottesmore	"	"
	Marham	"	"
	Coningsby	"	"
	St. Mawgan	"	"
	Lossiemouth	"	"
	Macrihanish	"	"
	Leeming	"	"
	Gaydon	"	"
	Finningley	"	"
	Valley	"	"
	Bedford	"	"
	Brawdy	"	"
	Yeovilton	"	"
	Lyneham	"	"
	Wyton	"	"
	Pershore	"	"
	Boscombe Down	"	"
	Kinloss	"	"
	Manston	"	"
	Ballykelly	"	"
	Filton	"	"
	Leconfield	"	"

TARGETS RELATED TO ALLIED NUCLEAR STRIKE CAPABILITY (65)

CENTRES OF CONTROL ETC. (32) (Cont'd)

(ii) USAF (6)	Missile Weapon yield per target	Aircraft Weapon yield per target
Alconbury	2 × 500 KT(A)	2 × 1 MT(S)
Bentwaters	"	"
Woodbridge	"	"
Wethersfield	"	"
Lakenheath	"	"
Upper Heyford	"	"

BASES ETC. FOR SEABORNE NUCLEAR STRIKE FORCES (12)

(i) Bases (5)		Missile Weapon yield per target	Aircraft Weapon yield per target
Garelock [i.e. Gareloch] (Clyde)	} Polaris	2 × 500 KT(A)	2 × 1 MT(S)
Holy Loch		"	"
Rosyth (SSBN Refitting Base)		"	"
Portsmouth	} Carrier	1 × ½–1 MT(A)	2 × 1 MT(S)
Devonport		"	"

(ii) Communication Installations (7)		Missile Weapon yield per target	Aircraft Weapon yield per target
VLF { Rugby		1 × 500 KT(A)	2 × 500 KT(A)
Criggion		"	"
Anthorn (NATO)		"	"
LF { Inskip		"	"
New Waltham	} US Navy	"	"
Londonderry		"	"
Thurso		"	"

MAJOR CITIES (20)

				Missile Weapon yield per target
Glasgow	4 ×	1 MT(A)		2 × 500 KT(A)
Birmingham		"		"
Liverpool			1 MT(A)	"
Cardiff	2 ×		"	"
Manchester			"	"
Southampton			"	"
Leeds			"	"
Newcastle			"	"
Bristol			"	"
Sheffield			"	"
Swansea			"	"
Hull			"	"
Middlesbrough			"	"
Coventry			"	"
Wolverhampton			"	"
Leicester			"	"
Stoke-on-Trent			"	"
Belfast			"	"
Edinburgh			"	"
Nottingham			"	"

TARGETS RELATING TO AID DEFENCES (18)

		Missile Weapon yield per target
CONTROL CENTRES (2)	Bentley Priory (HQ Fighter Command – after 1.3.68, Headquarters No 11 Group RAF)	2 × 1–3 MT(A)
	West Drayton (Southern Joint Control Centre)	"

FIGHTER BASES (4)	Coltishall	2 × 500 KT(A)
	Leuchars	
	Wattisham	"
	Binbrook	"

	Missile Weapon yield per target	Aircraft Weapon yield per target
TARGETS RELATED TO ALLIED NUCLEAR STRIKE CAPABILITY (65)		
CENTRES OF CONTROL ETC. (32) (Cont'd)		
SURFACE-TO-AIR Woodhall Spa (a)		2 × 500 KT(A)
MISSILE SITES (3)		
North Coates		"
West Raynham		"
BMEWS (1) Fylingdales		2 × 500 KT(A)
RADAR STATIONS (8) Boulmer (Master)		2 × 500 KT(A)
(See also footnotes Patrington (Master)		"
(c) and (d) below). Bawdsey (Master) (b)		"
Neatishead (Master, being rebuilt)		"
Buchan (Master) (Phases out 1970)		"
Saxa Vord (Satellite)		"
Staxton Wold (Radar site for Patrington)		"
Feltwell (Over-the-horizon radar)		"

(a) Delete when Woodhall Spa phases out as a SAM site end 1967.
(b) Delete when Bawdsey phases out as a radar station in 1970.
(c) Add Orford Ness when equipped with over-the-horizon radar about 1970.
(d) Add Oakhanger DCN Satellite Commuication station when it becomes fully operational early in 1969.[196]

'Government-Central' is described as 'London' (i.e. Whitehall) and Cheltenham (i.e. GCHQ). There is no mention of the alternative seat of government under any of its codenames. Note how the Regional Seats of Government have now become 'former' (i.e. stood down, part of the care and maintenance home defence policy). The Russians are thought, however, to know where they are, which is not surprising given that the 'Spies for Peace' distributed the list during the 1963 Aldermaston March. Among the military targets, as one would expect, were the very-low-frequency signals installations at Rugby and Criggion, whose purpose was (and is) to relay the Prime Minister's instructions to the commanders of the deterrent-bearing submarines. Seventeen major cities were thought to have two 1-megaton missile air bursts awaiting them, plus two 2,500-kiloton ones delivered by aircraft; Glasgow, Birmingham and Liverpool were thought to have four 1-megaton and two 2,500-kiloton; London was thought to have eight 1-megaton and two 2,500-kiloton respectively. That is, I reckon, 'breakdown' and more.

The major V-force bases and their dispersal fields (twenty-six in all) were likely to disappear beneath two 500-kiloton missile air bursts and two 1-megaton surface bursts delivered by Soviet bombers. Many of those on the list here had an all-too-vivid idea of what this would mean for the ground staff and their families as their V-bombers roared up and away flat out eastwards.

Bobby Robson's Vulcan would have risen into the sky from either Waddington or Scampton. He and his crew 'knew all the effects of an air burst and a ground burst'.[197] He knew where his targets were, too. He would not have needed to wait until 'positive control' was superseded by the order to attack as his aircraft approached the start-line over the Baltic just over an hour after clearing its Lincolnshire runway.

We had a canvas bag – the War Bag. When we were QRA [Quick Reaction Alert] we did target studies all the time, or 80 per cent of the time. We weren't allowed to leave the base. The only things you could do were eat, sleep and do target study and safety and escape drills.

You knew where you were going. You studied the routes. Minsk. Moscow. All the cities. Every significant city in the Soviet Union as far as you could go.[198]

In the 1960s the V-bombers would have gone in 'high-low-high' – 'high to the start line, dropping down low over enemy territory; you drop the weapon and then come out high because the theory is that there is then nothing there'.[199] Bobby Robson, like everyone else, wondered how many Vulcans like his would reach their target:

The satellite countries had left alleyways between the SAM [Surface-to-Air Missile] sites exactly where we would go. I thought they would be the equivalent of killing fields. But one getting through was almost unacceptable.[200]

Once approaching the start-line, the last ever order 'would have been a command signal from Bomber Command. The Pavlovian reaction would not have changed if the signal to continue had been received. We would have done it unhesitatingly. I really mean *unhesitatingly*.'[201]

Robson's last command would have come from beneath the Chilterns, on the western side of High Wycombe. If the nucleus of central government had rushed out of London using the emergency procedure, from where would the Commander-in-Chief of the Bomber Command have received *his* last order?

12 (*top*) TURNSTILE: the War Cabinet bunker entrance near Corsham if the Prime Minister came by road

13 (*above*) Q for Quarry: through the barrier and into the lift

14 (*below*) The author examining the tunnel entrance to the end of the world for those arriving by train. The eastern end of Brunel's Box Tunnel is on the left

15 The secret Cotswold Station ready to receive the last train

16 Along the old quarry workings and through Door 48 to the last redoubt

17 The kitchen for cooking the last supper

18 Makeshift accommodation for 210 people

19 Bizarre graffito on the bunker wall: one of several painted by workers during World War II when it was an underground aero-engine factory

20 The first-aid room: chipped white cups symbolizing the continuity of the state

21 The alert board for World War III

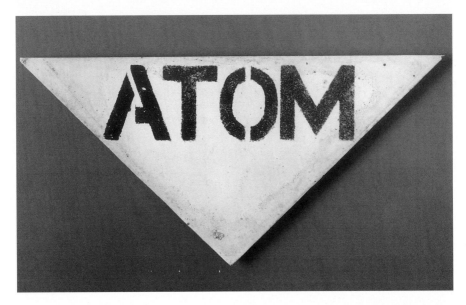

22 'ATOM': if this had been inserted into the bunker's slots, the world above would have been devastated by nuclear attack

23 Sir Frank Cooper: the Prime Minister can only authorize nuclear retaliation, not order it

24 HMS *Resolution*, a Polaris submarine in the Firth of Clyde, the Isle of Arran in the background: in a safe on board are the Prime Minister's wishes from beyond the grave to be opened only after a bolt-from-the-blue

5

To the Cotswold Station:
the Last Redoubt

*It is fundamental to all TURNSTILE planning that if its
location and purpose were known to the Russians it would
almost certainly be destroyed.*

United Kingdom Commanders-in-Chief Committee
memorandum, March 1963[1]

*The Chiefs of Staff never liked the idea of rushing to a bloody
quarry . . . people disappearing to the West Country.*

Sir Frank Cooper, former Permanent Secretary,
Ministry of Defence, recalling the 1960s in 1998[2]

STUCK HERE 4 ETERNITY
Undated graffito by unknown hand, TURNSTILE[3]

Where exactly was this ultra-sensitive nuclear bunker, this 'bloody
quarry' in the West Country, whose location had to be kept from
Soviet intelligence at all costs? It was a hundred feet *below* the top of
Box Hill and fifty feet *above* Brunel's celebrated Box Tunnel (towards
its eastern entrance) along which he drew his Great Western Railway
through the Cotswolds on the last stage of its run from Paddington to
Bath and Bristol. According to Sir Frank Cooper, 'the very few people
who were in on [the TURNSTILE secret] . . . always referred to it as
"The Quarry"'.[4] Others in the inner circle knew it as 'Corsham'.[5] The
military called it QOC (for 'Quarry Operations Centre').[6] Locals
simply referred to the old workings (for years the quarry had been the
place where that incomparable building material, Bath stone, had been
cut) as 'The Deep'.[7]

As far as is known, no Prime Minister has ever paid a visit either for real or out of curiosity[8] to what in the event of an East–West war would have been the last redoubt of the British War Cabinet. It was ready by 1962 when Harold Macmillan laid down a prime ministerial directive that 'Turnstile' was

(a) to act as the seat of Government in the period of survival and recon-struction.
(b) to be an alternative centre to London for authorising nuclear retaliation.[9]

Knowing that from the late 1970s, if not earlier, Russian intelligence had almost certainly located TURNSTILE (as a Soviet surveillance satellite was programmed to pass over it on each of its circumnav-igations of the earth),[10] and knowing, too, that by the turn of the twentieth century the bunker codenamed PINDAR, the Crisis Man-agement Centre beneath the Ministry of Defence in Whitehall, was the place from which, heaven forbid, nuclear retaliation would henceforth be authorized by the Prime Minister, I sought permission from the Cabinet Secretary, Sir Richard Wilson, early in 2001 to visit what remained of TURNSTILE.[11]

A member of the Cabinet Secretary's Private Office informed me that 'Box Hill, Corsham', as he called it, was now looked after by the Ministry of Defence who would be in touch.[12] The MOD duly was. Guy Lester, Private Secretary to the Permanent Secretary, Kevin Tebbit, said, 'we would be pleased to arrange for you to visit some of the site's more interesting historical areas. These include the Quarry Operations Area, the No. 10 Group wartime operations room, communications and stores areas, and the railway station . . .'[13] The site is now occupied by the ministry's Joint Support Unit, a communications installation administered by the Royal Air Force.

So, on a misty spring morning, three of us presented ourselves at the security gate of the JSU, Corsham – myself, my research assistant (my daughter, Polly) and a photographer (Jason Orton who took the TURNSTILE photographs in this book). There are, as it turns out, some sixty miles of tunnels beneath the JSU's patch. The quarry had been used during World War II as a huge ammunition depot in one section, an RAF operations centre in another and as a sizeable under-ground factory for making Bristol aero engines in a third.

Over the next few hours it was possible to reconstruct some of the elements which went into the making of TURNSTILE. Some (as Guy Lester had indicated), not all, because the files containing the plans, the layout and the operational drills have not been declassified, apart from a few, albeit very revealing, exceptions. And I am sure – I shall explain why in a moment – that not every bit of what once comprised TURNSTILE was laid open for our inspection. The reasons for this I can only guess at. Could it be that the facility, despite all the dereliction surrounding it, has not necessarily been pensioned off for ever? Whatever the remaining mystery, there is certainly a degree of sensitivity remaining about the early twenty-first-century 'Quarry'.

Since the RAF took it over in 1979 (they used it until 1990 as a Station Operations Room, part of RAF Rudloe Manor), new breeze-block walls and other adaptations have altered the site. In 1999 it ceased to be used at all for the last of its peacetime functions, the staff of the Service Communications Centre moving to the surface. So by the spring of 2001 TURNSTILE was a ghostly, dusty and slightly damp place, in striking contrast to the spick and span PINDAR with its hi-tech equipment, bright, modern furniture and clean, filtered air.

Some 210 people were earmarked to go underground at TURN-STILE during the last phase of a transition to nuclear war[14] (precisely who we shall see shortly). Very few would have been there before that. What would they have encountered first if the imminent catastrophe had propelled them west in the early to mid-1960s? It would have depended on their mode of transport from London.

It may be (this is speculation), that the senior figures destined for the last stand – the Prime Minister, members of the War Cabinet, the Chief of the Defence Staff, senior intelligence and security officers, top advisers to ministers in the War Cabinet – would have raced west down the A4. (The M4 was some years away from completion.) Who knows what the roads would have been like. Hopelessly clogged with the cars and vans of those seeking refuge beyond the obvious target of the metropolis? Passable for the ministerial, official and military limousines in convoy escorted by the police? Would certain trunk roads by this stage have been closed to all but essential, war-related traffic, the A4 included (much harder to do for an old road than a new motorway with few entrances and exits)?

Had they travelled by road, the top echelon would have turned off the A4 at the western end of Corsham just past the village of Pickwick (coincidentally the codename of Whitehall's secure telephone network in those days). But a short drive remained through the village of Rudloe to the Basil Hill barracks site, part of which is right above the Box Railway Tunnel. Once inside the perimeter, they would have entered a short, tower-like building and into a pair of lifts with only two buttons – 'G' for Ground and 'Q' for Quarry.

A few seconds later they would have left the lifts to pass along a corridor of offices built in the standard Ministry of Works style. Very quickly they would have emerged into a quarry gallery, oolitic limestone all around, the walls scratched with graffiti of many years' accumulation. One had an especially grim relevance – 'STUCK HERE 4 ETERNITY' – though it looks relatively fresh and could be post-1960s. A minute's walk later and they would turn right through a plain steel door marked only by the number '48'. This was the entrance to the Quarry Operations Centre – in its time perhaps the most secret installation of the UK's Cold War state.

Beyond here there is no cosy, Ministry of Works, Whitehall by-another-means feel. TURNSTILE was plainly improvised inside the eerie interlocking limestone chambers that once housed the aero engine workers. The murals left from those days add an air of utter surreality. There are sporting scenes of all kinds, with cricket and horseracing strongly represented. Bizarrely, an Anglican missionary being boiled in a pot by cannibals adorns one room. Nearby is the first-aid room. Stretchers on trolleys covered by long-since frayed blankets give a Dickensian, Miss Havisham feel. A rusty, red-cross-emblazoned tin helmet rests next to two white tea cups – enduring symbols of Britishness.

Some of the smaller rooms are crammed with army beds. Skeletal, uncomfortable-looking bunks are strewn around the larger gallery areas of the old quarry. The atmosphere here is part-pothole, part-dormitory. The cooking section is striking. Banks of huge ovens, an area of hotplates, a standard oblong canteen container for serving tureens. This might have struck those newly arriving at TURNSTILE, had it ever been activated, as it struck me, as the last supper area.

As a reminder of precisely what might be about to befall, an NBC (nuclear, biological, chemical) Room was nearby as were small, triangular metal discs with 'ATOM' and 'BIO' and 'GAS' stencilled on them for insertion into some unseen slot to signify conditions on Box Hill, a hundred feet above. These little triangles would have been ghastly indications of what had happened to wives and children, the world they had lost. TURNSTILE was a no-families zone.

How else might the TURNSTILE people, their files and their War Books have come from their mustering points in London? Two hundred-plus civilians and military and supporting impedimenta take some shifting and speed would have been of the essence. Rail is the obvious answer. Thanks to the efforts of Brunel in the nineteenth century and the Royal Engineers in the twentieth, everything needed for this lay a few hundred yards away. If you travel west from Chippen-ham to Bath on one of today's Great Western 125s that encounters a speed restriction in the Corsham area, you might see right next to Brunel's exquisite eastern arch at the mouth of Box Tunnel, a very different and infinitely shabbier entrance for a single branch line (this bit of track was lifted in the late 1960s). The approach is wet, over-grown and rubbish-strewn. The entrance is blocked by a large, rusted metal door.

From here poured out an endless series of ammunition trains during World War II and after when the Royal Ordnance Corps's Corsham Ammunition Depot was still operational. Nowadays, once through the metal door one encounters an impassable wall a few yards in. The other side of that wall, on the right of the track as you enter from London, are decontamination units, a series of through rooms contain-ing decayed shower facilities for washing off the nuclear particles. A little way beyond, the track divides, before running alongside two 800-foot-long platforms and terminating in a vast cavernous (in every sense) station. Once off the train, from the far end of the platform, it is a seven-minute walk *up* the quarry gallery, past the graffiti and into Door 48 and the Quarry Operations Centre.

The former RAF operations room I was shown (no doubt it was the one mentioned in Guy Lester's letter) was surprisingly small. It could be that the area which would have been used by the War Cabinet and the Chiefs of Staff was bigger and close by and not shown to us – that we were, in a manner of speaking, not taken through the final 'turnstile' to the last arena of British Central Government. I have no means of knowing for sure, but I think it very likely. Indeed I am virtually sure of it. Guy Lester used that phrase, 'some of the site's more interesting historical areas', with classic Civil Service care.

What of the room my team and I were admitted to that afternoon? Two things, above all, catch one's eye. The once-illuminable board beneath the ceiling listing the various alert states and the two murals on the wall, one of a tiny boxer knocking out a grinning and much larger opponent, the other of wrestlers in action. Just through the door was a large and very striking depiction of cricket on a village green. On the table lay a guide to radiation protection and some old maps. Like the furniture (standard Ministry of Works chairs) they were damp, dirty and mildewy. A train in Box Tunnel could be just heard beneath.

Somewhere nearby, towards the end of the transition (as outlined in the Stephens memo for the Queen) from MACMORRIS to VISITATION, it was planned that a human machine of 210 crown servants would swing into action. Who were they and what do their ranks and functions tell us about the overall purpose of TURNSTILE? The Queen herself was not to be with her Prime Minister and War Cabinet. She would not have had to wait for Stephens's brief in 1965 to know that. Planning for her evacuation to a safe place began in the time of her first Private Secretary, Sir Alan 'Tommy' Lascelles.[15] Once the royal yacht *Britannia* was commissioned in 1954, the plan was to get her aboard and out of danger during a period of international tension.[16] *Britannia* possessed good communications equipment (by the standards of the day) capable of reaching anywhere on the globe.[17]

The war planners realized, as one insider put it, that 'It made no sense to have the Queen with the War Cabinet in case the whole lot were wiped out together.' With an enduring sense of the personal royal prerogatives, it was appreciated that the Queen would need to appoint a new Prime Minister and senior ministers to replace the old set, if other politicians had survived, once it was safe for *Britannia* to sail back to her shattered kingdom.[18] But what would have happened if war came very swiftly with the Queen, say, at Balmoral and the royal yacht berthed in a southern port? There was a fall-back to rush her to a safe place somewhere on terra firma (almost certainly in Scotland)[19] but I have not yet been able to discover where.

So who *was* earmarked for TURNSTILE? Very few would have known, including 'Turnstilers' themselves, until shortly before the cars and the train set off west. Chapter III of the 1963 MOD War Book, entitled 'Alternative War Headquarters', is the best guide we have of the run-up period before the manning of TURNSTILE. It is worth reproducing in full, even though the sections of the Government War Book referred to remain classified. We do not know where the designated 'Check Point' was. We shall never know how many of those instructed to prepare for TURNSTILE would have obeyed rather than slipping into Whitehall and back to their homes and families ('Turnstilers', after all, would include some of the people best and most graphically informed of what hydrogen bombs do). It was, none the less, fascinating to read Appendix D to that 1963 MOD War Book when it was declassified in late 2000 and for the first time to see just what the World War III War Cabinet Organisation would have looked like. Here is the list.[20]

		Total numbers required
(1) *Prime Minister and War Cabinet*		
(a) *Prime Minister*	1	
Private Secretaries	2	
Executive Officers	2	
Clerical Officers/Shorthand Typists	4	9
(b) *Other Ministers of War Cabinet rank*	5	
Personal Staff	10	15
(2) *Chief of the Defence Staff and Staff*		
Chief of the Defence Staff	1	
Personal Staff	2	
D.C.D.S. or A.C.D.S.	1	
Staff Officers	4	
Clerical Officers	2	
Shorthand Typists	2	12
(3) *Civil Secretariat*		
(staffed by Cabinet Office)		
Secretary to Cabinet	1	
Private Secretary	1	
Deputy Secretary/Under Secretary	1	
Assistant Secretaries/Principals	2	
Clerical Officers (Secretaries)	3	8

		Total numbers required
(4) *Military Secretariat (Chiefs of Staff Secretariat)*		
Secretary	I	
Deputy Secretary	I	
G.S.O.1.	3	
G.S.O.2	3	
Clerical Officers	2	
Shorthand Typists	3	13
(5) *Ministry of Defence*		
(a) Deputy Secretary	I	
Under/Assistant Secretary	I	
H.E.O./E.O.	I	
P.A.	I	
Clerk	I	5
(b) *Directorate of Forward Plans*	2	2
(c) *Chief Scientific Adviser*	2	2
(d) *Co-ordinator, Communications-*	2	2
Electronics Policy		
(e) *British Communications-Electronics Board*		
Deputy Director	I	
Serving Officers	4	
Experimental Officers etc.	3	
Higher Clerical Officer	I	
P.A.	I	
Typist	I	11
(f) *London Communications Security Agency*	2	2
(6) *Joint Planning Staff*		
Deputy or Assistant Secretary	I	
Clerical Officer	I	
Team { G.S.O.1	I	
{ G.S.O.2 – F section	3	
Copy Typists	3	9
(7) *Joint Intelligence Committee*		
(a) *Secretariat*		
Secretary	I	
G.S.O.1.	I	
Principal	I	
Clerical Officers	3	6
(b) *Senior Representative*		
(Service Ministries.)		
J.I.B. (2), M.I.5		
M.I.6., G.C.H.Q.		8

			Total numbers required
(c) *Intelligence Staffs*			
Admiralty	2		
War Office	5		
Air Ministry	7		
M.I.6.	3		
G.C.H.Q.	2		
J.I.B.	5		
Security Service	1		
C.I.A. Representatives	2		
Canadian Liaison Offr.	1		
G.C.H.Q. Communications Staff	4		
F.O. Monitors	3		
M.I.6. Communications Staff	4		39

(8) *Combined Registry and Committee and Distribution Sections*

	From Cabinet Office	From Ministry of Defence	
H.E.O.	1		
E.O.'s	2		
C.O.'s	3	3	
Messengers	3	3	15

(9) *War Cabinet Signal Registry*
(staffed by Ministry of Defence)

H.C.O.'s		1	
C.O's		4	5

(10) *Typing Pools*

	From Cabinet Office	From Ministry of Defence	
Chief Superintendent	1		
Supervisors		2	
Typists	4	5	
Duplicator Operators	1	2	15

(11) *Prime Minister's Map Room*

(a) Captain R.N., Colonel, or Group Captain	1
(b) *Admiralty Component*	
Senior watchkeeper (Cdr.)	1

		Total *numbers* required
Watchkeepers (Lt. Cdrs.)	3	
Chief Clerk (FO)	1	
Clerks (typists)	2	
Orderlies	3	
(c) *War Office Component*		
Senior Watchkeeper (Lt. Col.)	1	
Watchkeepers (Majors)	3	
Supervising Clerk (WO1)	1	
Chief Clerk (Sgt.)	1	
Clerks (Typists)	2	
Draughtsmen	3	
(d) *Air Ministry Office Component*		
Senior Watchkeeper (Wg. Cdr)	1	
Watchkeepers (Sqn. Ldrs.)	3	
Chief Clerk (Sgt.)	1	
Clerks (Typists)	2	
Orderlies	3	32
GRAND TOTALS		210

This tally neatly describes the innermost circle of the Cold War secret state, those 'special areas of Whitehall', as Frank Cooper described them, 'which really concentrated on the immense problems that the rise of the Soviet state and its scientific and technological progress created' and those 'special mechanisms, limited to a smaller number of people who were there essentially to deal with this kind of problem. And, obviously, as it potentially involved war or peace, the Prime Minister was always the epicentre of it.'[21]

That war-or-peace decision, in the era when the British deterrent was carried by a manned V-bomber aircraft, as we have seen, had to be made in a matter of minutes to get the planes airborne, and slightly longer to authorize their flying beyond the start-line – the point-of-no-return. These were the kind of decisions a Prime Minister and a War Cabinet might have had to take very shortly after passing through Door 48 at TURNSTILE. Philip Allen of the Home Office, himself earmarked to go under Box Hill with the Home Secretary, pondered after his time on the Strath Committee just how the plans would work in practice if it came to a transition to war.[22] Like Allen, Frank Cooper, too, had his doubts when we talked about it for the BBC Radio 4's *The Top Job* programme in the summer of 2000:

HENNESSY: Can I ask you . . . about the planning for the dispersal of government if it really had looked that World War III was imminent and the management of the residual state – what would have been left, heaven knows, after the attack – from the dispersed governments in these bunkers around the country and, above all, the one that the Prime Minister and the inner group would have gone to in Wiltshire . . . ? Could you tell me about the exercising of all that? I know you were involved in it. Did British Prime Ministers ever go and sit in it [TURNSTILE] and play out their role?

COOPER: I'm a bit of a heretic about this dispersed government working smoothly under nuclear attack. I never really ever believed in it primarily because it was going to be such a shambles if anything like that did happen. And a picture of chaps sitting underground thinking calmly and clearly in the depths of some country shire just doesn't seem to me a likely picture . . . It was right to plan for this because it might have been possible – a big 'might' – over time to recover some degree of order through the country as a whole. And it was certainly right to have places all over the country from which you could hope to restore some kind of government and make all kinds of arrangements from medical to food. So that *did* make sense, but their sort of fingertip control over nuclear warfare seemed to me a contradiction in terms, quite frankly. I think some people certainly did practise . . . But the ministers practised in London as far as I know. I never knew a minister to go down.

HENNESSY: When you took ministers through this . . . how did it affect them?

COOPER: It was very confusing, I think, to most of them. It was very difficult to follow . . . They were awed with the responsibility of it and whether they'd get it right if it ever did happen . . . I certainly had doubts as to what would happen if it was for real and whether people would have the courage to do this, or the courage *not* to do it just as importantly – in fact, probably more importantly . . . It's the most horrifically awful decision you could possibly contemplate.[23]

It is worth examining carefully the mix of advisers a 1960s or 1970s Prime Minister compelled to contemplate such awfulness would have had at his disposal to help him 'get it right' in TURNSTILE had the whole set reached Box Hill in time.

I reckon one has to start with a cluster in the middle of the list in the MOD War Book. Under 'Intelligence Staffs' one finds space for two 'senior representatives of MI6', presumably 'C', the Chief of the Secret Intelligence Service, and a senior colleague, together with three MI6 staffers and an 'MI6 Communications Staff' of four. There were those among the war-planning community who thought that once the first nuclear weapon had been launched, by whichever side, irreversible escalation would take place until, the arsenals spent, the world would succumb to the Neville Shute *On the Beach* scenario. Writing in the mid-1950s, he predicted the consequence of 'The short, bewildering war [in the second half of 1961] . . . the war of which no history had ever been written or ever would be written now, that had flared all round the northern hemisphere and had died away with the last seismic record of explosion on the thirty-seventh day.'[24]

Others, however, thought that the process would neither be as rapid nor as teleological – that there would be time for hot lines to buzz between the bunkers containing the heads of government of the thermonuclear powers. As we have seen, the 1968 'INVALUABLE Exercise' was built around just such an assumption. It has been explained to me that the British Prime Minister, using MI6's separate and secure means of communication, could have instructed the MI6 Station Chief in Moscow to break cover, make contact with the Soviet leadership, announce plainly who he really was and convey the PM's message to Khrushchev, or later, Brezhnev.[25] The growing preoccupation about war-through-inadvertence made thinking about possible, last-minute procedures to prevent the first, limited nuclear exchange spiralling into the Neville Shute nightmare make sense in that world of desperate possibility.

One UK planner, whose experience spanned the 1960s and the 1970s, said of his craft:

In the end you had to do it because the other side might be irrational and one mustn't forget either the notorious flock of geese appearing on the radar as incoming missiles. What if, late at night with several vodkas inside them, Brezhnev and co. were approached by the Russian military saying 'you have but minutes to decide what to do.'?

The same applied to both sides. In the UK there was a difference between the V-force days, when you did only have minutes to decide [to get the bombers airborne], and Polaris when you could wait.[26]

As we have seen, the Royal Navy's Polaris submarines took over the deterrent role from the RAF's V-bombers in June 1969.[27]

Who would have been the Prime Minister's and the War Cabinet's chief military adviser in TURNSTILE? The Chief of the Defence Staff (CDS) with, no doubt, the Secretary of the Cabinet and the Chief Scientific Adviser to the MOD in close attendance.[28] In one sense the CDS would have been the second most important figure inside 'The Quarry' after the PM himself. For without the concurrence of the CDS, the V-bombers could not have raced towards their targets in the Soviet Union or the Polaris submarines launched their missiles out of the Atlantic, the Norwegian or the Barents seas. In other words, the CDS was Britain's protection against its head of government doing a 'Dr Strangelove'.

In the summer of 2000 I put such a scenario to Sir Frank Cooper (who in his days as the MOD's Deputy Secretary, Policy, 1968–70, had his own TURNSTILE slot[29]).

HENNESSY: Can I ask you a question which tends to lurk in people's minds about this? What if a Prime Minister went bananas ... at a period of high international tension and authorised the release of the British nuclear weapon and the military advisers concerned, and those small groups of civil servants who were involved as well, realised the Prime Minister was crackers – what would happen?

COOPER: Well, the key word is 'authorised'. The Prime Minister can only authorise the use of force or the use of nuclear weapons or anything of that kind, he cannot give an order. The only legitimate orders can be given by commissioned officers of Her Majesty's forces. And this is a fine distinction but not unimportant.

HENNESSY: So, what would happen if I was Prime Minister and you were my Chief of the Defence Staff and I said: 'Frank, I authorise the use of the British nuclear weapon' and you thought I was bananas? What would you do?

COOPER: Well, I'd argue with the Prime Minister for some time. You might not have a lot of time but I'd certainly argue with him and, in the last analysis, say: 'Well, I'm not going to do that' – which would probably mean you'd get court martialled if you survived. But it may be totally against your military judgment. Now the Prime Minister's response to that would be to fire me straight away and get a more pliant officer. [The plans envisaged either the Deputy Chief of the Defence Staff or an Assistant Chief of the Defence Staff being with the CDS behind Door 48.[30]][31]

Sir Frank went on to explain that 'this distinction between authorisation and the power to give orders is a very important one ... this is where you are into the royal prerogative basically. And, you know, there are many many cases where the royal prerogative [under which members are servants of the crown, not mere instruments of ministers] actually plays a very useful part in life and if you didn't have it you *would* need a written constitution.'[32]

It may be that other War Cabinet members had their doubts, too. Who would they have been? The plan allowed for five 'Other Ministers of War Cabinet rank' with two 'personal staff' apiece.[33] From Chiefs of Staff planning papers for 1959, when the possible future use of TURNSTILE was very much in mind (by the last months of that year 'Structural work for [the government's World War III] headquarters [was] almost complete, and the installation of communications [had] begun'[34]), we have precise information about which groups of ministers the very senior military would brief at the last pre-attack stage. On receipt of a 'tactical warning, i.e., when attack is imminent and the Allies have received definite information of an enemy attack having been launched, probably by the identification of enemy aircraft or missiles on the radar screens',[35] the Chiefs would proceed to a meeting with the Prime Minister and '(a) the Home Secretary, (b) the Foreign Secretary, (c) the Minister of Defence, (d) the Secretary of the Cabinet'.[36]

So, TURNSTILE planning allowed for two more *ad hominem* appointments to the War Cabinet by the Prime Minister. If the War Book drill had been followed, he would do this 'on the institution of a Precautionary stage'.[37] At which point:

(a) Secretary of Cabinet invites Prime Minister to select team of Ministers to proceed to TURNSTILE when order to man is given.

(b) Cabinet considers if staff designated for TURNSTILE should be warned.[38]

Three further Cabinet decisions were required before the microcosm of central government moved west to the Cotswold Station:

Cabinet decision to warn staff selected for TURNSTILE.

Cabinet decision to man TURNSTILE.

Cabinet decision to transfer control to TURNSTILE.[39]

The niceties of Cabinet government were to be preserved almost to the end.

I say 'almost' because it was a prime ministerial decision to authorize the launch of the 'Yellow Sun' or 'Blue Steel' H-bombs or, later, the Polaris missiles, as both Jim Callaghan and Alec Home have made plain to me.[40] Following the 1961 rethink, the Cabinet Office group on retaliation procedures listed among its assumptions that

(a) The Centre of Government, including the Prime Minister, would remain in the Whitehall area during a precautionary period, though the alternative seat of Government and the Regions would be manned by selected Ministers and officials . . .

(b) Two Deputies to the Prime Minister would be appointed in peacetime and one of them would be available to act as the Prime Minister's deputy for purposes of nuclear retaliation during any period, however short, when the Prime Minister was not immediately available.[41]

It is, I think, very likely (though not certain) that the Cabinet meeting Harold Macmillan planned for the afternoon of Sunday 28 October 1962 would have authorized a move to a Precautionary Stage had Khrushchev not backed down over Cuba that lunchtime. Indeed, at what was originally meant to be his pre-Cabinet meeting with the Chiefs of Staff, Peter Thorneycroft, the Minister of Defence, told his military professionals that in the changed circumstances he 'did not . . . consider that any immediate precautionary measures were necessary'.[42]

Had the crisis not eased and had the Cabinet agreed to the institution of the Precautionary Stage, who would have comprised the inner core of Macmillan's War Cabinet? His Foreign Secretary, Alec Home; his Home Secretary, Henry Brooke; plus Thorneycroft. It is likely that the First Secretary of State and Deputy Prime Minister, Rab Butler, would have filled the fourth slot. We do not know who was the number one designated deputy after Selwyn Lloyd had been sacked as Chancellor of the Exchequer the previous July as the most prominent victim of the 'Night of the Long Knives'.[43]

Within a couple of years Home was Prime Minister himself. Deep into his retirement (though not a word passed between us about TURNSTILE, a codename I did not know about at that stage), Alec Home talked to me about what one might call the last contingency of retaliation – 'Operation VISITATION'. The former premier told me the Soviet leaders could not bank on a British Prime Minister *not* pressing the button if there were 'great hordes marching right across Europe and demolishing European civilization as we know it'. I said this implied that retaliation might have been authorized before the Red Army's 'hordes' reached the Channel ports in Holland, Belgium and France. Lord Home acknowledged the possibility:

Terrible, isn't it, the thought; but reason, cold reason doesn't operate in those circumstances, quite often. And I'm not sure what cold reason would tell you either, if they were on the march.[44]

So, deep in 'The Quarry' – had they reached it in time – the PM and a small inner group of ministers primed by the Cabinet Secretary on the sequence of decisions to be taken in a matter of minutes, with the military and the intelligence channels rapidly feeding information (perhaps into the bespoke 'Prime Minister's Map Room' for which TURNSTILE allowed[45]), the Prime Minister would seek the final counsel of his political colleagues, his number one military adviser, the Chief of the Defence Staff, and, perhaps, his Chief Scientific Adviser. If the decision to authorize the implementation of VISITATION was taken, and the CDS did not decline to give the resulting orders, what did that mean in respect of the nuclear weaponry at the Prime Minister's sole personal disposal (as distinct from the forces assigned to NATO's Supreme Allied Commander Europe or operated under the dual-key with the United States, as were the Thor missiles at the time of Cuba)?

The sheer horror of the decision can never be properly reconstructed (and not just, mercifully, because VISITATION was never reached). And, as we have seen, we cannot know how much of the thermonuclear force would have got through to their targets. But this is what the plans envisaged. When the V-force was coming into full operation, the RAF converted its planned nuclear strike capacity to a '30–40 cities' policy[46] (though by the time Macmillan left office in October 1963, improved Soviet air defences had required this to be reduced to sixteen cities[47]). In more detail, the scale of estimated destruction was

(a) 35 bombs on 15 cities with populations in excess of 600,000;

(b) 25 bombs on 25 cities mostly with a population in excess of 400,000.

It [is] estimated that when the force is armed with megaton [hydrogen] bombs the casualties per bomb dropped would be of the order of:

(a) killed about 135,000 – total about 8,000,000;

(b) injured about 135,000 – total about 8,000,000.[48]

The successor system to the V-force was intended to enable a British Prime Minister to wreak havoc on a comparable scale. 'Polaris deterrent', the small group of ministers on Harold Wilson's Ministerial Committee on Nuclear Policy (PN) were told at the end of 1967,

has been planned to have a capacity, with three submarines on station, to threaten simultaneous destruction to thirty major cities in Western Russia, and we have hitherto considered that to constitute a deterrent credible in political and military terms.[49]

These are roughly the statistics that all premiers in post during what might be called the TURNSTILE years (that is from Macmillan to Thatcher) would have carried in their heads. The figures of eight million dead plus eight million wounded are what would have stuck in my mind if I had received that briefing during the first days of my premiership, and they would have been unbearably vivid had I found myself in TURNSTILE with but minutes in which to make the decision.

Other figures would have been searing me, too. I would certainly have known what Soviet nuclear weapons *could* do – and maybe by this stage *had* done – to my own country. If the little triangle marked 'ATOM' had been slotted into its 'Quarry' holder, would I have retaliated? I do not know. I cannot decide. Perhaps nobody could with absolute conviction until faced with it. And if I had authorized retaliation, would I ever have wanted to pass the other way through Door 48 along the quarry road and into the lift to the surface when (and if) radiation levels permitted? Only one Prime Minister from the TURNSTILE years (or any subsequent era) has admitted publicly what he or she would have done if confronted with the choice of authorizing or not authorizing VISITATION. It was Jim Callaghan, for the BBC Radio 4's *A Bloody Union Jack on Top of It* programme in 1988. If, he said, nuclear retaliation

had become necessary and vital it would have meant that the deterrent had failed, because the value of the nuclear weapon is, frankly, only as a deterrent. But if we got to that point, where I felt it was necessary to do it then I would have done it. I've had terrible doubts, of course, about this. And if I had lived after having pressed that button, I could never, never have forgiven myself.[50]

And had the Soviet Union discovered the whereabouts of TURN-STILE when the signals began to pour from it (the order to retaliate perhaps included), as the planners thought possible 'within a day or so' of it going operational,[51] all the quarry folk, from the PM down, probably would have been stuck there '4 ETERNITY'.

CONCLUSION

Buttons and Envelopes

When you become Prime Minister the first thing they do – after telling you how to launch the nuclear bomb – is to take your passport away from you, and then the rest of the time trying to get you to travel round the world.

Tony Blair to the 1998 Labour Party Conference[1]

The bolt-from-the-blue which takes out the seat of government and its communications – this became a real topic when the deterrent moved from the V-Force to the Polaris submarines. The subs were invulnerable, but not the command and control. The worry was, could you get the PM or an authenticated deputy into a hole-in-the-ground? The submarines could listen in to broadcasts but not broadcast back.

Senior civil servant recalling the early 1970s in 2001[2]

Within six months of that recollection in tranquillity from an old war planner, his successors in Whitehall – much to their surprise – found themselves preoccupied once more with what one of them called 'the continuity of the state' question.[3] The events of 'Black Tuesday' – 11 September 2001 – in New York and Washington led, in the subsequent days of intense activity in Whitehall, to a re-examination of the old Cold War drills for the chain of supreme decision-making should the Prime Minister be wiped out by a terrorist bolt-from-the-blue directed at the heart of British Government. The Prime Minister, the contingency planners of early autumn 2001 decided, needed to appoint at least one minister to be his deputy for such purposes, probably more.[4]

Comparisons between what Tony Blair called the 'war with terror-ism'[5] that would be waged 'for as long as it takes'[6], offering, in its wake, a chance to 'reorder this world around us'[7], and the Cold War should not be pushed too far. Yet the echoes were real enough – a long, hard, global struggle that would be punctuated by surges of anxiety on the part of large civilian populations regarding themselves, their cities and their public installations as possibly in the front line of future destruction.

Intelligence, too, moved to a position of centrality which it had not occupied since the more perilous moments of the Cold War. As the Permanent Secretary at the Ministry of Defence, Kevin Tebbit (himself a former Director of GCHQ and Deputy Chairman of the JIC), put it just over a month after the destruction of the World Trade Center, one of the principles of the secret state was once more of crucial relevance – 'the importance of timely, accurate intelligence of all kinds to narrow that vital gap between general knowledge of a terrorist group and knowing enough to engage it with confidence and success without damaging innocent civilians and societies, and, indeed, acceptable risk to our own forces'.[8]

There was another role of which Blair himself spoke in the early days after 11 September which would have resonated for Britain's Cold War practitioners. While in Washington for talks with President Bush, he talked of the 'huge and heavy responsibility' that falls upon a Prime Minister when British forces are sent into action.[9] And here he was speaking with a gravity derived from experience.

Nobody could have predicted when Tony Blair first entered No. 10 as Prime Minister in May 1997 the degree to which he would mutate into a war PM during the first four and a half years of his premiership. Gulf War II in December 1998 and the considerably larger two-and-a-half-months Balkans War in the spring of 1999 left him the only post-1945 premier to have presided over two wars in the space of six months (if you exclude the colonial emergencies that were running at the same time as Korea and Suez).[10]

Blair's first encounter with the grim theme of conflict that might affect the continuity of the state came on the sixth day of his first term in office when the Chief of the Defence Staff, Sir Charles Guthrie, briefed him on the nuclear deterrent, explaining where the Trident submarine was on patrol, what its armoury of missiles could do in terms of human and physical destruction and how swiftly it could do it. Insiders say that Blair 'went white' at the thought of such dreadful and awesome retaliatory capability.[11] I was relieved to hear this. It would be immensely disturbing if a new Prime Minister was *not* worried by this singular duty.

But since Ted Heath's time, the early nuclear briefing has been an even more sombre occasion, because a decision has to be taken swiftly about retaliation. In the V-bomber days, as we have seen, it was thought possible, should the thunderbolt arrive, to get at least the Vulcans on their Quick Reaction Alert pads at the end of the Lincolnshire runways, into the air and off to the start-line over the Baltic. But once Polaris became the chief carrier of the British bomb, drills had to change. The button remained but it had to be supplemented by envelopes. From the early 1970s, a Prime Minister could no longer say to himself or herself, 'I'll face this decision only when I have to and I'll decide according to the circumstances.' A decision from beyond the grave henceforth *had* to be on each Polaris submarine before it sailed on patrol from the west of Scotland.

This drill holds good today for the Trident system. Tony Blair, like John Major before him, had to place his instructions in a set of envelopes – one for each boat – with only Sir Robin Butler, the Secretary of the Cabinet, involved.[12] Butler did not see what either of them wrote and neither Blair nor Major have divulged what they decided. According to a senior figure familiar with the ultimate choice for several years, it came down to four options and one prior question, if 'the unthinkable had happened and the bulk of the UK was reduced to a cinder'.[13]

The prior question was: 'How could the submarine Commander persuade himself that an attack had happened?' He can scour the airwaves for anything being broadcast but cannot radio out seeking instructions for fear of giving their position away to enemy hunter-killer submarines. How could he be sure that the UK had suffered a catastrophic nuclear assault without an authenticated message from a bunker-protected premier or designated deputy? One of the very last tests – over several days – is that the BBC Radio 4's *Today* programme has been silenced (a pleasing last touch of national identity, in every sense, I have always thought).[14]

Today no more, the drill is for the Trident commander and his executive officer to go to the safe, retrieve and open the Prime Minister's envelope. According to the veteran nuclear planner, it can instruct one of four things:

1: Put yourself under the command of the United States, if it is still there.

2: Make your way to Australia, if it is still there.

3: Get on with it and take out Moscow [or the capital of whichever country has initiated the attack].

4: Use your own judgement.[15]

I have heard senior Royal Navy figures who have been fully indoctrinated into the end-of-the-world drills suggest that (4) is a real possibility even if the envelope contained (3).[16] Who knows – and deterrence rested (and may do again) on such ambiguity.

No Prime Minister I have talked to about these matters has remained anything other than affected by them. John Major, who carried this ultimate, button-and-envelope responsibility for six and a half years, acted in an unusual but intriguing way when first faced with it in the last weeks of 1990. When briefed by the Cabinet Secretary, Sir Robin Butler, on the need to file his instructions on the Trident submarines, he cancelled a planned weekend at Chequers and returned to The Finings, his home in Huntingdon.

He was said to have done so in order to consider the instructions he would give away from the apparatus of government. Apparently he wanted to make his decisions on a human basis and not simply as the dispassionate judgement of a head of government. He wrote them out by hand, sealed them and returned them to the Cabinet Secretary. It was, he once admitted privately, a most chilling introduction to the responsibilities of the premiership.[17]

Like his four predecessors in No. 10 during the buttons-and-envelopes years, and like his successor, Tony Blair, Mr Major wrote his wishes out in longhand on four separate sheets of paper before placing them in four envelopes – one for each boat. Neither Robin Butler nor anyone else read them. While in post, Prime Ministers can change their minds, recall the envelopes and alter the instructions. To the best of my knowledge, when they cease to be premier and their successor's instructions arrive, the envelopes and their contents are destroyed still unread.[18] Unless they choose to tell us, only they know the answer to the ultimate 'what if' question of British government. Rather them than me.

Notes

Headquotes

1. Michael Howard, 'Every Club in the Bag,' *London Review of Books*, 10 September 1992, p. 3.
2. Kevin Tebbit, 'British Security Policy from Cold War Through Peace Dividend To Force For Good In The World: A Personal Experience', the First Peter Nailor Memorial Lecture, 16 October 2001 (Gresham Society/Gresham College, 2001).

From Total War to Absolute War?

1. Reproduced in Arthur Koestler, *The Yogi and the Commissar and Other Essays* (Cape, 1945), p. 256.
2. Churchill spurned suggestions that even the three Service Ministers, let alone the War Cabinet or its Defence Committee, should be brought into the secret. Churchill alone took the decision to give the UK's consent (required under the secret Quebec Agreement of 1943) for the first atomic weapons to be dropped on Japan. Martin Gilbert, *Winston S. Churchill: Road to Victory. 1941–1945* (Heinemann, 1986), p. 715; Public Record Office (PRO), PREM 11/565, 'Record of Events Leading to Dropping of Bombs on Hiroshima and Nagasaki', Cherwell to Churchill, 28 January 1953.
3. For the contribution of the Soviet Union's atomic spies to the construction of the first Russian weapon see David Holloway, *Stalin and the Bomb: The Soviet Union and Atomic Energy, 1939–1956* (Yale, 1994), pp. 222–3.
4. George Steiner, *Grammars of Creation* (Faber, 2001), p. 2.
5. Macmillan quoted Kennedy to this effect during a Cabinet meeting in the early days of the Cuban Missile Crisis. PRO, CAB 128/36 CC (62) 61st conclusions, 23 October 1962.
6. Peter Hennessy, *The Prime Minister: The Office and Its Holders Since 1945* (Allen Lane The Penguin Press, 2000), p. 451.
7. Chairman of the Joint Intelligence Committee, 1984–92.
8. Permanent Secretary at the Ministry of Defence, 1988–92. Sir Michael conducted in

1994 a still classified review of the purposes and organization of the UK intelligence and security services in the post-Cold War period for the Major Government. Sir Michael Quinlan, 'The Future of Covert Intelligence', in Harold Shukman (ed.), *Agents for Change: Intelligence Services in the 21st Century* (St Ermin's Press, 2000), pp. 61–71.

9. Richard J. Aldrich, *The Hidden Hand: Britain, America and Cold War Secret Intelligence* (John Murray, 2001). See also W. Scott Lucas and C. J. Morris, 'A Very British Crusade: the Information Research Department and the Beginning of the Cold War', in Richard J. Aldrich (ed.), *British Intelligence, Strategy and the Cold War* (Routledge, 1992), pp. 85–110.

10. Percy Cradock, *Know Your Enemy: How the Joint Intelligence Committee Saw the World* (John Murray, 2002).

11. Michael Quinlan, *Thinking About Nuclear Weapons* (RUSI, 1997).

12. Michael Herman, *Intelligence Power in Peace and War* (CUP, 1996); Michael Herman, *Intelligence Services in the Information Age: Theory and Practice* (Frank Cass, 2001).

'The Queen Must Be Told'

1. Public Record Office (PRO), CAB 21/5655, 'Government War Book, 1964–68'.

2. *The Times*, 1 October 1938.

3. Mrs Tessa Stirling to Peter Hennessy, 26 January 2001.

4. PRO, CAB 21/5655, Grimble to Paget and Fraser, 2 November 1964; Paget to Hill, 3 November 1964.

5. Ibid., Grimble to Paget, 13 November 1964.

6. Conversation with Sir Derek Mitchell, 9 April 2001.

7. PRO, CAB 21/5655.

8. Ibid., Stephens to Laskey, 23 February 1965.

9. Ibid., Stephens to Laskey, 5 March 1965.

10. Ibid.

11. Ibid., McIndoe to Mitchell, 9 March 1965.

12. Ibid.

13. PRO, DEFE 2/225, 'Ministry of Defence War Book 1963', 15 August 1963.

14. Conversation with W. T. McIndoe, 9 April 2001.

15. Conversation with Sir Derek Mitchell, 9 April 2001.

16. PRO, DEFE 2/225, 'Ministry of Defence War Book. Appendix A – NATO Alert System'.

17. Ibid.

18. Ibid.

19. Ibid.

20. PRO, DEFE 2/225, 'Ministry of Defence War Book. Appendix F – Part 1 – Handling of Government War Book Messages within the Ministry of Defence'.

21. Ibid.

22. *The Works of William Shakespeare Gathered into One Volume* (Shakespeare Head Press/Blackwell, 1938), pp. 496–7.

23. Michael Howard, 'Military Experience in Literature', Tredegar Memorial Lecture to the Royal Society of Literature, October 1976, reproduced in Michael Howard, *The Lessons of History* (OUP, 1991), p. 180.
24. PRO, DEFE 2/225, 'Ministry of Defence War Book. Chapter IV – Mobilisation'.
25. PRO, CAB 21/5655.
26. Private information.
27. Eric Hobsbawm (in conversation with Antonio Polito), *The New Century* (Abacus, 2000), p. 51.

1: Secrets and Mysteries: the Intelligence Picture

1. Public Record Office (PRO), CAB 81/132, JIC (46) 1 (0).
2. PRO, CAB 158/1, JIC (47) 7/2.
3. Private information.
4. Anthony King (ed.), Robert J. Wybrow (compiler), *British Political Opinion 1937–2000: The Gallup Polls* (Politico's, 2000), p. 322. This poll was taken in October 1950.
5. House of Commons, *Official Report*, Session 1952–3, Vol. 518, Cols. 221–222 (HMSO, 1953).
6. David Butler and Gareth Butler, *Twentieth-Century British Political Facts 1900–2000* (Macmillan, 2000), p. 520.
7. Ibid.
8. Denis Healey, *My Secret Planet* (Michael Joseph, 1992), p. 83.
9. Michael Howard, 'Empires, Nations and Wars', the Yigal Allon Memorial Lecture, 1982, reproduced in Michael Howard, *The Lessons of History* (OUP, 1991), p. 47.
10. Private information.
11. See his Chapter 10, 'Up from the Country: Cabinet Office Impressions 1972–75', in Michael Herman, *Intelligence Services in the Information Age: Theory and Practice* (Frank Cass, 2001), pp. 164–79.
12. Michael Herman, 'The Role of Military Intelligence since 1945'. Paper delivered to the Twentieth-Century British Politics and Administration Seminar at the Institute of Historical Research, University of London, 24 May 1989.
13. Jeremy Black, *The Politics of James Bond: From Fleming's Novels to the Big Screen* (Praeger, 2001), p. xiii.
14. John le Carré, *Tinker Tailor Soldier Spy* (Hodder, 1974), p. 28.
15. Ibid., p. 125.
16. PRO, CAB 161/4, 'Cabinet Committee Organisation', 1949.
17. PRO, CAB 161/13, 'Cabinet Committee Organisation', 1962.
18. Percy Cradock, *In Pursuit of British Interests: Reflections of Foreign Policy under Margaret Thatcher and John Major* (John Murray, 1997), p. 40.
19. Ibid., pp. 39–41.
20. In conversation with Peter Hennessy on 29 August 2000 for the BBC Radio 4 programme, *The Top Job*.
21. Private information.
22. Cradock, *In Pursuit of British Interests*, p. 121.

23. Richard J. Aldrich, *The Hidden Hand: Britain, America and Cold War Secret Intelligence* (John Murray, 2001), p. 43.

24. Alex Danchev and Daniel Todman (eds.), *Field Marshal Lord Alanbrooke: War Diaries 1939–45* (Weidenfeld, 2001), p. 575. Diary entry for 27 July 1944.

25. Michael Herman, 'The Cold War: Did Intelligence Make a Difference?' Paper produced for the Royal International Affairs/BBC conference, *Cold War: Heroes, Villains and Spies*, 10 September 1998 and reproduced in Herman, *Intelligence Services in the Information Age*, pp. 159–63. For the distinction between 'secrets' and 'mysteries', I am grateful to Sir Michael Quinlan, 'The Future of Covert Intelligence', in Harold Shuckman (ed.), *Agents for Change: Intelligence Services in the 21st Century*, (St Ermin's Press, 2000), p. 65.

26. PRO, PREM 13/1343, 'Correspondence with Cabinet Office on Joint Intelligence Committee Current Assessments', anonymous JIC official to Michael Palliser, 31 October 1966.

27. PRO, CAB 158/45 Part I, JIC (62) 21, 'Indications of Sino–Soviet Bloc Preparations for Early War', 26 February 1962.

28. Ibid.

29. Ibid.

30. Ibid.

31. Private information.

32. PRO, CAB 158/45 Part 1, JIC (62) 21.

33. Ibid.

34. Private information.

35. PRO, CAB 158/45 Part I, JIC (62) 21.

36. Ibid.

37. Herman, 'Up from the Country: Cabinet Office Impressions 1972–75'.

38. Herman, 'The Cold War: Did Intelligence Make a Difference?'

39. Ibid.

40. I have taken an example at random. See PRO, CAB 158/23, 'Weekly Summary of Current Intelligence as at 5 January 1956'.

41. Herman, 'The Cold War: Did Intelligence Make a Difference?'

42. PRO, CAB 81/132, JIC (46) 1 (o).

43. Ibid., JIC (44) 466 (o).

44. Danchev and Todman (eds.), *Alanbrooke: War Diaries 1939–1945*, p. 697. Diary entry for 11 June 1945.

45. PRO, PREM 11/2418, 'Middle East 1957–58'. Brook to Macmillan, 6 December 1967.

46. Michael Howard, 'Every Club in the Bag', *London Review of Books*, 10 September 1992, p. 3.

47. Michael Dockrill, *British Defence since 1945* (Blackwell, 1988), Appendix IV, pp. 151–2.

48. PRO, PREM 13/2688, 'Reorganisation of Central Machinery for Politico-military Planning and Intelligence, 1967–1968', Trend to Wilson, 13 March 1967.

49. PRO, CAB 81/132, JIC (46) 1 (o).

50. Ibid.

51. Ibid.

52. Bradley F. Smith, *Sharing Secrets with Stalin: How the Allies Traded Intelligence, 1941–1945* (University Press of Kansas, 1996), p. 254.

53. PRO, CAB 81/132, JIC (46) 1 (o).

54. Smith, *Sharing Secrets with Stalin*, p. 154. Smith discovered the evidence for this in PRO, WO 208/4566.

55. PRO, CAB 81/132, JIC (46) 1 (o).

56. Oleg Tsarev, 'Intelligence in the Cold War', in Shukman (ed.), *Agents for Change*, p. 22.

57. Ibid., p. 41.

58. Ibid., p. 44.

59. Ibid., p. 32.

60. PRO, CAB 81–132, JIC (46) 1 (o).

61. Christopher Andrew and Vasili Mitrokhin, *The Mitrokhin Archive: The KGB in Europe and the West* (Allen Lane The Penguin Press, 1999), p. 156.

62. PRO, CAB 81/132, JIC (46) 1 (o).

63. Ibid.

64. Ibid.

65. Private information.

66. Andrew and Mitrokhin, *The Mitrokhin Archive*, pp. 180–81.

67. Christopher Andrew, 'The Venona Secret,' in K. G. Robertson (ed.), *War, Resistance and Intelligence: Essays in Honour of M. R. D. Foot* (Pen and Sword, 1999), pp. 203–26.

68. Ibid., p. 213.

69. Ibid., p. 209.

70. PRO, CAB 130/17, JIC (46) 70 (o), 'The Spread of Communism Throughout the World and the Extent of its Direction from Moscow', 23 September 1946.

71. PRO, CAB 130/20, GEN 183/1st Meeting, 16 June 1947.

72. PRO, PREM 8/1365, 'Proposed Activities Behind the Iron Curtain', Brook to Attlee, 30 November 1950; PRO, PREM 11/174, 'Request by Prime Minister for List of All Committees in Whitehall', Brook to Churchill, 20 November 1951. The minutes of these two official committees remain classified.

73. PRO, CAB 130/17, JIC (46) 70 (o).

74. Ibid.

75. Ibid.

76. Private information from one of the undergraduates who *did* become influential in public life but was certainly *never* a helper of Soviet intelligence.

77. Francis Beckett, *Enemy Within: The Rise and Fall of the British Communist Party* (John Murray, 1995), p. 221.

78. Private information.

79. PRO, CAB 158/1, 'Soviet Interests, Intentions and Capabilities – General', JIC (47) 7/2, 6 August 1947.

80. Peter Hennessy, *Never Again: Britain 1945–51* (Cape, 1992), p. 296.

81. PRO, CAB 158/1, JIC (47) 7/2.

82. Denis Healey, 'NATO, Britain and Soviet Military Policy', *Orbis*, Vol. XIII, No. 1, Spring 1969, p. 48.

83. PRO, CAB 158/1, JIC (47) 7/2.

84. Richard Aldrich and Michael Coleman, 'The Cold War, the JIC and British Signals Intelligence, 1948', *Intelligence and National Security*, Vol. 4, No. 3, July 1989, Appendix 2.

85. PRO, CAB 158/1, JIC (47) 7/2.

86. Peter Wright, *Spycatcher: The Candid Autobiography of a Senior Intelligence Officer* (Viking, 1987), pp. 362–72; Peter Hennessy, *The Prime Minister: The Office and Its Holders since 1945* (Penguin, 2000), pp. 372–4.

87. Dr Craig had in mind Aldrich and Coleman, 'The Cold War, the JIC and British Signals Intelligence, 1948'.

88. Alexander Craig, 'The Joint Intelligence Committee and British Intelligence Assessment, 1945–1956', unpublished PhD, Faculty of History, University of Cambridge, 1999, p. 260.

89. PRO, CAB 158/1, JIC (47) 7/2.

90. PRO, DEFE 4/14, COS (48), 97th Meeting, 12 July 1948.

91. I am grateful to Dr Craig for this information. Craig, 'The Joint Intelligence Committee and British Intelligence Assessment, 1945–1956', pp. 95–6.

92. Ibid., p. 90.

93. Ibid., pp. 91, 93.

94. PRO, DEFE 6/56, JP (59) 68, Final, 27 May 1959, 'Berlin Contingency Planning. Report by the Joint Planning Staff'.

95. For the Brownell Report on US SIGINT see Craig, 'The Joint Intelligence Committee and British Intelligence Assessment, 1945–1956', pp. 109–110. For the creation of the NSA see Aldrich, *The Hidden Hand*, pp. 401–2.

96. Christopher Andrew, 'Intelligence and International Relations in the early Cold War', *Review of International Studies*, 24 (1998), p. 329.

97. Aldrich, *The Hidden Hand*, p. 277.

98. Craig, 'The Joint Intelligence Committee and British Intelligence Assessment, 1945–1956', p. 109.

99. Aldrich, *The Hidden Hand*, p. 271.

100. Tom Dibble, 'The Missing Dimension? An Evaluation of the Intelligence Input into UK Policy Making During the Korean War in the Light of Recently Released Joint Intelligence Committee Files', unpublished MA research methods thesis, Department of History, Queen Mary, University of London, 1997.

101. PRO, CAB 158/11, Part 1, JIC (50) 77, 'The Likelihood of War with the Soviet Union and the Date by which Soviet Leaders Might Be Prepared to Risk It', 18 August 1950.

102. Ibid.

103. PRO, PREM 11/159, 'Paper by Vice-Admiral Longley-Cook entitled "Where Are We Going?" giving his views on the policies of US and Soviet Union, and UK attitude towards them', NID 7956, 6 July 1951.

104. PRO, CAB 158/11, Part I, JIC (50) 77.

105. PRO, PREM 11/159, 'Where Are We Going?'

106. PRO, PREM 11/669, draft Cabinet paper on 'Two-Power Meeting with Soviet Government', August 1954.

107. Neville Shute, *On the Beach* (Heinemann, 1957).

108. James Lees-Milne, *A Mingled Measure: Diaries 1954–1972* (John Murray, 1994), p. 68. Diary entry for 13 September 1957.

109. Martin Gilbert, Churchill's official biographer, mentions the episode but does not record any outcome. Martin Gilbert, *Never Despair: Winston S. Churchill 1945–1965* (Heinemann, 1988), pp. 1250–51.

110. PRO, CAB 81/132, JIC (4) 1 (0).

111. Ibid.

112. Ibid.

113. Jeremy Isaacs and Taylor Downing, *Cold War* (Bantam, 1998), pp. 146–7.

114. PRO, CAB 158/1, JIC (47) 7 (2).

115. PRO, CAB 158/4, JIC (48) 26 (0).

116. Lorna Arnold, *Britain and the H-Bomb* (Palgrave, 2001), p. 9.

117. Chapman Pincher, 'Fuchs Gave Bomb to Russia', *Daily Express*, 2 March 1950.

118. Andrew and Mitrokhin, *The Mitrokhin Archive*, p. 155.

119. Arnold, *Britain and the H-Bomb*, p. 23.

120. Andrew and Mitrokhin, *The Mitrokhin Archive*, p. 153.

121. David Holloway, *Stalin and the Bomb: The Soviet Union and Atomic Energy* (Yale, 1994), p. 222.

122. Arnold, *Britain and the H-Bomb*, p. 25.

123. For recent scholarship see Holloway, *Stalin and the Bomb*, p. 123. For Fuchs's interrogation by Michael Perrin see PRO, AB1/695, 'Perrin Interviews with Dr Fuchs, January–March, 1950'. 'Record of Interview with Dr. K. Fuchs on 30th January 1950 by M. W. Perrin.'

124. PRO, DEFE 41/126, 'Atomic Energy Intelligence', briefing 9–19 June 1952. I am very grateful to Professor Richard Aldrich for bringing this file to my attention.

125. PRO, CAB 158/11, Part 2, JIC (50) 111, 'Likelihood of Total War with the Soviet Union up to the End of 1954', 15 February 1951.

126. Ibid.

127. Ibid.

128. Arnold, *Britain and the H-Bomb*, pp. 6–31.

129. PRO, CAB 158/21, JIC (55) 58, 'Likely Soviet Courses of Action Up to 1st January 1957', 30 September 1955.

130. Ibid.

131. PRO, CAB 158/26, JIC (56) 136, 'The Extent to which the Present State of Tension Has Increased the Chances of Miscalculation which Might Lead to Global War', 13 December 1956.

132. Ibid.

133. PRO, CAB 158/29, JIC (57) 62, 'The Possibility of Hostilities Short of Global War up to 1965', 20 September 1957. Alban Webb's work is contained in 'An Analysis of the Joint Intelligence Committee's Assessment of the Soviet Threat and Input into the Cuban Missile Crisis and its Aftermath'. Unpublished undergraduate research project, Department of History, Queen Mary, University of London, 2001.

134. Taylor and Isaacs, *Cold War*, p. 182.

135. PRO, CAB 158/44, JIC (62) 10, 'The Likelihood of War with the Soviet Union up to 1966', 9 February 1962.

136. Ibid.

137. PRO, CAB 158/47, JIC (62) 101, 'Soviet Motives in Cuba', 6 December 1962.

138. PRO, CAB 158/44, JIC (62) 10.

139. Ibid.

140. PRO, CAB 158/47, JIC (62) 101.

141. PRO, CAB 158/47, JIC (62) 93, 'The Threat by Soviet Missiles in Cuba', 26 October 1962.

142. Len Scott, 'Intelligence and the Cuban Missile Crisis'. Paper read to the UK Study Group on Intelligence meeting at the Public Record Office on 15 September 1999. I am grateful to Dr Scott for permission to quote from it.

143. PRO, CAB 158/47, JIC (62) 101.

144. House of Commons, *Official Report*, Vol. 668, 5 December 1962, cols. 1463–8 (HMSO, 1962). The minister speaking these words, C. M. Woodhouse, Parliamentary Under Secretary at the Home Office, was answering a question about civil defence and the Cuban Missile Crisis.

145. His grandson, Lord Stockton, quoted in Hennessy, *The Prime Minister*, pp. 102–3.

146. Ibid., pp. 129–33.

147. Ibid., pp. 122–3.

148. PRO, CAB 158/47, JIC (62) 99, 'Possible Soviet Response to a US Decision to Bomb or Invade Cuba', 27 October 1962.

149. Ibid.

150. Ibid.

151. Craig, 'The Joint Intelligence Committee and British Intelligence Assessment, 1945-1956', p. 261.

152. Ibid.

153. See his *Who Is My Liege?* (Gentry Books, 1972).

154. See his *Spycatcher* (Viking Penguin Inc, 1987) .

155. Private information.

156. Private information.

157. Private information.

158. Private information.

159. Private information.

160. Hennessy, *The Prime Minister*, p. 130.

161. Private information. See Mr Cowell's obituary, 'Gervase Cowell. An Honourable Expulsion from Moscow', *The Times*, 8 May 2000.

2: The Importance of Being Nuclear: the Bomb
and the Fear of Escalation

1. Quoted in Peter Hennessy, *Muddling Through: Power, Politics and the Quality of Government in Postwar Britain* (Gollancz, 1996), p. 106.

2. Miles Jebb (ed.), *The Diaries of Cynthia Gladwyn* (Constable, 1995), p. 195. Diary entry for 12 December 1956.

3. Public Record Office (PRO), DEFE 10/402. 'Study Group', 1960. The paper's author was Group Captain Alan Shelfoon, a member of the Joint Inter-Services Group for the Study of All-Out Warfare.

4. PRO, CAB 134/3121, Part 2, 'Minority Report by Lord Rothschild' attached to the report from the Kings Norton Working Party on Atomic Weapons Establishments, 31 July 1968.

5. Private information cited in Hennessy, *Muddling Through*, p. 129.

6. Peter Hennessy, *The Hidden Wiring: Unearthing the British Constitution* (Gollancz, 1995), p. 204.

7. Chiefly in Peter Hennessy, *The Prime Minister: The Office and Its Holders since 1945* (Allen Lane The Penguin Press, 2000 and Penguin, 2001). See also Peter Hennessy, *Cabinet* (Blackwell, 1986), Chapter 4, 'Cabinets and the Bomb', pp. 123–62.

8. Timothy Garton Ash, *We the People: The Revolution of '89 Witnessed in Warsaw, Budapest, Berlin and Prague* (Penguin ed., 1999), pp. 65–9.

9. Margaret Gowing, *Britain and Atomic Energy 1939–1945* (Macmillan, 1964); Margaret Gowing, *Independence and Deterrence: Britain and Atomic Energy, 1945–1952, Vol. I: Policy Making, Vol. II: Policy Execution* (Macmillan, 1974).

10. PRO, CAB 130/3, 'GEN 75. Papers 1945–1947', GEN 75/1, 'THE ATOMIC BOMB. Memorandum by the Prime Minister', 28 August 1945.

11. Brian Cathcart, *Test of Greatness: Britain's Struggle for the Atom Bomb* (John Murray, 1994), pp. 8–25.

12. Michael Howard, 'Every Club in the Bag', *London Review of Books*, 10 September 1992.

13. PRO, CAB 130/2, GEN 75/8th Meeting, 18 December 1945.

14. Ibid.

15. PRO, AIR 2/5960, 'Draft Air Staff Requirement'. No. OR/230.

16. Sir Michael Perrin speaking on BBC2's *Timewatch*, 29 September 1982.

17. PRO, CAB 130/2, GEN 75/15th Meeting, 25 October 1946.

18. Ibid.

19. *Timewatch*, 29 September 1982.

20. PRO, PREM 8,911. 'Proposals agreed that research and development work on atomic energy be undertaken', 1947–1948. 'Note by the Controller of Production of Atomic Energy', 31 December 1946.

21. Hennessy, *Cabinet*, p. 127.

22. PRO, CAB 130/16, **GEN** 163/1st Meeting, 8 January 1948, 'Confidential Annex Minute 1. Research in Atomic Weapons'.

23. Francis Williams, *A Prime Minister Remembers* (Heinemann, 1961), pp. 118–19.

24. Ibid., p. 119.

25. Lorna Arnold, *Britain and the H-Bomb* (Palgrave, 2001), p. 235.

26. PRO, CAB 134/808, DP (54)6, 'United Kingdom Defence Policy. Memorandum by the Chiefs of Staff', 1 June 1954.

27. I am grateful to Alban Webb for finding this file when it was first released. PRO, CAB 130/101. The minute is simply entitled 'Note of a meeting' but it has 'GEN 465 1st' placed on it in handwriting and it forms part of the GEN 465 archive.

28. Ibid., 'NOTE of a meeting held in Sir Norman Brook's Room', 12 March 1954.

29. PRO, CAB 134/808, DP (54)6.

30. PRO, CAB 130/101, Note of Brook's meeting, 12 March 1954.

31. Ibid.

32. David Holloway, *Stalin and the Bomb: The Soviet Union and Atomic Energy 1939–1956* (Yale, 1994), p. 315.

33. Arnold, *Britain and the H-Bomb*, p. 30.

34. He did this for me on more than one occasion in the late 1980s especially when I was helping to prepare the BBC Radio 4 documentary, *A Bloody Union Jack on Top of It.*

35. PRO, CAB 130/101, Note of Brook's meeting, 12 March 1954.

36. Ibid.

37. Ibid.

38. The Macmillan Diary, Department of Western Manuscripts, Bodleian Library, University of Oxford, File d.19, diary entry for 26 January 1955.

39. Hennessy, *Muddling Through*, pp. 105–6. Lord Plowden described this scene when interviewed for the BBC Radio 4 programme, *A Bloody Union Jack on Top of It*, which was broadcast in two parts on 5 and 12 May 1988.

40. PRO, CAB 130/101, Note of Brooks's meeting, 12 March 1954.

41. Ibid.

42. Ibid., GEN 464/1st Meeting, 'Atomic Energy Development', 13 April 1954.

43. Ibid.

44. Hennessy, *Cabinet*, p. 137.

45. PRO, CAB 128/27, CC (54) 47th Conclusions, 7 July 1954.

46. PRO, CAB 134/808, DP (54) 6, 1 June 1954.

47. Ibid., DP (54) 2nd Meeting, 19 May 1954.

48. Ibid., DP (54) 6, 2 June 1954.

49. PRO, CAB 129/69, C (54) 249, 'United Kingdom Defence Policy', 23 July 1954.

50. Compare paragraph a of DP (54) 6 with paragraph 9 of C (54) 249 where the figures are replaced with 'x' and 'y'.

51. PRO, CAB 129/69, C (54) 249.

52. Ibid.

53. PRO, CAB 134/808, DP (54) 6, 1 June 1954.

54. Ibid., DP (54) 3rd Meeting, 16 June 1954, 'Confidential Annex. Atomic Weapons Programme'.

55. Hennessy, *The Prime Minister*, p. 199; Macmillan Diary, c.16/1, entry for 10 July 1954.

56. PRO, CAB 128/27, CC (54) 47th Conclusions, 7 July 1954.

57. Ibid.

58. Ibid., CC (54) 48th Conclusions, 8 July 1954.

59. Ibid. See also Christopher Driver, *The Disarmers: A Study in Protest* (Hodder, 1964), pp. 200–201.

60. PRO, CAB 128/27, CC (54) 48th Conclusions, 8 July 1954.

61. Ibid.

62. Ibid.

63. Martin Gilbert, *Never Despair: Winston S. Churchill 1945–1965* (Heinemann, 1988), p. 1092.

64. PRO, CAB 128/27, CC (54) 48th Conclusions, 8 July 1954.

65. PRO, PREM 11/747. 'Letter to HM the Queen from Prime Minister concerning UK Manufacture of a Hydrogen Bomb'. Churchill to the Queen, 16 July 1954.

66. PRO, CAB 128/27, CC (54) 53rd Conclusions, 26 July 1954.

67. *Statement on Defence: 1955*, Cmnd 9391 (HMSO, 1955).

68. Arnold, *Britain and the H-Bomb*, p. 84.

69. Ibid., pp. 131–64; 235–6.

70. Ibid., p. 209.

71. Victor Macklen, who was present at the meeting, speaking in 'A Bloody Union Jack on Top of It'. Hennessy, *Muddling Through*, p. 108.

72. Cmnd 537 (HMSO, 1958).

73. Hennessy, *The Prime Minister*, p. 113.

74. Cathcart, *Test of Greatness*, p. 273.

75. PRO, AIR 8/2400, 'Medium Bomber Force: Size and Composition', Defence Board, 'The V-Bomber Force and the Powered Bomb. Memorandum by the Secretary of State for Air', DB (58) 10, 29 October 1958.

76. Professor Nailor was speaking in 'A Bloody Union Jack on Top of It'. Hennessy, *Muddling Through*, p. 109.

77. For Blue Streak cancellation and Skybolt decision-making see Ian Clark, *Nuclear Diplomacy and the Special Relationship: Britain's Deterrent and America 1957–1962* (OUP, 1994), pp. 176–89, 251–64, 353–73.

78. Sir Philip de Zulueta was speaking in 'A Bloody Union Jack on Top of It'. Hennessy, *Muddling Through*, p. 110.

79. Peter Hennessy and Caroline Anstey, 'Moneybags and Brains: The Anglo-American "Special Relationship" since 1945', Strathclyde/*Analysis* papers, No. 1 (Department of Government, University of Strathclyde, 1990), p. 11.

80. Lord Home speaking in 'A Bloody Union Jack on Top of It'. Hennessy, *Muddling Through*, p. 111.

81. Ibid., p. 112.

82. Clark, *Nuclear Diplomacy and the Special Relationship*, pp. 409–15.

83. Hennessy, *Muddling Through*, p. 112.

84. The phrase is that of Denis Greenhill, former Head of the Diplomatic Service, who saw Macmillan in action with Kennedy on several occasions. Conversation with Lord Greenhill, 4 March 1996.

85. PRO, PREM 11/3689. 'Record of a Meeting held at Admiralty House at 5.00 p.m.

on Tuesday October 23, 1962'. FO telegram No. 7396 to Washington, Macmillan to Kennedy, 22 October 1962.

86. PRO, PREM 11/2718. 'Future of Berlin and Germany'. Brook to Macmillan, 28 July 1961, Macmillan to Brook, 29 July 1961.

87. PRO, CAB 158/47, JIC (62) 70, 'Escalation', 14 November 1962. It has emblazoned on it 'TOP SECRET – CAN/UK/US EYES ONLY'.

88. Ibid.

89. Ibid.

90. Ibid.

91. Macmillan Diary, file d. 42, entry for 25 June 1961.

92. PRO, CAB 158/47, JIC (62) 70.

93. Iverach McDonald, *A Man of The Times: Talks and Travels in a Disrupted World* (Hamish Hamilton, 1976), p. 184.

94. PRO, CAB 158/45, Part 1, JIC (61) 77, 'The United Kingdom Nuclear Deterrent', 23 January 1962.

95. PRO, CAB 128/36, CC (62) 76th Conclusions, 21 December 1962.

96. PRO, PREM 11/4147. 'Discussions on intermediate range ballistic missiles (IRBMs): Part 5', 1962–1963. Nassau Agreement', Paris to the Foreign Office, 2 January 1963.

97. PRO, PREM 11/4412. 'Summary of tasks ahead: Prime Minister wrote to Private Secretary and Ministers'. 'Polaris.' Prime Minister's Personal Minute M.343/62, 26 December 1962.

98. Hennessy, *The Prime Minister*, pp. 225–6.

99. PRO, PREM 11/4147, 'Record of a Meeting at Admiralty House at 6.00 pm on Monday December 31, 1962'.

100. Ibid.

101. PRO, PREM 11/4148. 'Discussions on intermediate range ballistic missiles (IRBMs): Part 6', 1963. Amery to Thorneycroft, 15 January 1963; Thorneycroft to Amery, 28 January 1963.

102. PRO, CAB 128/37, CC (63) 2nd Conclusions, 3 January 1963.

103. As Minister Resident in the Middle East he had explained to Richard Crossman that: 'We . . . are Greeks in this American empire . . . We must run the Allied Forces HQ as the Greeks ran the operations of the Emperor Claudius', *Sunday Telegraph*, 9 February 1964.

104. PRO, CAB 128/37, CC (63) 2nd Conclusions.

105. Ibid.

106. Ibid.

107. Michael Quinlan, *Thinking About Nuclear Weapons* (RUSI, 1997), p. 76.

108. PRO, PREM 11/4285. 'Development of nuclear disarmament movement; memorandum by Home Office; Prime Minister asked about views of Opposition'. Michael Fraser (Conservative Research Department) to John Wyndham (Macmillan's personal assistant in No. 10), 22 April 1963.

109. Ibid., 'Defence' attachment by Fraser.

110. *Let's Go with Labour for the New Britain* (Labour Party, September 1964),

available in F. W. S. Craig, *British General Election Manifestos 1918–1966* (Political Reference Publications, 1970). The section dealing with Labour's 1964 defence policy is on pp. 245–6.

111. PRO, PREM 11/4285, Fraser to Wyndham, 22 April 1963.

112. See Hennessy, *The Prime Minister*, pp. 61–3.

113. Hennessy, *Muddling Through*, p. 114.

114. PRO, PREM 11/4733, 'Talks on Defence Policy with Members of HM Opposition', Thorneycroft to Douglas-Home, 3 February 1964.

115. Richard E. Neustadt, *Report to J.F.K.: The Skybolt Crisis in Perspective* (Cornell University Press, 1999).

116. Conversation with Professor Richard Neustadt, 16 January 1997.

117. PRO, CAB 130/212, MISC 16/1st Meeting, 11 November 1964.

118. Ibid.

119. PRO, CAB 130/213, MISC 17/4th Meeting, 22 November 1964; PRO, CAB 128/39, CC (64) 11th Conclusions, 26 November 1964.

120. PRO, CAB 148/19, ODP (65), 5th Meeting, 29 January 1965.

121. Denis Healey, *The Time of My Life* (Michael Joseph, 1989), p. 302.

122. PRO, CAB 128/39, CC (64) 11th Conclusions, 26 November 1964.

123. PRO, CAB 134/3120, PN (66) 1st Meeting, 28 September 1966.

124. PRO, CAB 164/713, Healey to Wilson, 3 August 1967.

125. Ibid.

126. Hennessy, *Muddling Through*, p. 115.

127. PRO, CAB 130/212, MISC 16/1st Meeting, 11 November 1964.

128. Hennessy, *Muddling Through*, p. 116.

129. PRO, CAB 134/3120, PN (67) 4th Meeting, 5 December 1967. See also Matthew Grant, ' "Destined for the Junkyard of Steptoe and Son?" Polaris Improvement: The First Steps, 1965–70'. Unpublished undergraduate thesis, Department of History, Queen Mary, University of London, 2001.

130. Hennessy, *Cabinet*, pp. 148–53; Peter Hennessy, *What the Papers Never Said* (Politics Association, 1985), pp. 113–39.

131. PRO, CAB 134/3120, PN (67) 6, 1 December 1967, 'British Nuclear Weapons Policy'.

132. Hennessy, *The Prime Minister*, p. 291.

133. Driver, *The Disarmers*, pp. 52–3.

134. A. J. P. Taylor, *A Personal History* (Hamish Hamilton, 1983), p. 228.

135. Conversation with Air Vice Marshal Bobby Robson, 26 July 2001.

136. Ibid.

137. Hennessy, *Muddling Through*, p. 128.

3: Defending the Realm: Vetting, Filing and Smashing

1. Public Record Office (PRO), CAB 130/37, 'The Communist Party. Its Strengths and Activities: Its Penetration of Government Organisations and of the Trade unions',

attached as an appendix to a report prepared by a Working Party on 'Security Measures Against Encroachments by Communists or Fascists in the United Kingdom' for ministers in GEN 226, the Cabinet Committee on European Policy, and circulated to them on 26 May 1948.

2. Christopher Andrew and Vasili Mitrokhin, *The Mitrokhin Archive: The KGB in Europe and the West* (Allen Lane The Penguin Press, 1999), p. 209.

3. PRO, CAB 130/20, PV (50) 11, 'Committee on Positive Vetting: Report', 27 October 1950.

4. PRO, CAB 158/24, JIC (56) 41, 'Likely Scale and Nature of an Attack on the United Kingdom in a Global War up to 1960', 10 May 1956.

5. This is the title of the most recent history of the CPGB. Francis Beckett, *The Enemy Within: The Rise and Fall of the British Communist Party* (John Murray, 1995).

6. Ibid., pp. 1–8, 221.

7. Eric Hobsbawm, *The New Century* (Abacus, 2000), p. 159.

8. Eric Hobsbawm to Peter Hennessy, 8 March 2001.

9. PRO, CAB 130/37, 'The Communist Party'.

10. John Curry, *The Security Service 1908–1945* (Public Record Office, 1999), p. 82.

11. Ibid.

12. Ibid., pp. 350–51.

13. John le Carré, *Tinker Tailor Soldier Spy* (Hodder, 1974), pp. 97–115.

14. Curry, *The Security Service, 1908–1945*, p. 351.

15. PRO, CAB 130/20, 'Some Past Cases of Communist Espionage', Annex to GEN 183/1, Cabinet Committee on Subversive Activities, 'The Employment of Civil Servants Etc, Exposed to Communist Influence: Report of Working Party', 29 May 1947.

16. Curry, *The Security Service, 1908–1945*, pp. 354–5.

17. Ibid., p. 355.

18. Ibid.

19. Private information.

20. Private information.

21. Curry, *The Security Service, 1908–1945*, p. 357.

22. PRO, CAB 130/17, JIC (46) 70 (o), 'The Spread of Communism Throughout the World and the Extent of Its Direction from Moscow', 23 September 1946.

23. Curry, *The Security Service, 1908–1945*, p. 357.

24. PRO, CAB 130/37, 'The Communist Party'.

25. Ibid.

26. Ibid. See also Philip Deery, ' "The Secret Battalion": Communism in Britain during the Cold War', *Contemporary British History*, Vol. 13, Winter 1999, No. 4, pp. 1–28.

27. PRO, CAB 130/37, 'The Communist Party'.

28. PRO, CAB 130/17, JIC (46) 70 (o).

29. For the minutes and memoranda of GEN 183 see PRO, CAB 130/20.

30. Andrew and Mitrokhin, *The Mitrokhin Archive*, pp. 165–6, 184.

31. PRO, CAB 130/17, JIC (46) 70 (o).

32. Andrew and Mitrokhin, *The Mitrokhin Archive*, p. 180.

33. PRO, CAB 130/20, GEN 183/1, 'The Employment of Civil Servants, Etc, Exposed to Communist Influence'.

34. Ibid.

35. Ibid.

36. Ibid.

37. Ibid.

38. Margaret Gowing, *Independence and Deterrence: Britain and Atomic Energy 1945–1952. Vol. 2, Policy Execution* (Macmillan, 1974), p. 142.

39. PRO, CAB 130/20, 'The Employment of Civil Servants, Etc, Exposed to Communist Influence'.

40. PRO, CAB 130/37, 'The Communist Party'.

41. Andrew and Mitrokhin, *The Mitrokhin Archive*, p. 188.

42. PRO, CAB 130.20, 'The Employment of Civil Servants, Etc, Exposed to Communist Influence'.

43. Ibid.

44. Ibid. This careful formulation was probably drafted by S. J. Baker of the Home Office.

45. Ibid.

46. Ibid.

47. PRO, CAB 130/20, GEN 183, 1st Meeting, 16 June 1947.

48. Ibid.

49. Ibid.

50. Ibid., 'The Employment of Civil Servants, Etc, Exposed to Communist Influence'.

51. House of Commons, *Official Report*, Vol. 448, 15 March 1948, cols. 1703–8 (HMSO, 1948).

52. PRO, CAB 130/20, 'The Employment of Civil Servants, Etc., Exposed to Communist Influence.'

53. PRO, CAB 130/37, GEN 226/1, 'Security Measures Against Encroachments by Communists or Fascists in the United Kingdom. Report by a Working Party'.

54. Ibid., 'The Communist Party'.

55. Andrew and Mitrokhin, *The Mitrokhin Archive*, p. 151.

56. Ibid., pp. 203–4.

57. PRO, CAB 120/30, PV (50) 11, 'Committee on Positive Vetting. Report', 27 October 1950. For the 5 April meeting of GEN 183, see ibid., GEN 183/5th meeting.

58. Chapman Pincher, *Too Secret Too Long: The Great Betrayal of Britain's Crucial Secrets and the Cover-up* (Sidgwick & Jackson, 1984). See also Nigel West, *Molehunt: The Full Story of the Soviet Spy in MI5* (Coronet, 1987).

59. Richard Rovere, *Senator Joe McCarthy* (Meridian, 1960), p. 124. See also David Caute, *The Great Fear: The Anti-Communist Purge under Truman and Eisenhower* (Secker and Warburg, 1978).

60. Margaret Gowing, *Independence and Deterrence: Deterrence and Atomic Energy 1945–1952, Vol. 1, Policy Making* (Macmillan, 1974), pp. 241–72.

61. Peter Hennessy and Gail Brownfeld, 'Britain's Cold War Security Purge, the Origins of Positive Vetting', *The Historical Journal*, 25, 4 (1982), p. 965.

62. PRO, CAB 120/30, PV (50) 11.

63. PRO, CAB 120/30, GEN 183, 1st Meeting, 15 June 1947.

64. PRO, CAB 120/30, PV (50) 11.

65. Ibid.
66. Ibid.
67. Ibid.
68. Ibid.
69. Ibid.
70. Andrew and Mitrokhin, *The Mitrokhin Archive*, p. 188.
71. PRO, CAB 120/30, PV (50) 11.
72. Ibid.
73. Ibid.
74. Ibid.
75. Ibid., O'Donovan's *Observer* article is quoted in Kenneth Harris, *Attlee* (Weidenfeld, 1982), pp. 490–91.
76. PRO, CAB 130/20, GEN 183, 6th Meeting, 13 November 1950.
77. 'Making Whitehall Mole-proof', *The Economist*, 5 June 1982.
78. PRO, PREM 11/1585. 'Extension of positive vetting arrangements to non-civil servants', 1954–1956. Gwilym Lloyd George to Sir Anthony Eden, 24 January 1955.
79. Private information.
80. PRO, AIR 2/14582, 'Air Ministry Security Clearance of Civilian Staff: Notice to Directors and Heads of Division', 8 August 1962.
81. Ibid., 'Security Questionnaire'.
82. *Security Procedures and Practices in the Public Service*, Cmnd 1681, (HMSO, 1962).
83. PRO, PREM 11/5087, 'Officers of Civil Service Staff Associations with Communist Sympathisers', Chief Secretary to Prime Minister, August 1962–May 1963.
84. Private information.
85. Private information.
86. PRO, CAB 130/37, GEN 226/1, 'The Communist Party'.
87. Ibid.
88. Ibid.
89. PRO, PREM 11/1238, 'Communist Influence in Industry and Trade Unions', Brook to Eden, 28 April 1956.
90. PRO, CAB 158/25, JIC (56) 95, 'Discussion in Moscow between the British Communist Party and CPSU Representatives, May/June 1956', 3 September 1956.
91. Beckett, *Enemy Within*, p. 191.
92. Curry, *The Security Service 1908–1945*, pp. 352–4.
93. Andrew and Mitrokhin, *The Mitrokhin Archive*, p. 167.
94. Beckett, *Enemy Within*, pp. 86–7.
95. Andrew and Mitrokhin, *The Mitrokhin Archive*, p. 167.
96. Private information.
97. PRO, AIR 20/11367, 'Air Ministry. Notice to Directors and Heads of Division. Routine War Planning'. Extract from the Minutes of the Defence Transition Committee Meeting, 5 January 1949. For the wartime camps see Ronald Stent, *A Bespattered Page? The Internment of His Majesty's Most Loyal Enemy Aliens* (Andre Deutsch, 1980).
98. Curry, *The Security Service, 1908–1945*, p. 82.

99. Beckett, *Enemy Within*, pp. 9–17.

100. Ibid., p. 78.

101. House of Commons, *Official Report*, Vol. 450, 12 May 1948, col. 2117 (HMSO, 1948).

102. Peter Hennessy, *What the Papers Never Said* (Politics Association, 1985), pp. 23–7.

103. Christopher Driver, *The Disarmers: A Study in Protest* (Hodder, 1964), p. 18.

104. Ibid.

105. PRO, PREM 11/4285. 'Development of nuclear disarmament movement: memorandum by Home Office; Prime Minister asked about views of Opposition'.

106. Driver, *The Disarmers*, p. 149.

107. Ibid., p. 149. See also Richard Taylor, *Against the Bomb: The British Peace Movement 1958–1965* (OUP, 1988), p. 97.

108. Ibid., p. 258.

109. Ibid., p. 259.

110. Ibid., p. 260.

111. PRO, PREM 11/4285, Cunningham to Woodfield, 17 April 1963.

112. Ibid., 'The Development of the Nuclear Disarmament Movement'.

113. Driver, *The Disarmers*, p. 24.

114. PRO, PREM 11/428, 'The Development of the Nuclear Disarmament Movement'.

115. Lorna Arnold, *Britain and the H-Bomb* (Palgrave, 2001), p. 18.

116. Ibid., p. 19.

117. Driver, *The Disarmers*, p. 26.

118. PRO, PREM 11/4285, 'The Development of the Nuclear Disarmament Movement'.

119. Driver, *The Disarmers*, p. 27.

120. PRO, PREM 11/4285, 'The Development of the Nuclear Disarmament Movement'.

121. Ibid.

122. Driver, *The Disarmers*, p. 35.

123. Ibid.

124. ibid., pp. 354–6.

125. PRO, PREM 11/4285, 'The Development of the Nuclear Disarmament Movement'.

126. Driver, *The Disarmers*, p. 36.

127. For an interesting account of the environmental and civic version of single-issue pressure grouping see Mike Robinson, *The Greening of British Party Politics* (Manchester University Press, 1992).

128. Driver, *The Disarmers*, pp. 42–53.

129. PRO, PREM 11/4285, 'The Development of the Nuclear Disarmament Movement'.

130. Driver, *The Disarmers*, p. 74.

131. *Defence: Outline of Future Policy*, Cmnd 124 (HMSO, 1957).

132. Ibid.

133. Ibid.

134. Michael Foot, *Aneurin Bevan: 1897–1960* (Gollancz edition, 1997), pp. 554–5.

135. Driver, *The Disarmers*, p. 99.

136. Ibid., pp. 94–5.

137. 'Sir David Spedding', Obituary, *The Times*, 14 June 2001.

138. Private information.

139. Graham Payn and Sheridan Morley (eds.), *The Noël Coward Diaries* (Macmillan, 1982), p. 361. Diary entry for 4 August 1957.

140. P. G. Wodehouse, *Plum Pie* (Herbert Jenkins, 1960), pp. 119–39.

141. Beckett, *Enemy Within*, p. 148.

142. Ibid., p. 161.

143. Ibid.

144. Driver, *The Disarmers*, p. 72.

145. Ibid.

146. Ibid., pp. 65–6.

147. PRO, PREM 11/4285, 'The Development of the Nuclear Disarmament Movement'.

148. Anthony Hartley, *A State of England* (Hutchinson, 1963), p. 90. A. J. P. Taylor, *A Personal History* (Hamish Hamilton, 1983), p. 227.

149. Driver, *The Disarmers*, pp. 157–9.

150. Ibid., p. 35.

151. PRO, PREM 11/4285, 'The Development of the Nuclear Disarmament Movement'.

152. Ibid.

153. Driver, *The Disarmers*, p. 107.

154. PRO, PREM 11/4285, 'The Development of the Nuclear Disarmament Movement'.

155. Driver, *The Disarmers*, pp. 163–70.

156. George Blake, *No Other Choice: An Autobiography* (Cape, 1990), p. 223.

157. Ibid., pp. 222–47.

158. PRO, PREM 11/4285, 'The Development of the Nuclear Disarmament Movement'.

159. Ibid.

160. PRO, CAB 158/47, JIC (62) 104, 'Anti-Nuclear Demonstrations at RAF Airfields in a Period of Tension', 16 November 1962.

161. Ibid.

162. For the genesis of the quickly iconic CND symbol see Driver, *The Disarmers*, pp. 58–9.

163. Arthur Marwick, *The Sixties: Cultural Revolution in Britain, France, Italy and the United States c.1958–c.1974* (OUP, 1998), pp. 65–6.

164. Ibid., p. 635.

165. PRO, PREM 4/232, DP 32/68 (D), 'Security of the United Kingdom Base in Pre-Attack Phase of General War. Report by the Defence Policy Staff', October 1968.

166. Ibid., Annex A. The MI5 report was numbered D/DISSEC/7/3/1 and dated 9 September 1968.

167. Ibid.

168. Ibid.

169. PRO, CAB 148/83, 'FALLEX 68'. Paper circulated to the Defence and Overseas Policy (Official) Committee, 24 June 1968.

170. PRO, CAB 130/397, Cabinet INVALUABLE Committee, MISC 222 (68) 2, 'JIC Special Assessment as at 0800 (Z) Hours', 27 September 1968.

171. Ibid., MISC 222 (68) 20, 'JIC Special Assessment as at 1200 (Z) Hours', 27 September 1968.

172. Ibid., MISC 222 (68) 8th Meeting (CAB), 21 October 1968.

173. Ibid., MISC 222 (68) 6 'United Kingdom Background Situation Report at 1200 (Z) Hours,' 16 October 1968.

174. He later wrote a book about his activities. Jack Dash, *Good Morning Brothers!* (Lawrence and Wishart, 1969). See also Beckett, *Enemy Within*, p. 157.

175. PRO, CAB 130/397, MISC 222 (68) 6, 'United Kingdom Background Situation Report at 1200 (Z) Hours', 16 October 1968.

176. Ibid., MISC 222 (68) 5, 'JIC Special Assessment as at 1200 (Z) Hours', 16 October 1968.

177. Ibid., 'EXERCISE FALLEX 68, Joint Intelligence Committee (A). Special Assessment as at 1200 ZULU', 17 October 1968.

178. Ibid., MISC 222 (68) 8, 'United Kingdom Background Situation Report at 1200 (Z) Hours', 17 October 1968.

179. Ibid., 'EXERCISE FALLEX 68, Joint Intelligence Committee (A). Special Assessment as at 1200 ZULU', 18 October 1968.

180. Ibid., MISC 222 (68) 10, 'United Kingdom Background Situation Report at 1200 (Z) Hours', 18 October 1968.

181. Ibid., MISC 222 (68) 11, 'United Kingdom Background Situation Report at 0800 (Z) Hours', 19 October 1968.

182. Ibid., MISC 222 (68) 13, 'United Kingdom Background Situation Report at 0800 (Z) Hours', 20 October 1968.

183. Ibid., 'EXERCISE FALLEX 68, Joint Intelligence Committee (A). Special Assessment as at 0800 ZULU', 20 October 1968.

184. Ibid., MISC 222 (68) 15, 'United Kingdom Situation Report at 0800 (Z) Hours', 21 October 1968.

185. Ibid., 'EXERCISE FALLEX 68, Joint Intelligence Committee (A). Special Assessment as at 0800 ZULU', 21 October 1968.

186. Ibid., MISC 222 (68) 8th Meeting (CAB), 21 October 1968.

187. Ibid., 'EXERCISE FALLEX 68, Joint Intelligence Committee (A). Special Assessment as at 1200 ZULU', 22 October 1968.

188. Ibid., MISC 222 (68) 18, 'United Kingdom Background Situation Report at 1200 (Z) Hours', 22 October 1968.

189. Ibid., 'EXERCISE FALLEX 68, Joint Intelligence Committee (A). Special Assessment as at 1200 ZULU', 22 October 1968.

190. Ibid., JIC (68) (SA) JICX008, 'Special Assessment', 23 October 1968.

191. Ibid., 'EXERCISE FALLEX 68, Joint Intelligence Committee (A). Special Assessment as at 1200 ZULU', 17 October 1968.

192. PRO, DEFE 4/432, 'Security of the United Kingdom Base in the Pre-Attack Phase of General War', Annex A.

193. Ibid.

194. Andrew and Mitrokhin, *The Mitrokhin Archive*, p. 488.

195. Ibid., p. 499.

196. PRO, PREM 13/2009, 'Soviet Intelligence Activities in the UK', Stewart to Wilson, 27 September 1968.

197. Andrew and Mitrokhin, *The Mitrokhin Archive*, p. 499.

198. For details of this see G. Bennett and K. A. Hamilton (eds.), *Documents on British Policy Overseas, Series III, Vol. 1, Britain and the Soviet Union 1968–1972* (Stationery Office, 1997), pp. 359–96.

199. George Walden, *Lucky George: Memoirs of an Anti-Politician* (Allen Lane The Penguin Press, 1999), p. 146.

200. Ibid.

201. Andrew and Mitrokhin, *The Mitrokhin Archive*, p. 499.

202. Private information.

4: 'Breakdown': Preparing for the Worst

1. Public Record Office (PRO), CAB 130/41, GEN 253/1st Meeting, 1 October 1948.

2. PRO, CAB 158/20, JIC (55) 12, 'The "H" Bomb Threat to the UK in the Event of a General War', 13 January 1955.

3. PRO, DEFE 10/402. 'Study Group', 1960. SG (60) 35, 'Note on the Concept and Definitions of Breakdown', 10 June 1960.

4. PRO, CAB 21/4959, 'Sir Norman Brook: Miscellaneous Engagements and Personal Correspondence 1961–1964'. 'Cabinet Government', a private lecture to Home Office officials, 26 June 1959.

5. Ibid.

6. Ibid.

7. Ibid.

8. Richard Taylor, *Against the Bomb: The British Peace Movement 1958–1965* (OUP, 1988), p. 99.

9. Lord Allen of Abbeydale interviewed for the Channel 4/Wide Vision Productions programme, *What Has Become of Us?*, 31 May 1994.

10. PRO, CAB 21/4959, Brook to the Home Office, 26 June 1959.

11. PRO, PREM 11/3815, Prime Minister's Personal Minute M 243A/61, Macmillan to Brook, 29 July 1961.

12. Conversation with Air Vice Marshal Bobby Robson, 26 July 2001.

13. I am very grateful to my daughter Polly for finding this at the Public Record Office in July 2001.

14. PRO, CAB 21/4840, 'Nuclear Retaliation Consultative Procedures. Draft Memorandum for Discussion with US Government', L. J. Sabattini's MOD redraft of 16 May 1962.

15. Ibid., Abercrombie to Cary, 17 May 1962.

16. Ibid., Cary to Abercrombie, 21 May 1962.

17. Private information.

18. PRO, CAB 130/3. GEN 75/1. 'THE ATOMIC BOMB. Memorandum by the Prime Minister', 28 August 1945.

19. PRO, CAB 134/82, CDC (48) 10. Revise, 'Background and Policy for Civil Defence Planning', 7 July 1948.

20. PRO, CAB 134/2634, CD (o) (PC) (66) 3, Civil Defence Planning Committee, 'Home Defence Review'. Note by the Home Office, 4 February 1966.

21. Ibid., CD (o) (PC) (66) 7, 'The Home Defence Review. Presentation of Government Policy. Note by the Home Office', 25 May 1966.

22. PRO, DEFE 4/232, CIC 5/68, 'The Military Aspects of Home Defence of the United Kingdom. A Memorandum by the United Kingdom Commanders-in-Chief', 1 October 1968.

23. Nicola Bliss, 'The Role of Sir Norman Brook in the Construction of the Cold War State 1945–1961'. Unpublished MA in Contemporary British History thesis, Department of History, Queen Mary, University of London, 2000.

24. PRO, AIR 20/11367, 'Air Ministry. Notice to Directors and Heads of Division. Routine War Planning', 16 December 1948.

25. PRO, CAB 134/80, CD (M) (48) 1st Meeting, 16 September 1948.

26. PRO, AIR 20/11367. Extract from the Conclusions of DTC (48) 4th Meeting, 4 December 1948.

27. PRO, CAB 158/4, JIC (48) 26 (o), 'Russian Interests, Intentions and Capabilities', 23 July 1948.

28. PRO, CAB 134/82, CDC (48) 10. Revise, 7 July 1948.

29. Ibid.

30. Ibid.

31. Ibid.

32. PRO, PREM 8/1355. 'Civil Defence Expenditure', 1948–1951. Chuter Ede to Attlee, 29 September 1948.

33. PRO, CAB 134/82, CDC (48) 10. Revise, 7 July 1948.

34. PRO, CAB 134/80, CD (M) 48, 1st Meeting, 16 September 1948.

35. PRO, CAB 134/82, CDC (48) 10. Revise, 7 July 1948.

36. Ibid.

37. PRO, CAB 134/80, CD (M), 1st Meeting, 16 September 1948.

38. PRO, CAB 130/41, GEN 253, 1st Meeting, 10 October 1948.

39. Ibid.

40. PRO, CAB 21/1885, 'Situation in Berlin (June–July 1948)', Brook to Attlee, 29 June 1948.

41. PRO, CAB 21/1647, 'Structure of a War Cabinet, 1949–1951'. 'Note for the Record', Sir Norman Brook, 14 February 1951.

42. Ibid., Attlee to Shinwell, 12 March 1951.

43. PRO, AIR 20/11367, JP (49) 157 (Revised Final), 'Transition from Peace to War – Record of Decisions to Be Taken by the Chiefs of Staff. Report by the Joint Planning Staff', 4 May 1950.

44. Elizabeth Knowles (ed.), *The Oxford Dictionary of Twentieth Century Quotations* (OUP, 1998), p. 236.

45. Richard Weight, *Patriots* forthcoming (Macmillan, 2002).

46. PRO, CAB 134/942, HDC (53) 5 (Revise), Home Defence Committee Working Party, 'Estimates of Casualties and House Damage. Note by the Home Office', May 1953.

47. Ibid., HDC (WP) (53) 8 (Revise), 'The Distribution of the Population', 15 May 1953.

48. Ibid., 'Estimates of Casualties and House Damage'.

49. Peter Hennessy, *Never Again: Britain 1945–1951* (Cape, 1992), p. 99.

50. PRO, DEFE 13/45. 'The Defence Implications of Fall-Out from a Hydrogen Bomb'. Brook to Macmillan, 8 December 1954.

51. Ibid., Macmillan to Churchill, 13 December 1954.

52. Ibid., Strath's notes on 'Fall-Out'.

53. Ibid., Brook to Macmillan, 8 December 1954.

54. Ibid., Strath's notes on 'Fall-Out'.

55. Ibid.

56. Ibid. This is written on Macmillan's minute to him of 13 December 1954.

57. PRO, CAB 158/20, JIC (55) 12, 13 January 1955.

58. Ibid.

59. Ibid.

60. Ibid.

61. Ibid.

62. Ibid.

63. Ibid.

64. Private information.

65. PRO, DEFE 13/45, Brook to Macmillan, 7 March 1955.

66. PRO, CAB 130/109, GEN 491, 'Defence Implications of Fall-Out from a Hydrogen Bomb', 1st Meeting, 24 March 1955.

67. PRO, DEFE 13/45, Brook to Eden, 21 April 1955; PRO, CAB 130/109, GEN 491, 24 March 1955.

68. PRO, DEFE 13/45, Brook to Eden, 21 April 1955.

69. Ibid.

70. Ibid.

71. PRO, CAB 130/109, GEN 491, 1st Meeting.

72. Ibid.

73. PRO, DEFE 13/45, Brook to Eden, 21 April 1955.

74. Ibid.

75. PRO, DEFE 7/2056, 'Ministry of Defence War Book', August 1952.

76. PRO, CAB 130/109, GEN 491, 1st Meeting.

77. PRO, DEFE 7/731, 'Home Defence Committee: Working Party on Machinery of Government in War: Minutes of Meetings and Related Papers 1958–59', Day to Wright, 18 November 1959.

78. PRO, AIR 8/2376, 'UK Command Organisation in War, 1950–1957', 'UK

Command Structure in War: The Higher Military Organisation to Assist the Civil Authorities to Meet Thermo-Nuclear Attack. Report by the UK Commanders-in-Chief Committee', 6 June 1956.

79. Alban Webb, 'The Impact of the Strath Report: The Formation of Home and Civil Defence Policy in Thermo-nuclear Age and Its Development'. Unpublished undergraduate thesis, Department of History, Queen Mary, University of London, 2001.

80. PRO, CAB 134/1245, Home Defence (Ministerial) Committee, 'Shelter Policy: Memorandum by the Home Secretary'. 'Appendix: Report by a Group of Officials on "The Defence Implications of 'Fall-out' from a Hydrogen Bomb" ', 25 October 1955.

81. Ibid.

82. Private information.

83. PRO, CAB 134/1245, 'Shelter Policy: Memorandum by the Home Secretary', 25 October 1955.

84. Ibid.

85. Ibid., HD (M) (55), 2nd Meeting, 27 October 1955.

86. Ibid.

87. PRO, CAB 131/16, DC (55), 17th Meeting, 7 December 1955.

88. David Miller, *The Cold War: A Military History* (John Murray, 1998), p. 149.

89. Ibid.

90. Ibid., p. 153.

91. PRO, CAB 134/2634, CD (o) (PC) (66) 7, 25 May 1966.

92. PRO, CAB 134/2871, HDC (69) 5, 'The Care and Maintenance Decision', 17 June 1969.

93. PRO, CAB 134/1245, HD (M) (55) 12 (Final), 30 November 1955.

94. PRO, CAB 134/1206, Ministerial Committee on Civil Defence, CDC (55) 3, 'Evacuation and Peripheral Dispersal: Report by the Official Committee on Civil Defence with Notes by the Home Defence Committee', 29 December 1955.

95. PRO, CAB 134/1245, HD (M) (55) 12 (Final), 30 November 1955.

96. Ibid.

97. Ibid., 'Annex A: Defence Expenditure by Civil Departments: Report by the Home Defence Committee', 11 October 1955.

98. PRO, DEFE 7/731, 'Central Government in Global War: The Military Organisation', Annex to COS (59) 91, 28 April 1959.

99. PRO, CAB 21/4704, 'Plans for Censorship in Event of Emergency', Padmore to Brook, 4 January 1957.

100. PRO, DEFE 7/731, 'Central Government in Global War: The Military Organisation'.

101. Ibid.

102. PRO, CAB 21/4959, Brook, 'Cabinet Government'.

103. PRO, CAB 130/109, GEN 491, 1st Meeting, 24 March 1955.

104. PRO, AIR 8/2376, 'UK Command Structure in War'.

105. I am very grateful to Dr Edgar Anstey for taking me through the origins and functions of JIGSAW. Letter from Dr Anstey (and related conversations) in August 2001.

106. PRO, DEFE 10/402. 'Study Group', 1960. For the background to JIGSAW and

an appraisal of the nature of its work see Richard Moore, 'A JIGSAW Puzzle for Operational Researchers: British Global War Studies, 1954–1962', in *Journal of Strategic Studies*, Vol. 20, No. 2 (June 1997), pp. 75–91.

107. Jeremy Isaacs and Taylor Downing, *Cold War* (Bantam, 1998), p. 161.

108. PRO, DEFE 10/402, SG (60) 30, 'Some Thoughts on Deterrence or Lack of It', E. A. Lovell, 31 May 1960.

109. Ibid.

110. Moore, 'A JIGSAW Puzzle for Operational Researchers', p. 86.

111. PRO, DEFE 10/402, SG (60) 79, 'Breakdown in JIGSAW', 29 November 1960.

112. A summary of Dr Shaw's summary in ibid.

113. Ibid.

114. Ibid., SG (60) 13, 'Likely Effects of Nuclear Weapons on the People and Economy of a Country', 'Hypothesis I', E. Anstey, 20 May 1963.

115. Ibid., SG (60) 56, 'Birmingham Study', W. G. Weeks, 6 September 1960; SG (60) 13, 'Likely Effects of Nuclear Weapons on the People and Economy of a Country', 'Hypothesis II', E. Anstey, 20 May 1963.

116. Ibid., SG (60) 36. 'Effects of Damage on a Nation', A. G. McDonald, 13 June 1960.

117. Ibid., SG (63) 13, 'Likely Effects of Nuclear Weapons on the People and Economy of a Country', 'Hypothesis III', E. Anstey, 20 May 1963.

118. Letter from Dr Edgar Anstey, 17 August 2001.

119. Ibid.

120. PRO, DEFE 10/402, SG (63) 13, 'Likely Effects of Nuclear Weapons on the People and Economy of a Country', E. Anstey, 20 May 1963.

121. Ibid., SG (60) 39, 'A New Strategic Deterrent for the UK', A. J. Shelfoon, 17 June 1960; see also ibid., SG (60) 42, 'The Requirements for a UK Nuclear Deterrent', J. A. Randall, 27 June 1960.

122. PRO, CAB 134/2634, CD (0) (PC) (66), Cabinet Civil Defence Planning Committee, 'The Home Defence Review. Presentation of Government Policy. Note by the Home Office', 25 May 1966.

123. Ibid.

124. Ibid.

125. Moore, 'A JIGSAW Puzzle for Operational Researchers', pp. 86–7; letter from Dr Edgar Anstey, 17 August 2001.

126. Ibid.

127. PRO, AIR 8/2400, 'Medium Bomber Force: Size and Composition', Defence Board, 'The V-Bomber Force and the Powered Bomb. Memorandum by the Secretary of State for Air', DB (58) 10, 'Annex. Russian Capacity to Absorb Damage', 29 October 1958.

128. PRO, DEFE 25/49, 'Nuclear Retaliation Procedures – Communications.' Mountbatten of Burma, 'Note to the Government Communications Electronics Board,' 1 December 1960.

129. ibid., Mountbatten to Brook, 6 February 1961. I am grateful to Nicola Bliss for first bringing this correspondence to my attention.

130. Ibid., Mountbatten to Brook, 28 April 1961.

131. Ibid., 'Nuclear Retaliation Procedures: Communications'. Paper prepared by F. A. Bishop, 30 January 1961.

132. Ibid.

133. PRO, AIR 8/2238. 'Operational readiness of Bomber Command', 1958–1961', Hudleston to Cross, 11 August 1959.

134. Ibid.

135. Ibid. See also PRO, DEFE 25/49, GEN 743/10 (Revise), 'Nuclear Retaliation Procedures. Report from the Working Group', 23 January 1962.

136. Ibid.

137. Ibid.

138. Hennessy, *The Prime Minister*, p. 116.

139. PRO, DEFE 25/49, Mottershead to Playfair, 13 March 1961.

140. Ibid.

141. Neville Shute, *On the Beach* (Heinemann, 1957), p. 11.

142. PRO, DEFE 25/49, Mottershead to Playfair, 13 March 1961.

143. Ibid.

144. Ibid., F. A. Bishop, 'Nuclear Retaliation Procedures: Communications', 30 January 1961.

145. Ibid., untitled diagram.

146. Ibid., Brook to Mountbatten, 2 August 1961.

147. Ibid., Sir Norman Brook, 'Nuclear Retaliation: Alternative Procedures', March 1961.

148. PRO, CAB 21/4959, Bishop to Brook, October 1961.

149. PRO, DEFE 25/49, Brook, 'Nuclear Retaliation: Alternative Procedures'.

150. Ibid.

151. Ibid., Mountbatten to Brook, 28 April 1961.

152. Ibid., Brook to Mountbatten, 20 April 1961.

153. Ibid.

154. Ibid.

155. Ibid.

156. PRO, PREM 11/3815, 'Organisation of Government to Deal with a Crisis in Berlin'.

157. Ibid.

158. Ibid.

159. PRO, CAB 21/4840, 'Nuclear Retaliation Procedures', Brook to Macmillan, 6 March 1962; Bright to J. H. Robertson, 7 March 1962. On 6 March Macmillan had initialled 'I approve' on Brook's minute.

160. PRO, DEFE 25/49, GEN 743/10. (Revise), 'Nuclear Retaliation Procedures. Report'.

161. Ibid.

162. For the history and detail of this see Stephen Twigge and Len Scott, *Planning Armageddon: Britain and the United States and the Command of Western Nuclear Forces 1945–1964* (Harwood Academic Publishers, 2000), pp. 99–146.

163. PRO, DEFE 25/49, 'Nuclear Retaliation Procedures. Report', Annex B, 'Powers of Commander-in-Chief, Bomber Command'.

164. PRO, AIR 8/2530. 'Command directives', 1962–1965. 'Supplementary Directive' from the Chief of the Air Staff to the Commander-in-Chief, RAF Bomber Command, 25 September 1962.

165. Hennessy, *The Prime Minister*, pp. 117–36.

166. PRO, DEFE 32/7, Chiefs of Staff Committee: Secretary's Standard Files, 1962. Annex to COS 1546/29/10/62. 'Record of a Conversation between the Chief of the Air Staff, First Sea Lord and the Chief of the Imperial General Staff Held in the Ministry of Defence at 14.30, Saturday 27 October 1962'.

167. PRO, AIR 28/1657, 'Operation Record Book. RAF Waddington. January 1961– October 1962', Wing Commander O. E. Ness to RAF Waddington, 14 July 1961.

168. PRO, AIR 24/2688, HQ Bomber Command October 1962. 'Post-Exercise Report on Exercise Mickey Fin II'.

169. PRO, AIR 25/1703, 'Operational Record Book, Headquarters No. 1 Group, October 1962'.

170. PRO, CAB 21/4840, Cary to Abercrombie, 21 May 1962.

171. Hennessy, *The Prime Minister*, pp. 121–5.

172. PRO, DEFE 12/321, 'Government War Book 1963–1964', Trend to Thorney-croft, 21 May 1963.

173. Ibid., 'Review of Government War Book Planning in the Light of the Cuba Crisis', Cabinet Office, 20 May 1963.

174. Ibid. The draft bill is appended as Annex B.

175. Ibid., 'Review of Government War Book Planning in the Light of the Cuba Crisis'.

176. Ibid., Emergency Powers (Defence) Bill, Annex B.

177. Ibid., Emergency Powers (Defence) Bill. Draft, 19 March 1963.

178. Ibid., 'Government War Book Planning'. Brief for the Minister of Defence, 30 July 1963.

179. Ibid., Emergency Powers (Defence) Bill. Draft, 19 March 1963.

180. Sir Frank Cooper interviewed for the Wide Vision/Channel 4 series, *What Has Become of Us?*, 28 March 1994.

181. PRO, DEFE 4/232, 'Military Aspects of the Home Defence of the United Kingdom', 1 October 1968.

182. Ibid.

183. Ibid.

184. Ibid.

185. Ibid.

186. Ibid.

187. Ibid.

188. Ibid.

189. Ibid.

190. Ibid.

191. PRO, CAB 130/397, INVALUABLE Committee, MISC 222 (68) 2, JIC Special Assessment as at 0800 (2) Hours, 27 September 1968.

192. Ibid., MISC 222 (68) 5, Joint Intelligence Committee Special Assessment as at 1200 (2) Hours, 16 October 1968.

193. Ibid., MISC 222 (68), 8th Meeting (CAB), 21 October 1968.

194. Ibid.

195. Ibid., MISC 222 (68) 5, Joint Intelligence Committee Special Assessment as at 1200 (2) Hours, 16 October 1968.

196. PRO, DEFE 4/224, 'Nuclear Targets in the United Kingdom. Assumptions for Planning', COS 1929/2/11/67.

197. Conversation with Air Vice Marshal Bobby Robson, 26 July 2001.

198. Ibid.

199. Ibid.

200. Ibid.

201. Ibid.

5: To the Cotswold Station: the Last Redoubt

1. Public Record Office (PRO), DEFE 5/136, 'Chiefs of Staff Committee Memoranda, 20 February–28 May 1963', Annex to COS 96/63, 'United Kingdom Commanders in Chief Committee. Terms of Reference'.

2. Sir Frank Cooper in conversation with Tom Dibble and Peter Hennessy, 4 August 1998.

3. Seen by the author on a visit, 27 April 2001.

4. Conversation with Sir Frank Cooper, 18 May 2001.

5. Private information.

6. Briefing by Wing Commander Steve Greenwood, RAF, Commanding Officer, Joint Support Unit, Corsham, 27 April 2001.

7. Ibid.

8. Private information.

9. PRO, DEFE 5/ 136, Annex to COS 96/63.

10. Private information.

11. A small group of students and I were permitted to visit the Crisis Management Centre on 15 March 2001.

12. Conversation with Richard Abel, 21 February 2001.

13. Letter from Guy Lester to the author, 28 March 2001.

14. PRO, DEFE 2/225, 'Ministry of Defence War Book, August 1963, Appendix D – Turnstile Staff Requirements'.

15. Private information.

16. Private information.

17. Private information.

18. Private information.

19. Private information.

20. PRO, DEFE 2/225, 'Ministry of Defence War Book, August 1963, Appendix D – Turnstile Staff Requirements'.

21. Sir Frank Cooper interviewed for the BBC Radio 4 programme, *The Top Job*, 8 August 2000.

22. Lord Allen of Abbeydale interviewed for the Channel 4/Wide Vision Productions programme, *What Has Become of Us?*, 31 May 1994.

23. Sir Frank Cooper, 8 August 2000.

24. Neville Shute, *On the Beach* (Heinemann, 1957), pp. 3–4.

25. Private information.

26. Private information.

27. Peter Hennessy, *Muddling Through: Power, Politics and the Quality of Government in Postwar Britain* (Gollancz, 1996), p. 116.

28. PRO, DEFE 2/225, 'Ministry of Defence War Book, August 1963, Appendix D – Turnstile Staff Requirements'.

29. Ibid.

30. Ibid.

31. Sir Frank Cooper, 8 August 2000.

32. Ibid.

33. PRO, DEFE 2/225, 'Ministry of Defence War Book, August 1963, Appendix D – Turnstile Staff Requirements'.

34. PRO, DEFE 7/731, 'Home Defence Committee: Working Party on Machinery of Government in War: Minutes of Meetings and Related Papers, 1958–59', Day to Wright, 18 November 1959.

35. PRO, DEFE 7/737, 'Supplement to Ministry of Defence War Book', Annex to COS (59) 1.

36. PRO, DEFE 7/731, 'Action to Be Taken by the Chiefs of Staff on a Tactical Warning', Appendix II to Annex to COS (59) 12.

37. PRO, DEFE 2/225, 'Ministry of Defence War Book, August 1963, Chapter III – Alternative War Headquarters'.

38. Ibid.

39. Ibid.

40. Peter Hennessy, *The Hidden Wiring: Unearthing the British Constitution* (Gollancz, 1995), p. 90.

41. PRO, DEFE 25/49, 'Nuclear Retaliation Procedures'. Report from GEN 743/10 (Revise), 23 January 1962.

42. PRO, DEFE 13/212. MM/COS (62) 7, 'Record of a Meeting Between the Minister of Defence and the Chiefs of Staff on Sunday 28 October 1962'.

43. D. R. Thorpe, *Selwyn Lloyd* (Cape, 1989), p. 424.

44. Hennessy, *Muddling Through*, p. 129. The conversation took place in 1989 for the BBC Radio 3 *Premiership* series.

45. PRO, DEFE 2/225, 'Ministry of Defence War Book, August 1963, Appendix C – Turnstile Staff Requirements'.

46. PRO, AIR 8/2400, 'Medium Bomber Force: Size and Composition', 'Russian Capacity to Absorb Damage', Annex to DB (58) 10.

47. PRO, AIR 8/2201, 'UK/US Co-Ordination: Offensive Bomber Operations 1957–1962', 'Strategic Strike Planning by Bomber Command'.

48. PRO, AIR 8/2400, 'Russian Capacity to Absorb Damage'.

49. PRO, CAB 134/3120, 'Ministerial Committee on Nuclear Policy', PN (67) 6, 'British Nuclear Policy', 1 December 1967.

50. BBC Radio 4, *A Bloody Union Jack on Top of It*, Part 2, 12 May 1988.

51. PRO, DEFE 5/136, 'Chiefs of Staff Committee Memoranda, 20 February–28 May

1963', Annex to COS 96/63, 'United Kingdom Commanders-in-Chief-Committee. Terms of Reference'.

Conclusion: Buttons and Envelopes

1. 'The lighter touch', *The Times*, 30 September 1998.
2. Private information.
3. Private information.
4. Private information.
5. Andrew Grice, 'Blair declares Britain is "at war" with Terrorism', *Independent*, 17 September 2001.
6. Rupert Cornwell, 'British Forces in Action "within Days"', *Independent*, 21 September 2001.
7. The full text of Tony Blair's speech to the Labour Party Conference in Brighton on 2 October (in which this notion formed part of the concluding peroration) was reprinted as 'Work together to our brave new world', in *The Times* on 3 October 2001.
8. Kevin Tebbit, 'British Security Policy from Cold War Through Peace Dividend To Force For Good In The World: A Personal Experience', the First Peter Nailor Memorial Lecture, 16 October 2001 (Gresham Society/Gresham College, 2001).
9. Rupert Cornwell, 'British forces in action "within days"', *Independent*, 21 September 2001.
10. Peter Hennessy, *The Prime Minister: The Office and Its Holders since 1945* (Allen Lane The Penguin Press, 2000), p. 502.
11. Private information.
12. Private information.
13. Private information.
14. Peter Hennessy, *Muddling Through: Power, Politics and the Quality of Government in Postwar Britain* (Gollancz, 1996), p. 10.
15. Private information.
16. Private information.
17. Private information.
18. Private information.

INDEX

Figures in italics indicate tables and a diagram; those in bold indicate a map.

1. TARGETS RELATED TO ALLIED NUCLEAR STRIKE CAPABILITY (65)

(b) BOMBER BASES (including dispersal recovery and flight-refuelling bases) (32) (Cont'd)

    (ii) USAF (6)

        Alconbury
        Bentwaters
        Woodbridge
        Wethersfield
        Lakenheath
        Upper Heyford

(c) BASES ETC. FOR SEABORNE NUCLEAR STRIKE FORCES (12)

    (i) Bases (5)

        Garelock (Clyde)
        Holy Loch
        Rosyth (SSBN Refitting Base

        Portsmouth
        Devonport

    (ii) Communication Installations (7)

    VLF (Rugby
        (Criggion
        (Anthorn (NATO)

    LF   (Inskip
        (New Waltham
        (Londonderry) US Navy
        (Thurso   )

2. MAJOR CITIES (20)

        Glasgow
        Birmingham
        Liverpool
        Cardiff
        Manchester
        Southampton
        Leeds
        Newcastle
        Bristol
        Sheffield
        Swansea
        Hull
        Middlesbrough
        Coventry
        Wolverhampton
        Leicester
        Stoke-on-Trent
        Belfast
        Edinburgh
        Nottingham

The Joint Intelligence Committee's 1967 view of where the bombs would fall if war came.